Ricoeur and Theology

Ricoeur and Theology

Dan R. Stiver

B L O O M S B U R Y

LONDON • NEW DELHI • NEW YORK • SYDNEY

Bloomsbury T&T Clark

An imprint of Bloomsbury Publishing Plc

50 Bedford Square
London
WC1B 3DP
UK

175 Fifth Avenue
New York
NY 10010
USA

www.bloomsbury.com

First published 2012

British Library Cataloguing-in-Publication Data
A catalogue record for this books is available from the British Library.

ISBN: HB: 978-0-5671-3020-4
PB: 978-0-5675-3786-7

Typeset by Deanta Global Publishing Services, Chennai, India
Printed and bound in India

Dedicated to Iylan and Canyon
Grandchildren who constantly affirm
life and its possibilities

CONTENTS

PREFACE

Paul Ricoeur speaks of "a chance transformed into destiny by a continuous choice." This is an apt description of my interest in Ricoeur and his thought. I began studying his work in earnest in the mid-1980s and then wrote an earlier book on Ricoeur and theology, *Theology after Ricoeur*, published in 2001, a longer, more detailed work than this one. At the time, of course, Ricoeur was still alive, and even though he was approaching his nineties, he was still publishing books and articles. Also at the time there was little on the subject of Ricoeur and theology.

Things have changed, to put it mildly. Ricoeur passed away in 2005. Since then, there has been a veritable explosion of books and articles on or related to his work, and much more has been done on Ricoeur's significance for theology, particularly the book by Boyd Blundell, *Paul Ricoeur between Theology and Philosophy: Detour and Return* (2010). After my earlier work, I had turned to other interests, primarily in theology. I attended, however, perhaps the first conference on Ricoeur after his death, planned by Scott Davidson in Oklahoma City in the Fall of 2006. There was such attendance and energy that it prompted some to get together and project a Society for Ricoeur Studies. Soon George Taylor was the superb founding president, and I was the program chair. The first conference was held in Chicago in 2007, followed by conferences each year. I became vice-president and am currently president. I have to confess that I expected the attendance to fall off after the first year and perhaps we might then move to meet less regularly. To my surprise, in the midst of an economic downturn that has severely affected most university professional meeting budgets, the conferences regularly grew for several years and have attracted a broad international attendance. In addition, Ricoeur groups have sprung up in Europe and Latin America, all meeting now almost annually. For instance, there were well-attended conferences this Fall

2011, in the midst of finishing this book, in Moscow (September), Philadelphia (October), and Rio de Janeiro (November). In addition, an online journal has begun, *Études Riceourienne/Ricoeur Studies* and a Series on the Thought of Paul Ricoeur has been inaugurated. Many reasons could be given for this profusion of interest, most of which have to do with Ricoeur's own attractive hermeneutical persona, his work, and his international influence before his death. In addition, my sense is that the breadth of Ricoeur's thought that may have made it difficult to grasp his thought as a whole while alive and thus worked against him is now working for him. He draws attention from incredibly diverse scholars, who I think appreciate the stimulation and uniqueness of being brought together around a common person and corpus of work. Scholars have also been drawn, it seems to me, by the focus not only on Ricoeur's thought but also on the implications of his thought, often in areas he did not treat.

The conferences especially have afforded, as one might imagine, innumerable rich opportunities for hearing papers on many aspects of Ricoeur's thought as well as rich conversations. I cannot begin to acknowledge the contribution that so many scholars have made to my thought. Nor can I acknowledge adequately all of the burgeoning literature on Ricoeur that has helped me over the years. It would take a much longer book to be able to do that.

I would like to mention a few, however, who have been especially helpful. Those on the board of the Society for Ricoeur Studies have become friends who not only serve as board members but also have been stimulating conversation partners: John Arthos, Scott Davidson, Adam Graves, Molly Mann, Todd Mei, David Pellauer, Charles Reagan, Roger Savage, and George Taylor. This past summer of 2011, I was able to spend a summer sabbatical at Regent's Park College in Oxford, England, thanks to a Cullen grant for faculty development from Hardin-Simmons University, which has been a wonderful, supportive place to teach, learn from students, and do such research as this for more than a decade. I was able to work with Pamela Sue Anderson, who was also extremely hospitable in the midst of a busy summer term. She has written on Ricoeur and also cowrote the book in this series on Immanuel Kant with Jordan Bell. She read and discussed with me several chapters of the book, which were enormously helpful. I have fond memories especially of one long afternoon at a pub near Oxford with Pamela and my wife, Beth, debating several issues around Ricoeur's thought. In addition, I was able to attend a seminar that she and Paul Fiddes lead on Continental philosophy and theology. It was not per se about Ricoeur, but Ricoeur often came up in conversation and it provided helpful background. It was also delightful to engage in conversation again with Paul Fiddes, who had been a professor 35 years ago when I was a student for one year at Regent's Park College. Charlie Scalise also read chapters and offered incredibly invaluable feedback. Charlie has been a friend and colleague for several decades now who embodies for me the kind of lively dialogue that Ricoeur stands for: critical, appreciative, and insightful. Greg Johnson is the coeditor with me of the series on Ricoeur's thought, and he is also a friend of many years who embodies hermeneutical virtues and in ongoing discussions about Ricoeur constantly "gives rise to thought." My graduate assistant, Robyn Holtmeyer, read through the entire manuscript for style issues. Her speed and judgment was of enormous help to me during a very busy semester. All of these have helped; unfortunately, I cannot ascribe to them the responsibility for what I have written. The book, however, would be much less valuable without them.

I also thank Continuum press for their interest in the dialogue between philosophy and theology embodied in this series. I have been stimulated by other books in the series, and I appreciate their entrusting to me this project on Ricoeur and theology. Thomas Kraft initiated and spurred this process almost to the very end before leaving to take another position, but I appreciate all that he has done.

In addition, I would like to mention a close friend of mine, Tim Maddox, who suddenly passed away a little more than a year ago. Tim wrote a dissertation with me in the 1990s on Ricoeur and then came as a colleague to teach philosophy at Hardin-Simmons University in 2004. He was also a founding member of the Society for Ricoeur Studies and was on the program committee with me. We often joked about being the "Ricoeur Center for the Southwest" since it is unusual for any institution to have two Ricoeur scholars, much less a small liberal arts university with one philosophy professor (I am in the theology department). I cannot do justice to the influence of the constant conversations with Tim over many years, especially in a philosophy reading group that met at Monks Coffee Shop in Abilene year round for several years (whom I also acknowledge, especially long-time members Lisa Smith, Toby Taff, and Seth Maddox, Tim's son).

Such a project as this over a long period of time is not possible without the support of my family, especially my wife, Beth, who has put up with me working more than I would have liked through the Christmas holidays with unfailing good cheer and love.

Finally, I dedicate this book to my two grandchildren, Iylan (7) and Canyon (4). Our lives have been quite "interwoven," to use one of Ricoeur's terms, with them in Abilene almost all of their lives. Much of this book has been written in and around activities with them as well as with our daughter and their mother Carrie. I often think of Ricoeur's emphasis on a "primary affirmation" of life in their connection. They remind me in extraordinary ways of the gracious gift and value of life that he emphasized. At their age, also, they are brimming with "passion for the possible." I give thanks for them and the way they enrich both my life and my possibilities.

New Year's Eve, *2011*

1

A hermeneutical life

A young Paul Ricoeur, raised in a pious French Huegenot (Reformed) tradition, was facing a crossroad, one of those momentous decisions the impact of which unfolds only in retrospect. He was confronting an "inner conflict" between faith and reason along with his first serious encounter with the challenges of philosophy at age 17. He spoke later of being pulled in both directions and conducting an "internecine war, from one armistice to the next," between them (Ricoeur 1995a: 3–6, 1998: 6). The strong appeal of philosophy threatened his religious faith. His wise philosophy teacher, Roland Dalbiez, urged young Paul to face what he feared and so he did.[1] Thus began one of the most influential philosophical trajectories in the twentieth century, which in a teaching and writing career of almost 70 years made significant intersections not only with quite varied areas in philosophy but also with religion, literature, psychoanalysis, and sociology. In the end, Ricoeur became a philosopher, but he never left the religious issues behind and made major contributions in the religious area. His applications of his theory of symbol, metaphor, and narrative particularly to biblical studies are the kind that usually belong to experts in the field. He only made occasional intersections with theology, but his varied work in philosophy and his direct work in the philosophy of religion and biblical interpretation offer more stimulating connections than most. These connections are what we will explore.

Ricoeur's life

Ricoeur was born on 27 February 1913, near Lyons, France.[2] His mother died seven months later. His father was soon off to war and declared missing in action on September 26, 1915; his body was not to be found for almost 20 years. Ricoeur was raised by his Protestant Reformed (Huguenot) paternal grandparents, for whom his father was a war hero, and his aunt who lived with them. Ricoeur later made the poignant comment that he only experienced motherhood in his wife Simone's raising of their children. He was perhaps fated to deal throughout his work with the question of personal identity, where he made some of his most significant contributions.

Ricoeur was always reticent to discuss his personal life and for much of his career it was not particularly treated. Yet when one looks at its full scope, it is emblematic of the ups and downs of a life in the twentieth century. Besides the early loss of his mother and father and the vicissitudes of France during and after World War I, he lost his sister Alice, with whom he was very close, to tuberculosis when they were in their twenties. As we shall see, he was imprisoned as a Prisoner of War during World War II for almost five years. After being a highly popular professor at the Sorbonne, he helped launch reforms in education that ran aground in the chaos of the 1968 student revolts. He taught regularly in both France and United States for decades, all the while traveling and speaking throughout the world, which contributed to a wide international influence. He had personal contact and dialogue with many of the major figures of thought in the twentieth century, from Gabriel Marcel (1889–1973) and Karl Jaspers (1883–1969) through Emmanuel Levinas (1906–1995) and Jacques Derrida (1930–2004), and many others. And his long life of 92 years during which he was active as a philosopher right till the end, coupled with the unusual immersion into both Anglo-American analytical philosophy and Continental philosophy, meant that he experienced firsthand the twists and turns of philosophical and other intellectual currents for almost an entire century.

Ricoeur married Simone (Lejas), the childhood friend of his sister and himself, in 1935. His education also took him to Paris in the mid-1930s, where he engaged in the noted discussions in the famed French existentialist Marcel's home, with Marcel later writing letters to Ricoeur during Ricoeur's time in a prison camp. The discipline that Marcel inculcated is noticeable in Ricoeur's later creativity. Marcel instructed them to take up a topic and not repeat what others had said about it but to describe it anew in what Marcel called a "second reflection"; in effect, it was an early introduction to the phenomenological method of bracketing theory and tradition in order to gain a fresh perspective on lived experience. One of the refreshing aspects of Ricoeur's work throughout his life was just this tendency to take an experience, whether it might be an act of the will, of evil and suffering, of hope, of recognition, or of memory and describe it as if he were starting all over.

Ricoeur also became involved in the French socialist youth movements, advocating pacifism and Christian socialism (Ricoeur 1998: 11). Then World War II broke out and deeply affected him as it did the whole world. His pacifism rethought, he went to war and was quickly captured on June 7, 1940. Although he did not speak of it much, he spent almost five years in a German POW camp in very spartan conditions—an experience for most people that might dominate their entire lives. Despite the hardships, he and others actually conducted lectures and classes drawn from memory for which students received credit after the war; for example, Ricoeur gave a lecture on Nietzsche in the camp in July of 1940. During this time, Ricoeur also gained prized access to some of Edmund Husserl's (1859–1938) works and began a deep study of the father of phenomenology. He wrote out a translation, during these years, of a part of Husserl's important book *Ideas* on margins of the book, and his first international notoriety was as the author of that translation and as director of the Husserl Archives after the war. He also began work on his first major creative philosophical work, *Freedom and Nature*, also on the rationed amount of pen and paper that the prisoners were allowed, which was influenced by his intensive reading of Husserl and Karl Jaspers in the camp. Even though, as Charles Reagan says, "Intellectually, those years were not wasted," Reagan points out that "the surroundings were depressing and basic human needs were only minimally met" (Reagan 1996: 10).

They struggled with the varying reports about the war, hoping initially that it would be over soon and at other times wondering if they would ever be repatriated. On January 29, 1945, the prisoners were ordered to begin a march through snow to another camp over 200 miles away. At one point, Ricoeur and others stayed behind and hid in a barn, fearing that they might just be shot down by their captors. Their barn was shelled because of being so close to pitched battle between the Germans and the Russians. They eventually escaped to another farm where they stayed a week. As Reagan points out, "In eleven days, they had gone only 6 kilometers [3.7 miles]" (Reagan 1996: 13). They were then recaptured by the

Germans and sent by train to other camps, finally to be liberated by
the Canadians around April 23. He was not reunited with his family
until May 9, 1945, where he saw his five-year-old daughter, Noëlle,
for the first time. Ricoeur has said that it was important for him
to move forward, so he never really reflected on these experiences
in his writing, but they surely marked him in deep ways that he
would likely have acknowledged, especially for one steeped in the
workings of the unconscious through his Freud studies. One of his
first works after the war, notably, was on Jaspers, cowritten with
one of his fellow prisoners, Mikel Dufrenne.

After the war, Ricoeur began his family life and the ethos of a
young professor anew. He chose to live in Le Chambon sur Lignon, a
largely Protestant city noted for its courageous aid to Jews during the
war. Ricoeur was attracted by this context of pacifism and faith and
stayed there until 1948, recovering from the war and teaching at the
Collège Cévenol. They named their fourth child, born there in 1947,
Olivier to mark the peace after such a horrendous war. He also
met Albert Camus (1913–1960) at this time. Ricoeur then went to
teach at the University of Strasbourg for eight years, which he saw as
a particularly enjoyable and fruitful time. Ricoeur submitted *Freedom
and Nature*, published in 1950, for his major doctoral dissertation
and soon became noticed as a promising young philosopher. In the
Spring of 1956, he was asked to teach at the Sorbonne in Paris, where
his lectures became quite popular, at times with more than a thousand
students trying to squeeze into his classes.

At this time he became an outspoken critic of the nation's war
in the colony of Algeria. Ricoeur wrote and participated in protests
against the heavy-handed treatment of the supporters of nationalism,
especially against the use of torture against Arab prisoners. At one
point, he was arrested and his home searched; he was taken without
being allowed to communicate with his family, afterward being
released only under the condition of house arrest. Ricoeur's political
involvement went back to the early 1930s in his work with the
journal *Esprit*, dedicated to Christian socialism and pacifism that
had been initiated by the Roman Catholic personalist, Emmanuel
Mounier (1905–1950). Indicating his continuing involvement and
interest in these practical social issues, when Ricoeur moved to Paris
he was honored to be asked to live in an intellectual community
that Mounier had also initiated, called *Le murs blancs* (The White
Walls), in Chatenay-Malabray, a suburb in the south of Paris,

where the Ricoeurs lived until their deaths. Ricoeur could address social issues, often to Christian groups, in a popular, accessible, yet challenging way, which one can see in *Political and Social Essays* (Ricoeur 1974d).

The second volume of Ricoeur's philosophy of the will was published as two books in 1960, *Fallible Man* and *The Symbolism of Evil*. The first two, *Freedom and Nature* and *Fallible Man*, were more descriptive, phenomenological works, where the purpose is to describe in nontheoretical language the essence of certain experiences. In these books, Ricoeur described the components of action as involving all aspects of the embodied self, that is, holistically, which went beyond Husserl's more idealistic approach to the more embodied approach to phenomenology in Maurice Merleau-Ponty's (1908–1961) *Phenomenology of Perception* (published in French in 1945). In *Freedom and Nature*, Ricoeur stressed how the will always involves the body. His holistic approach also reflected the way that existential thinkers such as Martin Heidegger (1889–1976) and Jean-Paul Sartre (1905–1980) appropriated phenomenology.

Especially in *Fallible Man*, he characterized the self in existentialist terms as poised between heaven and earth, as it were, being rooted in the body and yet transcending through the imagination. Being pulled in many directions results in the human tendency toward falling into error and evil. Dealing with actual fault convinced him that such inherently irrational acts could not be described in terms of essential, rational description (the phenomenological method) and could only be depicted through symbol and myth, which led to his treatment in *The Symbolism of Evil*. From here he was led deeper into the vast field of hermeneutics, the theory and practice of interpretation, from which he never emerged and for which he is now most widely known.

He turned to the work of Sigmund Freud (1856–1939) in the early 1960s, which was much the rage in France at this time, to help with the interpretation of symbols, especially of course symbols of the unconscious. This work was a tour de force in the specialized field of Freud studies and led to painful controversy in part because he was a newcomer and not a therapist. He was engaged in a bitter tension with the most famed Freudian at the time in Paris, Jacques Lacan (1901–1981), whose seminar he had attended but whose work he did not utilize, saying that he did not understand it well. When he did not cite Lacan extensively in his work, Lacan and his supporters, including Ricoeur's son who was studying with Lacan, turned on him, which was another painful episode in his life. In the 1970s, Ricoeur turned to metaphor and wrote a magisterial book in this area, *The Rule of Metaphor*. Then in the 1980s, after the age of 65, he began a prodigious literary output in its own right, beginning especially with a major three-volume work on narrative, *Time and Narrative*.

In the meantime, the revolutionary student unrest of the 1960s had engulfed Ricoeur. Ricoeur actually left the Sorbonne against the advice of many colleagues to become dean at the new University of Nanterre because of his sympathy with the need for reform in favor of students. For example, at this time in Paris there were an estimated 120,000 students for a university built for 20,000, with no resident students, no faculty offices, obviously large classes, and little contact between professors and students. As he acknowledged, Ricoeur and a few others set out on his own utopian venture, interesting in light of his later work on utopia, to bring about a smaller, residential campus with greater communication and reciprocity between faculty and students (Ricoeur 1998: 28, 39). As Reagan comments, "Nanterre would be an attempt to create the atmosphere of the best American and British residential universities" (Reagan 1996: 33). Unfortunately, the radical movements of 1968 swept over him and the university, and he found himself trying to maintain stability in the midst of students and even other youths near the campus attempting, by violence if necessary, to take over the university. At the height of the conflict, Ricoeur was attacked by a student on horseback with a lance in the hall. As Dean of the Faculty of Letters, Ricoeur had little power. In a move to provide protection in light of the violence and some attacks on female students, Ricoeur asked for the police to provide protection. They came in earlier than he desired, and in conflict with the rioters themselves exacerbated the situation by their excesses. Ricoeur, shaken by these events and experiencing failing health, resigned on March 16, 1970. He asked for a three-year leave of absence from the French university system and saw his star fade in France for nearly two decades even as he continued a momentous practice of teaching annually at the University of Chicago Divinity School in the John Nuveen chair previous held by Paul Tillich (1886–1965).

During this time, he became renowned as an international philosopher, though not a major presence in France. In fact, Ricoeur is unusual as a philosopher in bringing together at some depth

Continental and Anglo-American analytic philosophy, which is especially seen in Part 1 of his Gifford Lectures, perhaps the major lectureship in the world on religion and philosophy, published as *Oneself as Another* in 1990 (Eng. 1992). Much of his later influence in religious studies, after *The Symbolism of Evil*, was due to his influence in the Anglo-American world. A published book of essays on philosophy of religion, *Essays on Biblical Interpretation*, and a treatise on applying the philosophy of metaphor to the parables of Jesus had a major impact (Ricoeur 1975, 1980a). It is very unusual for a major philosopher to have such influence directly, for example, in biblical studies and biblical interpretation.

It was *Oneself and Another* and his major work on narrative combined with the fading of the influence of structuralism and poststructuralism in France that led to a renewal of Ricoeur's influence in France in the late 1980s and lasted until his death. Ricoeur's new reception in France led to political involvement that resulted in two small books on legal hermeneutics, *The Just* (1995; Eng. 2001) and *The Just Revisited* (2001; Eng. 2007). They address philosophical issues but often are addressed to specific issues of just treatment of minorities. These reflected the long-standing interest in political philosophy throughout his life. Besides his more well-known works on hermeneutics in the 1970s, his *Lectures on Ideology and Utopia*, originally given in the 1970s, also represent a fresh perspective from the side of political philosophy that offer rich possibilities for connections with theology (Ricoeur 1986b).

Even in the new millennium, in his late 80s and 90s, he brought out a fascinating small book, *On Translation* (2004; Eng. 2006) and a major book bringing together several of his loves—hermeneutics, phenomenology, justice, narrative and history, and self-identity—in *Memory, History, Forgetting* (2000; Eng. 2004). His last published book in his lifetime brought together his lifelong preoccupation with phenomenology, personal identity, and political philosophy—and word studies—in an analysis of the concept of "recognition" in 2004 (Eng. 2005).

His son Olivier committed suicide, sadly after a meaningful time together with Ricoeur and his wife in connection with his Gifford Lectures, again marking him as a person acquainted with many great griefs of life, from the loss of parents at a young age, to war, to civil strife, and to personal loss.[3] His wife and companion Simone died in 1992, to whom he dedicated the books *Thinking Biblically* and *Memory, History, Forgetting*. With these griefs and the pains of advancing physical decline, Ricoeur grappled seemingly anew with death in his journal, which was actually not written for publication, published posthumously as *Living Up to Death* in 2009. At the same time, Ricoeur was receiving numerous accolades for a lifetime of contributions, notably the Balzan Prize in 1999 and the John W. Kluge Prize for Lifetime Achievement in the Humanities in 2004.

As one can see even from this brief sketch of Ricoeur's life and work, he had an impressive range of interests and expertise, which also has made it notoriously difficult to access his work. Many times I have been asked where to begin in Ricoeur by students and colleagues, and there is not an easy answer. Ricoeur does not have one *magnum opus*, and it is difficult to avoid adding to a brief recommendation of a few books, "Oh, you also need to read that one in that area." Ricoeur himself at one point commended a commentator for tying together threads in his thought of which he himself was not fully aware (Ricoeur 1980a: 41). This situation certainly makes it difficult for theologians who are aware of Ricoeur's influence and who want to study further but who are daunted by the task—a reason for this kind of book!

Fortunately, at this time, with his full life's work in hand, we also have many who have stepped in to discern underlying order to his work, a kind of phenomenology of the essence of his work, as it were. A Society for Ricoeur Studies arose shortly after his death and has flourished in North America, along with developing Ricoeur societies in Europe and Latin America. These have provided a forum for many scholars from multiple disciplines to continue to work out the themes and implications of Ricoeur's work, including theology, which is an ongoing and incomplete task. In fact, with the rise of what is commonly seen as a new postmodern context for theology, Ricoeur's thoroughgoing but balanced critique of modernity in some ways is just being appropriated at a deep level as a conversation partner for theology.

Primary themes

A rich tapestry with many threads runs through Ricoeur's work, all of which impinge on theology. A brief look at some of these will prove useful in setting up our more sustained dialogue with theology.

Phenomenology

As we saw, the phenomenological method as an attempt to provide an accurate but not jargon-laden description of the essence of various experiences is manifest throughout Ricoeur's career, but Ricoeur's approach is a revision of the idealist and objective approach that Husserl hoped would be the foundation of a "rigorous science" (Husserl 1965). Ultimately, Ricoeur followed Maurice Merleau-Ponty in seeing that an accurate description—phenomenology—of phenomenology ironically reveals that one cannot be presuppositionless.[4] Ricoeur developed further the sense in which all such description is inescapably interpretive or hermeneutical. Moreover, it ran into its limits in describing phenomena such as evil and even hope, whose essence is not possible or available. Nevertheless, as a fresh approach to the phenomena, not unduly influenced already by theory, Ricoeur showed again and again its productivity. His first major work of phenomenology, *Freedom and Nature*, was a phenomenology of the will, but it was already a mixed, "diagnostic" approach that related description of felt experience with what can be learned about the body by science and external observation, much as a doctor combines a patient's subjective reporting with scientific knowledge of the body. This mixed approach led Ricoeur sometimes to call his approach a "phenomenological hermeneutics" or "hermeneutic phenomenology."

Hermeneutics

This leads us to a second major theme, hermeneutics. As mentioned, Ricoeur's approach could be called "hermeneutic philosophy," even though he did not explicitly take up hermeneutics as a theme until the 1960s.[5] Nevertheless, even his earlier work that involved his lifelong pattern of setting various approaches that are in tension in a dialogical or dialectical way represents hermeneutics in action, such as in *Freedom and Nature*. He drew on Martin Heidegger's and Hans-Georg Gadamer's (1900–2002) emphasis that people do not just interpret or do hermeneutics from time to time but are hermeneutical all the way down, as it were, which Ricoeur saw as ontological hermeneutics (Ricoeur 1991a: 63). This is the basis for a powerful critique of modernity's desire for a presuppositionless beginning, which we saw in Husserl, as well as the Cartesian demand for "clarity and distinctness." We always start reflection too late, as Ricoeur put it. The unconscious, the involuntary, and our immersion in culture and tradition always already accompany the conscious and voluntary. Thus, Ricoeur early rejected the tradition of idealism that saw knowledge and understanding as transparent to the self; rather, he emphasized the "wounded *cogito*," where such understanding always involves interpretation, and interpretation involves a "surplus of meaning" that cannot lead to absolute certainty. Even with his affinity for Heidegger in phenomenology and hermeneutics, Ricoeur characteristically distinguished his "long route" that must traverse other disciplines, preeminently the mediation of language, and further explanations using critical methodologies in contrast with Heidegger's "short route" that moved more directly to the grasp of Being and of human beings (Ricoeur 1974b: 10–11).

Ricoeur did place himself in the tradition of what he called "reflexive philosophy," which he traced from René Descartes (1596–1650), Immanuel Kant (1724–1804), Edmund Husserl (1859–1938), and Jean Nabert (1881–1960). Unlike Descartes and Kant, however, Ricoeur saw reflection as mediated through the displacement of the independence of the self through the phenomenological turn to the world and through the hermeneutical turn to language. Ricoeur's reflexive philosophy then understands self-knowledge as inherently involving dialogue with others and interaction with the world—a clear rejection of Descartes' inward turn to the individual self whereby one could start anew all by oneself (Ricoeur 1991d: 12–15). Similarly, Ricoeur characterized his view somewhat playfully as a "post-Hegelian Kantianism." Deeply influenced by both philosophers, Ricoeur rejected Hegel's (1770–1831) grasping at absolute knowledge, preferring the Kantian limits on knowledge of the thing-in-itself. Yet Ricoeur appreciated Hegel's much richer sense of the context of knowledge in tradition and community in ongoing dialogue and historical understanding. Ricoeur's hermeneutical spiral allowed, like Hegel, complex dialectical thought for greater grasp of reality and even the Absolute but always with a sense of Kantian limits and mystery that precluded Hegelian closure and completeness. In the end, Ricoeur rejected even the kind of clarity and certainty that Kant thought one could have with phenomenal knowledge relating to objects, viewing such knowledge also as hermeneutical. This radical hermeneutical turn in reflexive philosophy placed hermeneutics at the foundation of knowledge, meaning that the Enlightenment dream of objective certainty could never be fully realized. On the other hand, Gadamer and Ricoeur were not as skeptical as some postmoderns who seem to question the possibility of knowledge at all, seeing it dissipated in the play of power, the fragmentation of the self, or multiple interpretations.[6] Ricoeur expressed this *via media* clearly in *Oneself as Another*, "The hermeneutics of the self is placed at an equal distance from the apology of the cogito and from its overthrow" (Ricoeur 1992: 4). At this point, Ricoeur did not hesitate to speak of "the gap that separates the hermeneutics of the self from the philosophies of the cogito," further distancing reflexive philosophy from philosophies of the subject such as Descartes (Ricoeur 1992: 18).

The self

As mentioned, Ricoeur was concerned with the nature of the self throughout his life. Besides Ricoeur's understanding of the self as deeply hermeneutical, his emphasis on the self not as primarily a thinker but as a doer was also a crucial theme. As much as he always saw himself as a phenomenologist, rather than the focus on perception of Husserl's and Merleau-Ponty's phenomenologies, Ricoeur was interested in the acting and responsible self, which he later called the "capable self" *(homo capax)*. Reagan reports that Ricoeur was contemplating another major work on the capable self before he died, and one can deduce such a book from his many works. Drawing on Spinoza (1632–1677) throughout his life, Ricoeur stressed the self's embodied desire (*conatus*) to exist, so significant for Spinoza, that stretches toward transcendence. Related to this desire was his sense of a primary affirmation of the being of the self.[7]

At the same time, as one living in war-torn Europe, he also deeply saw the fragility of the self. He reflected, "My departure from Husserlian phenomenology was largely due to my disagreement with its theory of a controlling transcendental *cogito*. I advanced the notion of a wounded or split *cogito*, in opposition to the idealist claims for an inviolate absolute subjectivity." And in a note of interest to theologians, he added, "It was in fact Karl Barth who first taught me that the subject is not a centralizing master but rather a disciple or auditor of a language larger than itself" (Kearney 1984: 27).

As his work developed, Ricoeur increased his emphasis on the significance of the imagination in self-understanding and understanding of the world. Such imagination underlies his creative work on metaphor, where unlike the historical tradition on metaphor, he understood "live metaphor" (the translation of the French title, *La metaphore vive*) as irreducible to literal explanation and in many ways more powerful than prosaic language. He argued that metaphor allows us to create new meaning, and he thus praised the "ontological vehemence" of metaphor. Along with metaphors and symbols, he added that human identity is formed by narratives and myths, which likewise are irreducible to theoretical prose.

The hermeneutics of the self hence becomes more and more complex, moving from the diagnostics of *Freedom and Nature* to the hermeneutics of symbol and story. Self-identity is inherently an open-ended story that is interwoven with all of the stories that we encounter. In light of his later work, there is here a "course of recognition" that involves the treacherous task of right memory, relationships with others, and inevitably a demand for "difficult forgiveness." Again, the self-possessed or unencumbered self of modernity is left behind.

Yet Ricoeur did not sympathize with the total loss of the self as in some postmodern thinkers. His typically balanced and dialectical approach is seen in the way that he regarded the self as wounded and suffering, yes, and often lost in the desert of criticism and ideology, to be sure, but it is still a responsible and capable self. Ricoeur also engaged the turn to see the self as inescapably a social self, "oneself as another." This meant that the self could not only not be understood as a solitary self but also not even exist as such a self— although such an individualistic view of the self lies at the root of much modern philosophy and political theory. The self, moreover, in Ricoeur's view is a self not only in dialogue with personal others but is inescapably enmeshed in larger communities that call for a sense of justice. Hence, the political works of his later years.

The just

Early and late Ricoeur was interested in ethics and political philosophy, although the themes were muted in his middle period. Ricoeur's "little ethic," as he termed it, in *Oneself as Another*, has won high praise for its adroit synthesis of the two great ethical traditions that usually compete sharply with one another: Aristotelian teleology and Kantian deontology. In this area, he thus offered another example of his hermeneutical and dialogical approach to issues that often resulted in a fruitful new position. Ricoeur placed priority on the former and its tradition of the "good" as providing a basis, however, for a sense of demand in the "right" stemming from the deontological tradition. He thus shared the communitarian emphasis that ethics calls for some imaginative idea of the just society to get going, so to speak. On the other hand, within such a vision, there is a place for obligation, law, and the moral. As in his hermeneutical arc, the story is primary but it necessitates explanation. Toward the end of his life, Ricoeur emphasized that self-identity is forged in dialogue with personal others and also lives in the states and world of impersonal others, where issues of equality, obligation, and legal responsibility are inherent. Here one must address justice in particular ways, as he did, toward the stranger, the marginalized, and the victimized. One cannot but think also of his own childhood and early life formed without father or mother but with an extended family in a state caught up in two world wars. He summed this up as each of us having a primary aim to live justly with and for others in just communities. While Ricoeur had a positive place for the utopian, as with much of his thought, he also stressed the inadequacy, even tragedy, that is inherent in striving for this goal. In fact, the last word in his last large, major book *Memory, History, Forgetting* is "incompletion" (Ricoeur 2004: 506).

Method

Ricoeur does not particularly explicate a method, apart perhaps from his hermeneutical arc; rather, he shows it. In part, his hermeneutical emphasis, like Gadamer, is that a tight, rigid method is inadequate. One of his characteristics therefore is a sense of the brokenness, woundedness, and thus partiality of our grasp on truth and reality. Sometimes in frustrating ways, his works end with a meditation on what has not been shown—and what needs still to be done. A striking example is his three-volume work on time and narrative that ends with such a meditation on its incompleteness. When one gets to the end, one is also struck by how limited was its focus—despite its breadth. This careful concern to move cautiously perhaps also reflects his deep sense of Kantian limits and also his religious, Reformed sensibilities that reflect the mystery and majesty of God, and the Pauline limits that "we know in part." In his own way, he deconstructed much as Jacques Derrida, his erstwhile student, does, but it is also true that he sees the dialectic going in terms of reconstruction, which he once described in dealing with the parables of Jesus as "reorientation by disorientation" (Ricoeur 1975: 114). Despite the possibilities of affirmation of which he never lost sight, sometimes there is almost a greater sense of negation and limit. For instance, in *Time and Narrative*, volume 1, Ricoeur brings Aristotle and Augustine into dialogue on the self's narrative as a discordant (Augustine) concordance (Aristotle)—or is it a concordant discordance?[8]

Mentioning this approach in *Time and Narrative* reveals another major aspect of Ricoeur's method: it was historical and dialectical. Unlike a Husserl or a Wittgenstein, Ricoeur explicitly engaged the history of interpretation on any theme, and he did it in a dialectical or dialogical way. The extent and patience with which he engaged so many thinkers and traditions is difficult to capture apart from seeing it over and over in many texts. He was widely known throughout his career for his generous practice of interpretation that sought to do justice to the strengths of the other's position, a practice that often as much as content has been meaningful to those drawn to the Society for Ricoeur Studies and other Ricoeur groups worldwide.[9] Richard Kearney describes Ricoeur as having an approach of mediation and translation, "a diplomat of philosophical exchange," and adds, "In his philosophical role as translator, Ricoeur was, I believe, unrivaled in his time."[10]

Ricoeur's view was framed typically in dialogue with two approaches that initially seemed to be in great tension, such as Aristotle and Augustine on time or, as we saw above, Aristotle and Kant on ethics. Other examples are the voluntary and involuntary in *Freedom and Nature*; the finite and the infinite in *Fallible Man*; explanation and understanding; metaphor and narrative; Kant and Hegel; chronological time and existential time; ideology and utopia; phenomenology and hermeneutics; structuralism and hermeneutics; and forgetting and remembering. Ricoeur's approach was to read all that he could on a subject and bring it together in a dialectical synthesis that was not wooden but quite creative. Boyd Blundell emphasized Ricoeur's own characterization of his work as "detour and return" to his main interests (Reagan 1996: 133; Blundell 2010: 2). Perhaps another aspect of the dialectic is that he combined the emphasis on phenomenology of going "to the things themselves," without prior interpretation, and yet also delving deeply into the history of a subject and its interpretation.

A parallel dynamic that one finds in Ricoeur is intensive engagement with major philosophers of the Western tradition, the classic philosophers. His wont was to take a major philosopher's corpus each summer and read through it. One sees then the intensive commentary and influence of such philosophical luminaries as Plato, Aristotle, Augustine, Spinoza, Kant, Hegel, Husserl, Marcel, and Heidegger, who reappear again and again. Some names are missing in terms of extensive treatment such as the pre-Socratics and Stoics and Anglo-American modern philosophers such as John Locke (1632–1704), David Hume (1711–1776), Bertrand Russell (1872–1970), and Ludwig Wittgenstein (1889–1951), but he has treated many of these authors extensively in lectures, however, that are unpublished and preserved at Le Fonds Ricoeur in Paris.

Concerning the Anglo-American analytical philosophers, however, one should notice that a striking aspect of Ricoeur's work is that he does bridge the analytical-Continental divide in an unusual way. He does not engage the major figures as he does a Kant or a Hegel, but on specific issues, his American teaching led him to extensive dialogue with issues on self and grammar in *Oneself as Another* and with political philosophers like John Rawls and Michael Walzer in his later works. Such intensive preoccupation with classical Western philosophy makes his works both rich and forbidding. Although he is careful to engage in studied summaries of what he is doing, he does not write "introductory" works. It is often mentioned that he writes as one participating in an ongoing complex conversation, and one must also have some grasp of the conversation to enter it. This is why some of the published interviews, which are more informal and introductory, are a good place to begin in moving into Ricoeur's thought. In fact, at one place where I was teaching, I was discouraged from offering a class on Ricoeur because it might be too narrowly focused on one person. When I finally did teach a class on Ricoeur, I found that, to the contrary, we had to engage almost the whole history of philosophy to provide the context for his works. It turned out to be one of the broadest classes that I taught.

Religion and theology

For a major philosopher who is not primarily a philosopher of religion, Ricoeur is unusual in the breadth and depth of his engagement with religion, primarily the Judeo-Christian tradition. He not only writes upon themes that have immediate implications for religion but also explicitly addresses such themes at great depth. His earlier work, *The Symbolism of Evil*, was a standard read by seminary students throughout the 1960s and 1970s. It dealt with other traditions such as the Orphic, but it profoundly treated the biblical text and the theological interpretation of sin and the fall. His work directly on the parables rivals other major biblical interpreters and contributed to a major revision of the understanding of the parables. His biblical interpretation is also seen in a later collaboration with a prominent Hebrew Bible scholar, André Lacocque, in *Thinking Biblically* (LaCocque and Ricoeur 1998). His emphasis on the significance of the various genres of Scripture in the sense of the medium being the message is a major contribution to narrative theology. His work in philosophy of religion in English is primarily seen in the essays collected in *Essays on Biblical Interpretation*, which includes the essay on the genres of Scripture, and *Figuring the Sacred*. These essays represent significant accounts of the relationship of philosophy, theology, and faith.

And then, there are oddities for someone so interested in issues of faith. He wrote three volumes on narrative but never particularly applied his emphasis on the interweaving of history and fiction to the Gospels particularly at a time when these options represented polar approaches.[11] Ricoeur was careful to disclaim that he was a biblical scholar, theologian, or preacher. He called himself a "listener" to the biblical message and at one point an "apprentice theologian," although he especially seemed to refrain from identification with doing theology per se (Ricoeur 1965b: 5, 1998: 152). Although his work tracks many theological themes, he did not directly engage theologians to the extent that he did biblical scholars. He himself reflected on his "biblical faith that is nourished by exegesis more than by theology" (Ricoeur 1995a: 53). He indicated that he preferred the first-order expressions of faith before they are worked up in systematic theology; for example, he had great appreciation of Augustine's phenomenology, one might say, but not his theology. Even here, though, he related to theologians in writing primarily as a philosopher, of which he said, "The philosopher is not a preacher. He may listen to preaching, as I do; but insofar as he is a professional and responsible thinker, he remains a beginner, and his discourse always remains a preparatory discourse" (Ricoeur 1974e: 441).

Similarly, there was his strong insistence throughout most of his career until just to the end on his prominent gap between philosophy and theology, which sits in some tension with his general dialectical approach. The French context for philosophy had something to do with this, where a strong identification as a Christian philosopher could count strongly against one as a philosopher. He admitted as much in later reflections where he also questioned this gap. On the other hand, his emphasis on their disciplinary integrity also protects them. Perhaps this represents yet another of his detours and returns, as mentioned by Blundell. Of course, this opens up several questions for us: How do we relate Ricoeur to theology? Do we take Ricoeur's scattered theological comments as the theological consequences of his philosophical thought? Or are they just one possible direction to go? Are we limited to those particular areas in appropriating his philosophy? Was Ricoeur as interested and knowledgeable in theology as in other areas? What are the strengths and limitations of his philosophy and his approach for theologians? These are questions that will accompany us as we proceed.

2

The context for theology

The terrain for philosophy and theology has dramatically shifted in the last 50 years, and Paul Ricoeur himself has contributed to these changes. The most common rubric for this altered landscape is now "postmodernity," but it comes with heavy baggage. On the one hand, Ricoeur was uncomfortable with the phrase, and most of those considered major postmodernists did not use the phrase about themselves. On the other hand, it is a widely used term that connects these thinkers in their common criticisms of "modernity," also a freighted phrase. In this sense, it is not unlike the term "existentialism," which is widely used and yet difficult to define, where the leading thinkers often did not identify themselves as existentialists. The biggest drawback for the productive use of the term is that it is sometimes seen as a passing French fad or as a synonym for relativism or perhaps even nihilism. Nevertheless, as a term that describes a common critique of modernity, it has been widely appropriated among some circles of philosophers and theologians, especially in the United States. And used loosely, it points toward theologies that are developed in light of these criticisms that often include postliberal theology associated particularly with Yale, emergent churches, postconservative theologies, liberation theologies, and a host of other individual theologians.[1] For instance, one can see a range of such theologians in *The Cambridge Companion to Postmodern Theology*, which presents seven different kinds of postmodern theologies in the first part of the book. One could actually add more from the topical articles in the second half (Vanhoozer 2003). Interestingly, none of them would espouse relativism.[2] I agree with Graham Ward in distinguishing between a more constructive and a deconstructive postmodernism, the latter of which implies relativism.[3] In this sense, Ricoeur acknowledged at one point that his "enterprise could be called postmodern if this qualification can apply to reconstruction and not (or not only) to deconstruction" (LaCocque and Ricoeur 1998: 116). In actuality, most theologies who would affirm the postmodern label fit the constructive type.

Conversely, if that term is simply too identified with relativism and a denial of reason altogether, perhaps it is judicious just to observe that we are in a transitional period where deep assumptions that reigned for several centuries are now commonly questioned if not rejected. The disunity and even chaos appears in terms of alternatives, where numerous trajectories of thought have pointed the way toward the future. It is reminiscent of the huge shift in theology marked by what is now called the Neo-Orthodox movement in the 1920s, spearheaded by Karl Barth, Emil Brunner, Paul Tillich, and Rudolf Bultmann. At the time, their criticism of the liberalism that they had inherited left them similarly in what they called "between the times" (*Zwischen den Zeiten*).[4] It is only in retrospect, decades later, that they can be identified as participating in a similar and radical shift in theology—but also to see that, while they were seen as closely united at the beginning, they represent major different responses to that shift. We are just now beginning to identify some of the major different responses to the crumbling of the modernist paradigm in philosophy and theology in the late twentieth century.

As one of the major philosophers of the twentieth century, Ricoeur's own critique of modernity is especially trenchant yet also critical of relativism. In this sense, he offers a philosophical reference point for theologians that avoids a common dilemma in modernity that Richard Bernstein termed objectivism versus relativism (Bernstein 1985). In other words, Bernstein argues that modernity oscillates between a longing for an extreme standard for knowledge (objectivism) and a despair of attaining it (relativism). In this sense, relativism haunts modernity in some ways more than postmodernity. Ricoeur provides a philosophical discussion partner who, while sympathetic to theology, represents a distinctively different direction from this tendency in modernity, which has provided the framework and even underpinnings for theology for several centuries. At the same time, Ricoeur's Aristotelian moderation has kept him from stepping into the extreme rapids of some of the postmodern responses that tend toward relativism, utter skepticism, and nihilism. "Attestation," he said at one point, "defines the sort of certainty that hermeneutics may claim, not only with respect to the epistemic exaltation of the cogito in Descartes, but also with respect to its humiliation in Nietzsche and its successors" (Ricoeur 1992: 21).

Ricoeur was engaged throughout his career in an onslaught against what one might call the citadel of modernity, the self-sufficiency of the thinking self, a *"disembedded* and *disembodied* being"* who is atomistically detached from situation and context who can arrive at a God's-eye point-of-view. This is a view of the self that not only lies at the root of modern epistemology but also forms a basis for the social contract in political philosophy (Benhabib 1992: 152). René Descartes, often considered the father of modernity (in this sense dated in the 1640s), famously inscribed the thinking self, the *cogito*, as the ground of certainty to deal with radical doubt. In search of a certain, indubitable foundation, he found the formula (already in Augustine) that he could not doubt that he was thinking or doubting, *cogito ergo sum* (Descartes 1952: 51; Augustine 1971: XI, 26). From there, he was able to bring back a trustworthy God and much else besides. Ricoeur took aim at this powerful French legacy.

The subject: The wounded cogito

First, Ricoeur underscored other skeptics in questioning the transparency of the self, which reputedly allowed Descartes to be clear about grasping his own self and to be indubitably certain about some beliefs. This grounding of reality upon the self or ego was followed by other idealist philosophers in the Continental tradition even beyond Descartes, such as Johann Gottlieb Fichte (1762–1814). Ricoeur argued, however, that the understanding of the self is a lifelong task, not an accomplishment—certainly not a starting point. He thought of it in terms of what his teacher Gabriel Marcel called a "mystery" as opposed to a "problem" (Marcel 1956: 18–19). A problem is something that we cannot yet explain, but we potentially can. A mystery refers to a reality that can be understood better but can never be fully grasped. The self is a prime example of a mystery. David Hume beginning from empiricist premises looked for the sensory experience of a self—but to no avail. Later thinkers who influenced Ricoeur such as Immanuel Kant and Edmund Husserl saw the self not as an entity that one can grasp directly but, only by indirection, as a presupposition or an implication. Ricoeur gave this indirection a sharp hermeneutical and social turn, yielding the self as a matter of inherent interaction with and interpretation of a world that is also mediated through texts. A common statement for Ricoeur is, "For us, the world is the ensemble of references opened up by the texts" (Ricoeur 1981f: 202).

Second, Ricoeur also questioned Cartesian certainty. His first major work pointed out that the self is not purely mind but a mixture of the voluntary and the involuntary, freedom and nature. There is a realm of the unconscious and barely conscious that is central to human thought and action that cannot fully or easily be brought into conscious awareness. This work as a phenomenology of the will was consciously building upon Maurice Merleau-Ponty's phenomenology of perception (Ricoeur 1995a: 11). Both moved beyond Husserl's desire for phenomenology to yield "apodictic" or certain results or a rigorous science, based on what Husserl called an "eidetic reduction," which supposedly allowed one to transcend any presuppositions or influences and thus to see things, Cartesian-like, clearly and with certainty. Merleau-Ponty, who like Ricoeur greatly appreciated Husserl, nevertheless frankly stated, "The most important lesson which the reduction teaches us is the impossibility of a complete reduction" (Merleau-Ponty 1962: xiv). Ricoeur then especially turned to Sigmund Freud's work as a kind of hermeneutic of the self, which recognizes the ongoing work of uncovering and deciphering the subterranean depths of the self through an archeology of the self's past as well as what Ricoeur added, namely, a teleology of the self (Ricoeur 1970). This backward and forward orientation itself leads to an ongoing conversation, as it were, about who the self is. Ricoeur's later work on narrative further pointed to the self as an ongoing story that is being constantly written and rewritten (Ricoeur 1988, 1992), which he characterized as an odyssey of interpretation in *Memory, History, Forgetting* (Ricoeur 2004: 470). From this vantage point, one can see how far removed we are from Descartes' being "shut up alone in a stove-heated room" where in one day he grasped himself with certainty (Descartes 1952: 44). Ricoeur contrasted such a philosophy of consciousness or immediacy with the tradition of reflexive philosophy, implying continual reflection. Ricoeur thus in distinction from the Cartesian tradition understood the self in terms of temporality, mystery, and ongoing fallible interpretation.

Ricoeur's erstwhile student, Jacques Derrida, prominently underscored this point, and arguably went further than Ricoeur, by criticizing what he saw as a common "metaphysics of presence" that pervades Western thought (Derrida 1974: 16–17, 49). Derrida highlighted a common assumption that face-to-face presence is better than distance, thus speech over writing. This emphasis goes back not just to the father of modern philosophy but to the father of philosophy, Plato himself. In Plato's *Seventh Letter*, Plato notoriously excoriated the attempt to put his teaching into writing in favor of face-to-face teaching; of course, the irony is that all we have of Plato's teaching is in his writing (also in dialogue form that he thought was not as valuable as his lectures, which we do not have) (Plato 1952). In a series of insightful essays, Derrida built upon this irony to bring this Western assumption into question.[5] He pointed out that even face-to-face speech involves language that must be interpreted, and the record shows that speech can be mischaracterized just as much and sometimes more than writing. While Ricoeur continued to maintain a relative distinction between the immediacy of direct speech and the distantiation involved in writing, Derrida's emphasis carried out the universality of hermeneutics in Ricoeur perhaps more consistently at this point. Ricoeur later pointed in this direction in suggesting that the dynamics of translation that involves adequacy but not equivalence must be applied even within a language (Ricoeur 2006: 10, 24). In some ways, interestingly, writing can be more precise, this point being made in terms of Derrida's neologism, *différance*, which in writing can be distinguished from the French *différence*, meaning both the state of differing or deferring in English (Derrida 1973: 82, 129). In speech, one cannot tell the "difference" (and he is also stressing that in both speech and writing, meaning is not transparent and must be interpreted; one has to gauge from context which meaning). Sometimes later reflection, which Ricoeur emphasized in a number of essays in terms of "distanciation," can lead to greater understanding than the immediacy of presence. So why is presence privileged? Was Descartes' immediate awareness of himself so "clear and distinct"?

Third, in a related way Ricoeur questioned whether one can start from scratch, so to speak, as Descartes thought. Ricoeur especially pointed here to the rehabilitation of tradition by Hans-Georg Gadamer. Gadamer playfully chided the Enlightenment prejudice against prejudice (Gadamer 1991: 270). In doing so, he was not denying that preunderstanding can often be destructively prejudicial, but he was also making the serious observation that preunderstandings enable understanding. In other words, they may go wrong, but they are also a key to going right; either way, we cannot do without them. Humans are unavoidably shaped by tradition. Our preunderstandings are what enable us to be interested, to ask questions, to begin looking, and to have some idea of what an answer would look like. This critique of the modernist ideal of a presuppositionless starting point is an aspect of the way that Gadamer, Martin Heidegger, and Ricoeur all emphasize that humans are hermeneutical beings, always beginning with something to be interpreted rather than with nothing at all, as Descartes sought. As Ricoeur put it once in relation to symbols:

> In contrast to philosophies concerned with starting points, a meditation on symbols starts from the fullness of language and of meaning already there; it begins from within language which has already taken place and in which everything in a certain sense has already been said; it wants to be thought, not presuppositionless, but in and with all its presuppositions. Its first problem is not how to get started but, from the midst of speech, to recollect itself. (Ricoeur 1974g: 287–88)

Fourth, Ricoeur chimed in with a number of other philosophers in placing action before thought. One may well think of Karl Marx's well-known saying, "The philosophers have only interpreted the world, in various ways; the point is to change it" (Marx 2011: Thesis 11). In fact, Ricoeur gave a careful analysis of Marx's contribution to a hermeneutic of suspicion in a series of lectures that we will examine later. One can also think of the later Ludwig Wittgenstein's approving quotation of Wolfgang Goethe's *Faust* in the *Philosophical Investigations*, "In the beginning was the act" (Wittgenstein 1958: par. 402). As we shall also see in Ricoeur's hermeneutical arc, it ends not in reflection but in action or appropriation (which involves, to be sure, a greater understanding). In both philosophy and theology, there has been a great shift toward praxis or practice, not just as an alternative to a problematic split between theory and practice but as the sense in which this split is overcome. It represents a realization that comprehension cannot be separated from the practices that undergird it and may best be realized in practice. As such, Ricoeur's thought joins a major turn toward practices in theology.[6] An example in narrative theology is the focus upon biography as giving meaning in the practice of life to theological doctrines, as in James McClendon's *Theology as Biography* (McClendon 1974). Ricoeur expressed this relationship in another way: "The mystery of personhood is not capable of being resolved *speculatively*, which means in a Cartesian, objectivist sense; it can however be put to work productively or *practically*" (Ricoeur 1992: 147). He especially saw this as manifest through narrative.

Fifth, in the end Ricoeur did not dissolve the self but maintained it, as fragile and contested as it is. Here he parted ways with some of the more extreme postmodernists, such as Michel Foucault who at one point proclaimed the death of the self (Foucault 1973). In fact, despite Ricoeur's own roots in existentialism, he already questioned Jean-Paul Sartre's dualism toward the self, "Sartre's *Being and Nothingness* produced in me only a distant admiration, but no conviction: could a disciple of Gabriel Marcel assign inert things to the dimension of being and reserve only nothingness of the vibrant subject of affirmations of all sorts?" (Ricoeur 1995a: 11). Ricoeur pointed rather toward a holistic existentialism, one might say, represented more by the incarnational tradition of Marcel and Merleau-Ponty than of Sartre, who despite his prominence in discussions of existentialism, remains here in the Cartesian dualistic tradition. This dialectical balance that is typical of Ricoeur corresponds with a more recent and surprising poststructuralist return to a singular self, given the way that structuralism and poststructuralism began in much opposition to the existentialist preoccupation with the singular self (McSweeney 2008). Such an attempt at affirming a self, however frail, is especially crucial in feminist philosophy and theology, which we will explore more in Chapter 5. At this point, it suffices to mention that the postmodern critique of the self has been welcome in part to feminist critique of the privileged masculine self, but Susan Hekman laments that just as women are finding themselves, the postmodernists of which we are speaking sometimes dissolve the self, yielding a disputatious relationship between the two (Hekman 1990: 136, 189). As Hekman goes on to suggest, however, such an approach to the self belongs to a certain interpretation of the more radical poststructuralist types of postmodernity such as those of Derrida and Foucault. These, she argued, can actually be helpful, as well as hermeneutical philosophy, Gadamer's being the one she appropriates as a conversation partner—and one can add Ricoeur as well (Hekman 1990: 62–73).

The object: Inextricably entangled in the world

Descartes' doubt ran all the way through the self, leaving behind a questionable world of objects, raising the question not only of the subject but also of the object.[7] While he reestablished a substantial self, which other philosophers such as Hume were to question, he himself left a legacy of doubt concerning knowledge of the external world of objects. Likewise, as Nancey Murphy points out, empiricism in the modern period has been imprinted with a perceptual model of knowledge, whereby the challenge has been to determine whether the sense impressions ever "get out" of the body and correspond to anything real, leaving no end of problems in its wake (Murphy, Kallenberg and Vanhoozer 2003: 28–29). Others such as Foucault and Richard Rorty (1931–2007) have also strongly criticized this spectator model for philosophy (Foucault 1973; Rorty 1981). For those interested in maintaining a sense of validity in knowledge, such as Heidegger and Gadamer, the response has been not to tweak the model but to throw it out, noting that it is difficult to give a good answer to a bad question.

Ricoeur first followed here the Heideggerian prompt of a critique of Cartesian skepticism in favor of an emphasis on human embodiment. According to Heidegger's existentialist turn from his mentor Husserl's phenomenology, humans are first beings-in-the-world before being thinkers. When people approach "objects," this is not the first reality but a secondary reality (which Heidegger expressed as things being "ready-to-hand" rather than "present-to-hand"). As Heidegger picturesquely expressed it, "What we 'first' hear is never noises or complexes of sounds, but the creaking waggon, the motor-cycle. We hear the column on the march, the north wind, the woodpecker tapping, the fire crackling. It requires a very artificial and complicated frame of mind to 'hear' a 'pure noise'" (Heidegger 1962: 207). Merleau-Ponty in his own extension of Husserl's phenomenology went much further in his emphasis on human embodiment, saying, "We are involved in the world and with others in an inextricable tangle" (Merleau-Ponty 1962: 454). Rather than being an impediment, he stressed the body as "the pivot of the world" (Merleau-Ponty 1962: 82). Ricoeur, as noted, began his own work on *Freedom and Nature* by presupposing Merleau-Ponty's work on the phenomenology of perception. In this light, skepticism about the "world" outside of oneself cannot get any traction. We are already "inextricably entangled" in the world.

This does not mean that the world is "clear and distinct," however, nor does it finally yield to Cartesian indubitability or Baconian domination. Rather, an aspect of "starting too late" because of our being-in-the world is that before we begin to reflect we are enmeshed in the world of things. In fact, separating out "things" is already an arbitrary act that comes second, as Heidegger and Merleau-Ponty noted. The process of identifying discrete objects is already an abstraction from primary experience. Alfred North Whitehead (1861–1947), who was a master of abstraction as a coauthor with Bertrand Russell of *Principia Mathematica*, regarded by some as the greatest work on logic since Aristotle, nevertheless called such abstraction "the fallacy of misplaced concreteness," where scientists and mathematicians confuse their abstractions with the "real" world (Whitehead 1953: 64, 72). One could say with the contemporary emphasis on practice and action that our primary engagement with the world is one of holistic action, involving all aspects of the self-enmeshed in the world, from bodily perception (Merleau-Ponty) to bodily willing (Ricoeur).

This underscores as a second point the irreducible hermeneutical relation to the world. We start reflection already on the journey and interpret a complex whole that involves the involuntary aspect of our bodies as well as holistic integration of action and practical thought. It is striking then that Ricoeur's first major work is a phenomenology of the will (not of thought or even of perception as in Merleau-Ponty) that already discerned the impossibility of a pure intuition that transcends the body, which Husserlian phenomenology desired. He of course quickly moved on to tackle Freud himself on the unconscious and to the irreducible nature of figurative language in relation to more precise prose.

As Ricoeur's thought developed, he was inspired by Heidegger's hints, and perhaps more by his colleague Emmanuel Levinas, to consider that it is not just the body, then objects along with "books," but more deeply, other people as a third aspect of the world. In other words, the development of an identity capable of philosophical reflection, contra Descartes and most social contract philosophers, already includes other people. Heidegger had delineated this sphere in *Being and Time*, but did not develop it, as in so many cases, with the category of a "with-world" (*Mitwelt*) (Heidegger 1962: 154). Ricoeur had adumbrated this point in *Freedom and Nature* with the emphasis on birth (rather than Heidegger's preoccupation with death as the signal hermeneutical key to existence) where humans are given so much from others, especially parents and caregivers, that is central to shaping the personality long before one is capable of abstract thought (Ricoeur 1966: 433–43). Levinas deeply influenced Derrida and others not only with his emphasis on the unavoidability of continuing commentary on the traces in thought and communication but also with his emphasis on the priority of the "face" of the other before the abstractions of metaphysics and even ethics as disciplines (Levinas 1969). Ricoeur later developed this theme at great length in *Oneself as Another*. Even the "object" that was often so transparent, especially in science, in modern thought yields to a holistic complex of self, body, other, in practical engagement with the world.

At this point, the kind of reductionism on which the skeptical empiricist tradition especially concentrated is totally reversed. Bertrand Russell was an exemplar, who at one time assumed that the primary reality is irreducible atomistic "bits" of sensory data that are "later" worked up into dubious larger concepts.[8] Merleau-Ponty sharply criticized this atomistic approach to reality and indicated how actually "secondary" and abstract it is (Merleau-Ponty 1962: Chs. 1–4). The later Wittgenstein himself sharply contended with his own earlier work that followed in Russell's wake and shaped the Logical Positivist movement by pointing out similar themes as we have seen in the Continental tradition of Heidegger, Merleau-Ponty, and Ricoeur concerning the priority of action and of holistic engagement with the world. The later Wittgenstein also emphasized something similar to this latter tradition by indicating how language also inserts itself almost unconsciously into all of our dealings with the world (Wittgenstein 1958: par. 19, 1963: par. 173). This is the point that Gadamer has made so well in terms of the primordial "linguisticality" of the world (Gadamer 1991: 389). Gadamer was not saying, as some have understood, that there is nothing but words (any more than Derrida meant that there is nothing but books in his saying that there is nothing but the text). What Gadamer did mean was that by the time we can reflect upon the world, we are as "inextricably entangled" with language as we are with the body and the rest of the world. And when one adds with hermeneutical philosophers and the deconstructionists that language is essentially a matter of interpretation, the clear and distinct self, as well as clear and distinct object so assumed and desired by modernity, dissolves.

The complex whole that is the mystery of the self intertwined with the world then becomes the challenge of philosophy and theology for the twenty-first century. Theology was shaped by the assumptions of modernity, perhaps best seen in the Scottish Common Sense Realism that so permeated the foundations of fundamentalism and evangelicalism in the nineteenth century. In this view, as seen particularly in the Old Princeton Theology of Charles Hodge, nature was understood as a collection of discrete objects and uninterpreted facts, and so the Bible similarly must be an inductive collection of uninterpreted "facts" that can be seen clearly by those with "common sense" (Marsden 2006: 56; Murphy 1996: 32–5). At the time, much of Anglo-American Christianity was positive about the growing prestige of science and desired theology to reflect that prestige. It was a shock then when it was actually the philosophy of science that challenged such simple understanding of facts and objects. Rather, all facts came to be seen as "theory-laden," or in other words, "hermeneutical" (Barbour 1997: 108). While many dissimilarities abound, the "language games" of science and of religion began to veer toward what had been perceived to be the weaknesses of religion in relation to science: its subjectivity, the role of the community and tradition, and, despite Common Sense Realism's attempt to transcend interpretation, religion's seemingly irreducible hermeneutical dimension. Mary Hesse, a philosopher of science, in fact pointed out in the 1970s that the characteristics given of religion earlier could now almost exactly describe science (Hesse 1980: 171–2). Ricoeur's starting point is this breakdown of the ideas of the substantial, unencumbered self and the transparent object.

The conflict of interpretations

Ricoeur then added the hermeneutical turn in language per se. The title of one of his first major collections of essays, most of them from the 1960s, is *The Conflict of Interpretations* (Ricoeur 1974f). Hermeneutical philosophy in general, going back to Friedrich Schleiermacher, has been provoked by the pervasiveness of "misunderstanding" and disputed interpretations. Ricoeur put this more positively in the subtitle of one of his most widely read books, *Interpretation Theory: Discourse and the Surplus of Meaning* (Ricoeur 1976a). Rather than being a disadvantage, the surplus of meaning points to the richness of the "object," so to speak, and how it can be approached from many, virtually inexhaustible, angles. Especially when one is thinking about religious texts and religious experiences, such an approach respects this rich mystery rather than attempting to dissolve it, which some rationalist and then the empiricist Common Sense Realist approaches tended to do by reducing its diversity and claiming to grasp too much.

 One of the attractions of hermeneutical philosophy for theology is that they are seemingly natural allies. They both start for the most part from the basic dynamics of interpretation of texts and trade on both the potential and vagaries of language. They both point to texts that can be interpreted but which also lead to multiple interpretations, many of which can be well supported. They wrestle with the conflict of interpretation and also the surplus of meaning. They grapple with the fact that no easy resolution of differing interpretations is in sight. Increasingly, both have come to recognize that they are not just dealing with literal, propositional language but also, if not largely, with symbolic language and multiple genres, which are largely irreducible to prosaic language.

Despite attempts to stabilize theology, various theologies have existed from the beginning. Several factors led, however, to a greater awareness of this plurality in theology in the latter half of the twentieth century. The breakdown of the dominance of German theology, the rise of the many forms of liberation theology, such as Latin American, black, and feminist, now often transmuted into postcolonial theology, and the increasing globalization of the church and the world, all have led to an upsurge of theologies from many differing perspectives. From a context where the expectation was to have a universal theology that represented all viewpoints, this near cacophony of voices has felt like a "shattered spectrum" (Kliever 1981). On the other hand, it has given rise to fresh new perspectives. Kevin Vanhoozer has argued that the centrality of the Incarnation, the Word becoming flesh (John 1:14), in theology actually implies not one theology for all time but a continually contextualized and recontextualized theology that is actually more adequate to the richness of revelation.[9] A hermeneutical philosophy that is attuned to the surplus of meaning and also to a hermeneutics of suspicion has been a resource for this pluralization of theology. In one sense, it supports it by underscoring that interpretation is always perspectival and that many interpretations are possible. It has also supported, for instance, liberation theology's suspicion of much traditional theology as protecting the vested interests of church and state. Ricoeur's own turn to a critical hermeneutics in particular, going beyond Gadamer, has been widely appropriated in this regard.[10] In another sense, however, hermeneutical philosophy provides a nuanced supplement or corrective by providing a broader framework for dealing with the richness of language, texts, and experience. As we shall see in the next two chapters, Ricoeur's noted hermeneutic arc allows for a first naïve reading and then a push forward to a critical reading. It does not stop there, however, but calls for a postcritical appropriation that challenges the tendency toward being hypercritical or reductionistic. His hermeneutics also underscores the differences in genres between prose, metaphors, and narratives—and the differences in narrative between historiography and fiction.

In many ways, this natural alliance between hermeneutical philosophy and theology is a contested work in progress. Many theologians still draw on nineteenth-century rationalist and propositional approaches; others do not see the two as supplemental but as competitive. There is dispute between critical and fiduciary approaches and between those who emphasize one genre over another, such as metaphor or narrative. Some are leery of any close relationship with philosophy, ironically seeing such an alliance as too modern even though the philosophical side is quite critical of modernity. Others see hermeneutical philosophy as too "affirming" and look for more ideology critique.

An example is the earlier dispute between the so-called Chicago and Yale Schools of narrative theology, in which Ricoeur was caught.[11] Hans Frei and George Lindbeck pulled Gadamer and Ricoeur into Lindbeck's category of liberal "experiential-expressive" theology, which Lindbeck saw as positing a common universal experience of religion behind the differences in expression (Lindbeck 1984; Frei 1993: 127). They criticized David Tracy for allowing the modern world to absorb the biblical world rather than the other way around. The irony for both Tracy and Ricoeur, both hermeneutical thinkers, especially the latter, is that Lindbeck saw such a liberal theology as very nonhermeneutical. In the end, the criticisms were not very valid for any of the three associated with the University of Chicago, and the two movements were much closer than was originally thought in the heat of controversy (Placher 1987, 2007; Tracy 1985; Wallace 1990). Yet for some time, the division was seen as a gulf between two of the most influential theological movements in the United States in the latter part of the twentieth century. Both Gadamer and Ricoeur's emphasis on the horizon of the text became "eclipsed," to use a term of Frei's, by seeing them as allied with a liberal theology that emphasizes the modern horizon.

For our interests, another significant confusion was collapsing Ricoeur's philosophy into his "theology," usually interpreted through his colleague David Tracy's theology. The Yale theologians were very influenced by their interpretation of Karl Barth as a postcritical theologian, which was seen especially as a concern to keep theology from being dominated by philosophy (Frei 1981). They pointed to an ad hoc approach to philosophy that keeps it from being in the driver's seat (Werpehowski 1986). In practice, however, they also drew upon philosophers such as Wittgenstein and even Derrida as well as anthropologists like Clifford Geertz. The very emphasis they were making, however, is one that Ricoeur, as a hermeneutical philosopher, insisted upon, namely, that one cannot subsume all regional hermeneutics into a universal hermeneutics (Ricoeur 1976b). Ricoeur stressed that theology particularly should not be dominated by general hermeneutics, and sometimes the dominating influence would stream from theology. Ricoeur's own position indeed represents a shift from the tendency to "eclipse the biblical narrative" with a master philosophical narrative about which Frei worried (Frei 1974). Ricoeur's carefully worked out position, sensitive to the internal dynamics of biblical and theological interpretation, in many respects revealed the kind of fruitful relationship for which the Yale School theologians called. Vanhoozer has described Ricoeur as a philosopher listening with a cupped ear to revelation (Vanhoozer 1990: 275). This aptly describes the stance that Ricoeur took toward not only Scripture and theology but also to life experiences in general. He took such sources as giving rise to philosophical thought in essence funding and shaping philosophical thought more than the other way around. In turn, though, such philosophical thought could offer resources to the theologian and exegete. The positions of Frei and Lindbeck turned out to be far more complex than a simple rivalry suggests; they actually differ significantly from one another (DeHart 2006). When Frei later elaborated a typology for theology, Ricoeur's approach is actually quite close to his own.[12] In the end, from the vantage point of some distance, there is more of a family resemblance between these two approaches, both of which are critical of modernity, than conflict.

Some major shifts in theology especially over the last century have also resonated with themes that Ricoeur and other philosophers have tackled. A major change is an emphasis on a holistic self rather than a dualistic self. This came about through a remarkable confluence of rethinking in several fields. Biblical studies began to question whether the Hebrew Bible and even Paul with his language that could be read through Platonist lenses could finally be seen as dualistic. In psychology and biology, the separation of mind from brain and reason from emotions began to be erased. And in philosophy, the movements of phenomenology, existentialism, and hermeneutics also stressed the interweaving of mind, body, and language. The more recent development of ecological theology supports a stronger immersion of the self in nature. The various quests for the historical Jesus are also related as they moved toward setting Jesus within his Jewish milieu and have stressed the "fully human" side of the creedal confessions more than ever in Christian history.[13]

The "linguistic turn" in theology and biblical studies has emphasized a renewed sense of the way the "medium is the message" in Scripture and preaching. The related rise in narrative and metaphorical theologies has contributed to a "postpropositionalist" turn in theology. Ricoeur himself has contributed, as we shall see, to these movements, directly and indirectly. The rise of various liberation theologies has appropriated Ricoeur's emphasis on the hermeneutics of suspicion and relates to his own rethinking of the Marxist critical tradition. Ricoeur touched base also with the upsurge of hope and eschatology in theology, connecting especially with Jürgen Moltmann's "theology of hope."[14]

For a variety of reasons, Ricoeur practiced a "conceptual asceticism" between philosophy and religion, segregating carefully

these writings in his own work (Kearney 2004: 45). The value of
this division is that it renders his philosophy open to a variety of
appropriations in theology, across the spectrum from liberal to
conservative. As we shall see when we examine his thought more
closely in the following chapters, his own ad hoc theological and
religious reflections are not tightly integrated with his philosophy
nor do they represent the one and only application of his philosophy
to theology. On the other hand, Ricoeur did not refrain from
directly tackling religious issues. These theological and exegetical
forays do give some hints, more than one has in most philosophers,
without being systematic, of how his philosophy can be in dialogue
with theology. His own philosophy of the holistic self itself actually
undermines the possibility of such a compartmentalization, a
dynamic that he himself saw toward the end of his life, seeing such a
distinction that he had drawn as no longer tenable (Kearney 2004:
45). Despite his own division of the disciplines, his writings, in one
of his favorite expressions, "give rise to thought," much thought,
in relation to the current situation of theology. He himself, in part
due to his lack of interest in theology per se, did not spell all of
this out, although some would look favorably on his occasional
theological reflections.[15] He was the kind of thinker who did not
even necessarily carefully integrate all of his philosophical thought
but tended to make one detour after another without clearly
making the return. The growing interest in his thought after he
died reflects the interest in both the promise and the challenge of
working out those connections.

3

The framework
for theology

Ricoeur did not particularly treat theology itself in a thematic way, but my argument in this chapter is that his philosophy nevertheless offers a fruitful framework for doing theology. His hermeneutical philosophy has an affinity for theology, as we have mentioned, because theology is also deeply hermeneutical and focuses on the interpretation of texts, events, and experiences. Ricoeur's careful development of a distinctive hermeneutical arc that deals with all of these provides a backdrop for considering the challenges for revisioning theology in the kind of transitional context considered in the previous chapter. In this chapter, therefore, I will treat first the hermeneutical arc and its related sequel, the narrative arc, and then their implications for theologizing.

The hermeneutical arc

After Ricoeur's engagement with Freud and with critical theory in the 1960s, he published extensively on the philosophy of metaphor in the 1970s and began considering the implications for narrative. In the process, he worked out a hermeneutical arc that was largely a response to two challenges (Ricoeur 1976a, 1981f). In general, he dealt with the divide in Continental philosophy between explanation (*Erklärung*) and understanding (*Verstehen*) (Ricoeur 1981f: 209). Second, he responded to the emergence of structuralism as a powerful movement in the 1950s and 1960s in France (Hawkes 1977; Stiver 1996: 163–80).

The legacy of hermeneutics after Wilhelm Dilthey (1833–1911) was to see it as the privileged approach to human studies

(*Geisteswissenschaften*) as opposed to the studies in the natural sciences (*Naturwissenschaften*) (Ricoeur 1991a: 58–63). In the Anglo-American world, the humanities and social sciences correspond to the *Geisteswissenschaften*, while the natural sciences correspond to the *Naturwissenschaften*. Gadamer's *Truth and Method*, which was published in 1960 and very influential on Ricoeur, defended the value of hermeneutics for the *Geisteswissenschaften* as opposed to the heavy reliance on objective method in the *Naturwissenschaften*. The prestige of the natural sciences has continually worked on the one hand to draw the *Geisteswissenschaften* into a scientific, objective approach that minimizes the human element. On the other hand, this pressure has tended to marginalize these other approaches as either "soft" sciences or not as science at all—and thus perhaps not even counting as knowledge. Gadamer was dealing with the tendency especially to see art or aesthetics as not saying anything about truth or reality (Gadamer 1991: Part 1). This tendency on the Continent was matched by New Criticism in the United States that made a similar point about the autonomy of the text concerning poetry and other artistic texts (Hawkes 1977: 151–3). One may note here that theology has experienced the same kind of bifurcation due to the privileging of scientific or instrumental rationality in modernity. On the one hand, theology has been pulled toward making itself objective or scientific. This is not only true in liberal attempts to justify the truth of religion in science or philosophy, for example, in David Tracy's use of process philosophy in *Blessed Rage for Order* (Tracy 1979) but also among evangelicals, who especially in the nineteenth century saw themselves as treating the Bible as an encyclopedia of facts that are studied objectively and scientifically (Marsden 2006: 56, 110–11). On the other hand, there has been a tendency toward fideism on the conservative side, and on the liberal side a Kantian split between scientific findings on the one hand and religious truth on the other that is in a category or realm immune from scientific and historical investigation.[1]

Dissatisfied with this kind of dichotomous approach to the *Naturwissenschaften* and the *Geisteswissenschaften*, Ricoeur developed a dialectical relationship between the two in a creative hermeneutical arc that at the same time undermines paradigmatic themes in modernity (Ricoeur 1980c). Reflecting his and Gadamer's stance in the hermeneutical tradition, Ricoeur affirmed that the first stage of the hermeneutical arc is one of hermeneutical "understanding." To take a text as the example, this represents an initial, holistic grasp of the meaning of the text, which would include the full human dimension of purpose and emotions. Ricoeur is clear that such an understanding is not a detached, neutral appraisal since the attempt to understand always comes "too late" for such detachment. Following Heidegger and Gadamer, he affirms that we are immersed in tradition and language long before we are critically self-conscious. Our understanding of a particular text at a first reading includes much that is unconscious and which occurs without much reflection, just as we understand our native language quickly without having to think about it. In one of Gadamer's prominent images, it is especially at this point that we are "played" by the game as much as we play, or are in control, of the game (Gadamer 1991: 101–10). In light of Ricoeur's phrase about a later stage of the arc, this stage could be called a naïve understanding. If one thinks of a fictional work like Mark Twain's *Huckleberry Finn* or even a philosophic work like Plato's *Republic*, this first understanding may represent a surface level grasp or perhaps even intimation of wider significance such as a critique of racism in the former and a critique of democracy in the latter. Nevertheless, even such insights remain as intimations to be further tested.

Where Ricoeur differs from a typical hermeneutical appeal to reread the text is in the second stage or moment of "explanation." Here Ricoeur allows for "methods" to be utilized in analyzing texts. It is at this point that he went beyond both Heidegger and Gadamer in preferring a "long route" to understanding (Ricoeur 1974b: 11). At the time, his main example was structuralist methodology (Ricoeur 1981f: 216, 1981g: 153). Structuralism looked for "deep," underlying codes, often binary oppositions, such as light and dark or native and foreign that could even be pervasive through a range of a culture's customs or folk tales. It represented a kind of objective, more scientific analysis appropriate to texts. Ricoeur was perhaps too engrossed in the idea of structuralism at the time to spell out other kinds of methods, but one can easily imagine here in biblical and theological studies the full range of "criticisms" at the time, including structuralist, literary, form, redaction, sociological, and tradition criticism (Ricoeur 1980a: 44; Scalise 1994: 70). One would now also draw on ideological, deconstructionist, postcolonial, and liberationist criticisms.

Ricoeur had earlier spoken of a "hermeneutic of suspicion" in his Freud studies, where one especially looked for covert ideology. This emphasis was continued in his adjudication of the debate between Gadamer and Jürgen Habermas, where Ricoeur affirmed Habermas' emphasis on ideology critique as long as it did not assume to transcend the impact of tradition and hermeneutical preunderstanding, which Gadamer emphasized. Interestingly, in Ricoeur's further discussion of ideology critique around the time he was explicating this hermeneutical circle, he thought that ideology is best countered by utopia, which points in a different direction than "explanatory," scientific methods.[2] This approach involves the imagination and figurative language as a means of critique, which has implications for considering systematic theology as a form of critique. With these approaches in mind, the second stage is a critical phase where the emphasis is on analysis by means of various methodologies, or in the sense of utopia, in terms of alternative imaginative schemes. In the end, these test one's initial grasp of meaning and help to expand the understanding. On this point, Ricoeur said, "To explain more is to understand better" (Ricoeur 1984: 5). If one adds his dialectic of ideology and utopia, the second stage can also be seen sometimes as involving an imaginative, metaphorical alternative that is critical while also being figurative. In other words, the critical mind is also imaginative, which is easier to see when one does not play off the explanatory methods, say in science, against the configurative aspects of the humanities. As science has also come to be seen as involving metaphors and models as deeply embedded in its critical, explanatory work (Barbour 1997: 115–24), theology can be seen as both prosaically systematic (methodological) but also imaginative, metaphorical, and configurative—but more on this later.

If one understands the complex dynamic between different kinds of thinking as understanding and explanation, then it is easier to see Ricoeur's breakthrough suggestion that goes beyond Gadamer in bringing distantiation into the picture as a complement—and not a detriment—to hermeneutics. Ricoeur stressed that Gadamer's distinctive emphasis is on the way that "belonging" is essential to hermeneutics (Ricoeur 1981a). We belong to a tradition and a culture in what Gadamer called a historically effected consciousness (*Wirkungsgeschichtliches Bewusstseins*) (Gadamer 1991: 301). Ricoeur agreed with Gadamer that we cannot escape this fundamental hermeneutical situation, which helps us get the interpretation going.

On the other hand, Ricoeur thought that criticism at a deep level is also intrinsic to hermeneutics, and not extrinsic to it as Habermas thought, especially in the situation of written texts. Ricoeur points out that in written texts the writing is disconnected from the author in significant ways. In many cases, we do not even know the author, as in folk tales and most of the scriptural writings. In others, the text may be the result of multiple authors and editors such as a constitution or, again, many of the biblical writings. The span of time and culture offers an unavoidable gap, which some have thought cannot be bridged.

In Ricoeur's criticism of the meaning as the author's intent, seen as the Romantic view of Friedrich Schleiermacher (1768–1834), Dilthey, and in more nuanced ways by more recent thinkers such as Emilio Betti (1890–1968), E. D. Hirsch, and Nicholas Wolterstorff, Ricoeur argued, first, that we cannot know the mind of the author. Second, the public nature of the way that speech is fixed in writing means that the meaning is again distanced from the author's intent. Ricoeur here made the kind of point that the later Wittgenstein emphasized, namely, that language is not something that people privately control but is something that precedes us and transcends us (Wittgenstein 1958; Kerr 1986; Labron 2009). Gadamer made this point provocatively in saying that it is as true to say that language speaks us as we speak language (Gadamer 1991: 463). The words, grammar, and also larger structures of genre are means of expression in language that are not entirely under the control of the author. Ricoeur said:

> The spirituality of discourse manifests itself through writing, which frees us from the visibility and limitation of situations by opening up a world for us, that is, new dimensions of our being-in-the-world.
>
> In this sense, Heidegger rightly says—in his analysis of *verstehen* in *Being and Time*—that what we understand first in a discourse is not another person, but a project, that is, the outline of a new being-in-the-world. Only writing, in freeing itself, not only from its author, but from the narrowness of the dialogical situation, reveals this destination of discourse as projecting a world.[3]

Against other misunderstandings, Ricoeur does not deny that texts are "authorless" and actually says that authors are still relevant but the relationship becomes complex. He clarified, "Not that we can conceive of a text without an author; the tie between the speaker and the discourse is not abolished, but distended and complicated."[4] His point is that knowing an author is not crucial to understanding a text, which is a good thing, or the understanding of much ancient literature, such as the Bible, would be impossible. If one does know an author, however, and the context of the author, it can contribute to understanding the fuller meaning of a text.

At this point, Ricoeur distinguished between the presence of speech and the distantiation of writing, but we can take cues from his later work and also the work of Jacques Derrida to point out that many of the same distantiating dynamics are involved in speech as well. In one of Ricoeur's last works, *On Translation*, he says that translation is never exact and always involves more or less adequacy. He goes on to say that one can think of discourse *within* a language as a kind of translation (Ricoeur 2006). This means that interpretation is involved in any communication. Derrida went further, as we saw in the last chapter, in his critique of a "metaphysics of presence," which he saw pervading Western philosophy, in showing how the interpretation involved in speech contains the dynamics of interpretation that are more clearly seen in writing.[5] This distantiation (Ricoeur) or absence (Derrida) makes room for and calls for interpretation—and critique—at the heart of hermeneutics itself. In light of this, we might modify the above quotation to read that writing especially reveals distantiation—but not that it is only revealed in writing. One can certainly imagine narration and oral storytelling, if not virtually all communication, as involving a degree of the distantiation that is more clearly seen in writing, especially of ancient texts where the author or authors are not known.

In terms of the virtual denial of any extratextual reference often found in structuralism and in New Criticism, however, Ricoeur both argued for the value of these methodologies and also resisted their closure to the "world of the text." Like Gadamer, who affirmed the "truth of the work of art," Ricoeur thought that the energy expended in analysis was somewhat fruitless without referential implications for grasping the world outside of or in front of the text. In speaking of the way that texts actually refer to an existential world outside the text, Ricoeur said, "Structural analysis merely represses this function. But it cannot suppress it" (Ricoeur

1981f: 217). Ricoeur points out that structuralism can hardly move from deep structures to meaning, much less from the text to the world. In fact, Ricoeur's emphasis to the contrary lay on the power of texts through human imagination to convey a "world." Texts can describe or recreate a world through the "reproductive" imagination, but Ricoeur was more interested in the power of texts to redescribe or project a creative world through the "productive" imagination (Taylor 2006). His common reference to the way that our identity is the result of all the books that we have read picks up on the way that we are shaped by these literary "worlds" (Ricoeur 1984: 80). And in considering the impact of the Scripture, we can think of the way that not just individuals but whole communities are shaped by the worlds or world portrayed in the Scripture. Ricoeur sometimes used the language of sense and reference, drawn from analytical philosophy, to make this point. He related "sense" to the way that structuralism uncovers the specific structure of a text and "reference" to the way of being in the world that a text projects. As we shall see, he soon found this terminology cumbersome. "Reference" helped him move beyond the strictures of structuralism to an extratextual implication, but structuralism's stress on the deep structures of a text did not fully convey the constructed sense of a text. This terminology was developed in terms of propositions, but Ricoeur's turn to narrative and figurative language in general inclined to a different terminology.

In more apt terminology, this power of projecting a world points to the third stage of the hermeneutical arc, namely, a second understanding or as he variously called it, application, appropriation, or a postcritical naïveté. It is a rich point that involves numerous facets, some more credible than others. The fact that it is an "understanding" means that it is again holistic. In contrast to the emphasis upon analysis, even dissection, in the second stage, this is a synthetic appropriation of the world of the text for oneself. The emphasis upon application means that the text is not an inert object lying upon the table upon which one has operated but becomes a living part of oneself in some way. It makes a difference. It again calls not only for the will engaged in action but also for bodily, emotional appropriation. It is thus holistic like the first understanding and gives rise to one of Ricoeur's most apt phrases, a "postcritical" understanding, which he had enunciated already in the closing chapter of The Symbolism of Evil (Ricoeur 1967: 352).

The "postcritical" can perhaps be seen in terms of the modern-postmodern dynamic (Ricoeur 1967: 352). Ricoeur at times correlated these moments of the hermeneutical arc with epochs. He actually goes back to the premodern to correlate with the first naïveté before the advent of the Enlightenment, the rise of modern science, and the rise of modern biblical criticism. He sees the "modern" emphasis on explanation as valuable. In reaction to the withering criticisms of modernity, there is a reactionary tendency to avoid criticism. Ricoeur did not make this point, but the extensive study of fundamentalism now tends to see it as a modern reaction, one which avoids criticism of its foundations (although fundamentalists may well criticize extensively modernity and now postmodernity) (Barr 1981). Even with Ricoeur's trenchant criticisms of modernity, he stressed that we must move into the critical moment. At this point, one can see that people are not compelled to move through all three stages but may remain at any level. Ricoeur, however, urges that we should not remain "stuck" either in the precritical or the critical stage, which in this analysis implies an inability to be critical and then an inability to commit or to appropriate, in other words, to act. The latter malady is often seen in academia, among students and professors, where "paralysis by analysis" comes from seeing the holes that can be poked in virtually any large-scale position. Theology students often struggle with relating the understanding of profuse approaches to the biblical text and theology to their faith affirmations. Scientists themselves have struggled with the problem of "anomalies" in virtually any large-scale theory and wonder whether they totally discount a theory. The common conclusion at this point is that such criticisms or anomalies have to be taken seriously but should not paralyze further investigation and use of theories (Murphy 1990: Ch. 3). Ricoeur similarly urged that one should be willing to "wager," one of his favorite words, on taking a position, despite difficulties. The fact that it is a "postcritical" position, however, means that it is not a fideistic "leap in the dark," disconnected from extensive method, arguments, and evidence, as we shall see in Chapter 6. What it does mean is that such holistic judgments invariably go beyond such objective evidence; in other words, the objective evidence and arguments "underdetermine" the conclusions.

At this juncture, Ricoeur is taking up Gadamer's point that method does not suffice to lead to conviction. In the words of a later book of interviews with Ricoeur, Ricoeur desired to take up Gadamer's emphasis on conviction but combine it with critique by setting them within the dynamics of his hermeneutical arc (Ricoeur 1998). At the same time he was working out the hermeneutical arc, Ricoeur was developing a "hermeneutics of testimony," which also points to the way in which affirmations of the Absolute are based on evidence but transcend it in a wager to which one's life is a witness (a martyr) (Ricoeur 1980c). In essays on the subject where he surprisingly drew on Hirsch whose emphasis on authorial intent he was rejecting, Ricoeur likened this hermeneutical appropriation to making a "probable guess" at the meaning, a kind of calculus of probability for validation appropriate to texts just as science uses a calculus of probability for verification (Ricoeur 1981c:175, 1981f: 211–12).

The fact that this is a second "understanding" also means that its dynamics changes from the distantiation involved in explanation to the kind of "subjectivity" that Soren Kierkegaard (1813–55) would emphasize in terms of personal truth. Kierkegaard was not necessarily implying, in saying that "truth is subjectivity," that such a truth affirmation is not valid or based on nothing, but he meant that it is what we would now call an existential affirmation (Kierkegaard 1941: 169–79). It is my own, as in the difference between a study of cancer and hearing the verdict that "You have cancer."

In passing, this is one of the common misunderstandings of Ricoeur by numerous theologians. In emphasizing this subjective, existential nature of appropriation of texts, some have thought that he countenanced no objective reference at all. In this sense, one appropriates a world in which God gives meaning to life, but that does not necessarily mean that there is a God. As long as a text has subjective effect, that is all that is necessary. This interpretation would place Ricoeur with noncognitive approaches to religion.[6] Ricoeur, however, expressly rejects such an interpretation in his insistence upon reference over against structuralism's denial of it. One could say that personal, existential appropriation is a *necessary* condition of the second understanding, but it is not a *sufficient* condition. If the "world" one appropriates implies the Absolute of a certain nature, it is a testimony, a wager, to that effect. To be sure, the objective evidence would far underdetermine the conclusion, but it does not negate the conclusion. Ricoeur at this time also thought that philosophy of religion could not by itself make the theological affirmation; that was a testimony that belonged to faith. In the end,

Ricoeur emphasized the existential dimension, but his uniqueness, one could say, is that he includes and integrates the objective in a postcritical way. Conviction is reached *through* critique, even suspicion, and not *in spite of* it.

The word "naïveté" in the postcritical appropriation also underscores holistic, existential appropriation. It indicates that the way of thinking is different than in criticism, as Dilthey saw so well. One can perhaps grasp this by other examples that Ricoeur does not use. For instance, one can think of the way in performances such as drama and sports that playing primarily in the critical, analytical mode inhibits good performance. There is a time for criticism, but usually after the performance. It is a well-attested phenomenon in sports by the epithet of "choking" where falling into the critical mode at the wrong time can be disastrous to performance.[7] Similarly, in the postcritical naïveté, one might say that there is a delicate balance of focusing on the holistic, existential appropriation while having the benefits of all of one's criticism in the background. While this may sound odd, again, in performances such as drama and sports, it is common. One studies one's lines and critically practices and scrutinizes one's performance beforehand, but in the moment, one acts without the focus being on the criticism—yet benefitting from all the criticism. One swings a bat or shoots a basketball with all of the benefit of watching a film, but in the moment, one cannot be thinking about the film and the piecemeal breakdown of each aspect of such actions. Action is holistic; Ricoeur implies that the full range of interpretation is an action in that respect.

In fact, Ricoeur significantly turned the hermeneutical arc to events and not just texts, which has had an influence in sociology (Ricoeur 1981f). Events are also interpreted. We grasp them with an initial understanding, critically reflect upon them, and critically appropriate them. Ricoeur revealed here a way in which hermeneutics is enlarged in the way that Gadamer sees the "universality of hermeneutics" but with more specificity.

With the basic picture of the hermeneutic arc in mind, we can further extend it in various ways. Ricoeur pointed out that it should not be understood always as three distinct actions that temporally follow in sequential fashion. They sometimes occur closely together and can only be distinguished conceptually. Also, as Ricoeur himself noted, often the actions of the arc continue in a spiral, where even with a postcritical appropriation, one may continue to reflect on it critically and perhaps modify or reject it (Ricoeur 1981c: 171).

Despite Ricoeur's treatment in other contexts of a hermeneutics of suspicion, in these contexts, he usually thought in terms of a basically positive appropriation, however critical and nuanced. One can, however, also think of a negative appropriation. For example, one may see *Gone with the Wind* and appreciate some dimensions of it but reject its nostalgic racism of a lost South. One is still, in a way, impacted by the work. In Gadamer's terms, there is still a "fusion of horizons" (Gadamer 1991: 306). One understands the work, perhaps very extensively due to a deep ideology critique, and one's horizon is widened thus not by appropriating the work positively but negatively in broadening one's understanding and rejection of racism. One might think here of Ricoeur's own critical appreciation of Marx or structuralism where he offers major criticism of both but it is clear that they contribute to his conclusions. In this sense, the world projected by the text in front of the text is rejected as a whole, but it is also possible to appropriate the world in front of the text in a nuanced and partial manner. For example, one might take up Augustine's *Confessions* as a way that God works intimately in one's life but not in the strong, controlling sense of meticulous providence that Augustine assumes, even to the point that God finally determines the elect. In other words, an Arminian Open Theist, who rejects any kind of irresistible grace (in Augustine or Calvin), could still find value in the intimate, engaged interaction with God implicit in Augustine's work but reject the more specific portrayal of divine providence that is presented there as a "possible world in which we might live." Another example is the way that Ricoeur scholar Pamela Anderson, drawing on Luce Irigaray's work, points to the way that myths such as Antigone can be creatively reconfigured or "mimed" to undergird a feminist interpretation.[8]

This discussion points to a certain ambiguity in Ricoeur's writings on this subject. He did not always distinguish clearly between the world "of the text" and the world "in front of the text."[9] At other times, he seems to distinguish between the world of the text and the world in front of the text, where they correspond to moments of explanation and appropriation, respectively. The latter use is helpful especially in considering a work of fiction, for one can

distinguish clearly between the task of understanding the fictional
"world," say of *Huckleberry Finn* or *Gone with the Wind*, and the
way that world might refer and be appropriated by a much later
reader. Structuralism, for example, operates on the world of the
text in the former sense. Ricoeur, however, is best read as implying
that "the world of the text" opens up a possible world "in front of
the text" in which we might live and which we might appropriate,
in partial or full ways. This is more transparent in the case of
fiction, but it can also be applied to nonfictional works such as
history. For example, the account of the Civil War in the North
and the South in the United States often varies. The history may
be largely accurate, but the emphasis and nuances of vocabulary
point to a world in front of the text as a way for later generations
to regard the issue of race. In Ricoeur's later work on narrative,
he sees both fiction and historiography as highly "configured,"
having significant artistic—and ideological—elements. Both in this
sense portray a world. Both can be appropriated in ways that go
beyond the world of the text itself. Another example is Ricoeur's
own consideration of the contentious history of the Vichy regime,
which collaborated with Nazi Germany and the other Axis powers
after France's defeat in World War II. Ricoeur dealt with this under
the heading of "Forgetting and Manipulated Memory" in *Memory,
History, Forgetting* (Ricoeur 2004: 448–52). One can easily think
here also of biblical narratives, seeing, for example, a narrative
about Abraham or the more highly developed Gospel narratives
as reflecting a world of the text that points toward ways in which
they might be appropriated in very different contexts. In fact, this
is the way that biblical scholars would say that they functioned
in the Bible, usually being written at a much later time for a later
audience. The writings were passed down and later canonized for
the purpose of being appropriated by yet later generations who
lived in quite different conditions and who thus could not simply
take over literally the "world of the text." In this more explicit
sense, the "world in front of the text" is a creative appropriation
of "the world of the text." For example, Kevin Vanhoozer's book,
The Drama of Doctrine, which emphasizes that the biblical text is
more like a script (the world of the text) that must be performed
or enacted in creative, improvisatory ways in new contexts (the
world in front of the text), expresses this relationship well in a way
quite consistent with Ricoeur.[10] The "script" has to be performed

in Vanhoozer's language, or appropriated in Ricoeur's language, before it can be said to be fully understood.

The narrative arc

In order to deal further with these narrative "worlds," however, we can draw on Ricoeur's own further delineation of a later kind of arc that he developed in treating narrative in the 1980s. In his three-volume *Time and Narrative*, published in English from 1984–88 (French 1983–85), Ricoeur was treating multiple themes, and given its length he did not apply it broadly. In a sense, the completion of *Time and Narrative* is *Oneself as Another* (1992). The English translator, David Pellauer, notes that Ricoeur actually developed the idea of narrative identity, which is so prominent in *Oneself as Another*, in the course of writing *Time and Narrative*; the term does not appear until the third volume.[11] As the title suggests, *Time and Narrative* is dealing with making sense of the human experience of time, a quest that is reminiscent of Heidegger's incomplete famous work, *Being and Time*. In the process, Ricoeur especially envisaged narrative as the way that humans bring together the linear, cosmic time of clocks and physics with experiential, lived time. In turn, in dealing with narrative, he especially engaged the vexed relationship of historiography and fiction in terms of their common nature as narratives, challenging especially the modern view that would distinguish them almost entirely with historiography relating to reality and fiction with fantasy (nonreality). Ricoeur concluded that both historiography and fiction involve configuration or are "mimetic." They are both constructive works of the imagination, involving artful selection, focus, and emplotment. He thus saw both as involving a three-fold mimesis or "figuration," which he delineated as mimesis$_1$, mimesis$_2$, and mimesis$_3$ (Ricoeur 1984: Ch. 3).

He also named these perhaps more straightforwardly as prefiguration, configuration, and refiguration. Ricoeur is following Aristotle here more than Plato in his appropriation of mimesis (imitation) (Ricoeur 1984: 45). Art for Aristotle is not in Plato's terms an "imitation" of the real but in a sense a revelation of the real or in more contemporary terms, a creative interpretation if not creation of the real. Understanding is thus not primarily a work of the analytical reason beloved by the Enlightenment but is an act of imagination. Ricoeur, of course, in terms of his earlier hermeneutical arc saw such analytical reason in terms of method as working congruently with the creative imagination, just in a different way in the narrative or "mimetic" arc.

The fact that one again has something of a three-fold hermeneutical arc and shares at least the last term—refiguration being used in relation to the earlier "application" or "appropriation"—raises the question of how they are related. Ricoeur himself did not explain their connection and the tendency is to collapse them together. A closer look reveals significant differences, however, but both arcs, so to speak, can interact in fruitful ways.

Ricoeur saw prefiguration as involving what one brings to the text, so to speak, as writer or reader. It is one's preunderstanding, in Heideggerian terms, and the influence of tradition, in Gadamerian terms. It draws on experience that is already symbolically shaped, already a nascent story, as Ricoeur indicated, "If, in fact, human action can be narrated, it is because it is always already articulated by signs, rules, and norms. It is always already symbolically mediated" (Ricoeur 1984: 57). It thus includes the influence of one's language and also more specifically expectations of genre and forms of speech. For example, in modern terms, one expects historiography to be more objective and not an apologetic for a larger point of view, as many ancient "histories" were. One expects fiction also to fulfill certain expectations and would not be looking particularly for accurate historical figures. In postmodernity, one could say, we have seen these expectations modified by realizing that historiography, while attempting to be objective and faithful to documents and evidence, still always reflects a certain point of view, some more obvious than others. Conversely, the popular genre of historical fiction blurs the same lines by attempting to be true to the broad lines of historical data but freely creates characters, situations, and dialogues. Still, it would be a blunder for such fiction to make large mistakes of history, for example, getting the winner of the Civil War in the United States wrong. This prefiguration is therefore already "figured" in significant ways and colors the way we approach any text.

The second stage of "configuration" reveals especially the creative imagination at work. Whether fiction or history, a narrative is constructed among a virtual infinity of possibilities. Particularly, a plot is constructed, which Ricoeur follows Aristotle in conceiving as bringing a "synthesis out of the heterogeneous" (Ricoeur 1984: 66). As Ricoeur said of Augustine, "In short, the act of narrating, reflected in the act of following a story, makes productive the paradoxes that disquieted Augustine to the point of reducing him to silence" (68). Even as Ricoeur desired to move, with the help of Aristotle, beyond Augustinian silence, he continued to stress the fragility and incompleteness of the synthesis.

The creative act of emplotment is best understood in terms of an author. An author configures a narrative out of multiple resources, which is as true of the historian as of the fiction writer. After bringing the two types of authors closer together, much closer than many more modern-oriented thinkers would like, Ricoeur wanted nevertheless to distinguish the two in a relative sense. Historians, he emphasizes here and also later in *Memory, History, Forgetting*, must pay "a debt to the past" (Ricoeur 1988: 157). They are responsible to be faithful to the traces, archives, and documents of the past in a way that fiction is not. While still being basically mimetic, histories attempt to portray accurately the evidence that we have of the past. On the other hand, while fiction's configurative dimension is larger, Ricoeur pointed out that there is also an attempt to portray a possible world accurately, which bears a connection to the lived world (177). We saw this in the above example of historical fiction, but it is also true in the sense of a fiction writer trying to convey experiences of sadness and tragedy. There is a verisimilitude that has to be maintained to human experience or the attempt fails. Ricoeur is insistent that both are imaginative and revealing, "This critique of the naïve concept of 'reality' applied to the pastness of the past calls for a systematic critique of the no less naïve concept of 'unreality' applied to the projections of fiction. The function of standing-for or of taking-the-place-of is paralleled in fiction by the function it possesses, with respect to everyday practice, of being undividedly revealing and transforming" (158). Both therefore have a referential sense, which points to the third stage, refiguration.

The third stage of refiguration is perhaps best conceived in terms of a reader. Ricoeur continues to assume his earlier language of a text "projecting a possible world in which we might live." Another way in which he expressed it is, "What is interpreted in a text is the proposing of a world that I might inhabit and into which I might project my ownmost powers" (Ricoeur 1984: 81). Here in the mimetic arc as in the hermeneutical arc, the third moment of the arc is one of appropriation that he terms refiguration to place emphasis on the creative imagination. This projection of a possible world is perhaps more clearly seen in terms of the narrative arc than the hermeneutical arc. A narrative imaginatively implies or "refers" to a way in which it can be appropriated, a way of life as it were. As one can see, Ricoeur has dropped his earlier language of "sense and reference," which belonged to a logical discourse somewhat inappropriate to narrative in favor of figuration or mimesis (Ricoeur 1988: 158). He nevertheless still saw that a text must be holistically appropriated in a second understanding in terms of its claim upon reality. Refiguration involves a wager about what is "true" of a text, whether history or fiction.

In light of this narrative arc, Ricoeur has drawn both historiography and fiction together, while still allowing for them to be relatively distinct—no mean achievement in itself. In the next chapter, we will consider how this approach may fruitfully be applied to the Gospel genre in the New Testament, which has been caught in the buzz saw between scholars oriented either to them as history or as fiction. In the larger sense, he has indicated how both cosmic and human time can be drawn together and made meaningful through narrative, thus overcoming the complete discordance between them as seen in Kant and Heidegger—again, no mean achievement.

For our purposes, however, he has offered an elaboration of his hermeneutics in some tension with his earlier hermeneutical arc. First, however, there are some tensions in the narrative arc. As mentioned in the explanation, he seemed most clearly to envisage the second moment of configuration in terms of a writer and the third moment in terms of a reader—yet without signaling clearly the relationship between the two. The first moment of prefiguration could fruitfully apply to both (Gorospe 2006). Or one could think of authors all the way through. The authors bring their prefiguration to the creative task of configuration and intend through the text to convey a possible world for the reader's refiguration. Perhaps they refigure themselves in the process! One might apply this process, for instance, not just to fiction or history but to systematic theologies.

Conversely, one could think of the reader all the way through. The reader brings preunderstanding to a text and then must configure the world of the text, following the cues of the text. At the point of refiguration, especially, Ricoeur himself brings in "reader-response theory," which grew out of phenomenology as a description of the experience of reading (Ricoeur 1984: 70–87, 1988: Ch. 7). Often people assume that the text is complete in itself, but actually a text artfully includes some things and leaves out others. A movie similarly focuses on a shot that implies much else besides. It leaves the rest to the reader's imagination, we say. A good book or movie neither conveys too little nor too much, which may be the difference between pornography and art. Wolfgang Iser points out how texts intentionally leave gaps that are clues to be filled in by the reader (Iser 1974: 96). The biblical writer known as J in the Pentateuch, for example, Genesis Chapters 2–4, is recognized for being a master of understatement. In the story of Cain and Abel, for example, Cain's wrong is never actually stated, being left to the imagination of the reader. Such a writer places a great deal of responsibility, one might say, on the reader's imagination even to be able to read the story, much less theologize extensively about it.

Reader-response theory applies especially at the point of refiguration, but it applies as well, as in Iser, to configuration of the world of the text in the cases of fiction and history.[12] In the J narrative above and in the fictional world of *Huckleberry Finn*, the reader must imagine much that is only suggested in the books, especially if one is quite unfamiliar with the Middle Eastern context or the pre-bellum south and the Mississippi River. Nevertheless, since the novel is ironic in using racist language to criticize racism, the reader must especially be creative at the point of refiguration. The distinction here between the world of the text and the world in front of the text is rather sharp. In the Cain and Abel story, one brings one's prefiguration to the reading, which may involve a high view of the Scripture and an expectation to find trustworthy meaning, based on one's being traditioned into the Bible as the Holy Scripture. This likely also involves one's experiences of temptation, generosity and jealousy, cheerful and uncheerful giving to God, and even of sibling strife. Then one must imaginatively engage the story at a high level, since the J writer is so suggestive. One may alternately take on the role of Cain and Abel, as in the process of *lectio divina*. The refiguration may involve appropriating the story in terms of a personal struggle with temptation "crouching at the door" (Gen. 4:6, NIV) at home in the twenty-first century.

When one thinks of a genre such as systematic theology, the story is more complex. In the case of a contemporary theologian such as Jürgen Moltmann, there may be little difference between the world of the text and the world in front of the text. Realizing that systematic theology is a modern genre, there is perhaps more of a difference in reading the work of Augustine or Calvin in search of a systematic theology. One has to take into account not only the difference in genre but also their context generally, which differs radically from the contemporary context, for instance, their reliance on church-state alliance long before modern democracies rather than separation of church and state in a contemporary democracy, leading both to use the sword of the state to enforce religious beliefs, against the Donatists in Augustine's (354–430) case and against Servetus in Calvin's (1509–64) case. So even here, one can distinguish between a world of the text and a way in which that world might be appropriated in a quite different context.

In this sense, the world in front of the text likely goes far beyond any putative intention of the author, who could not have imagined a twenty-first century world. This is a point that underscores the previous discussion of the hermeneutical arc as not focusing on authorial intent. The world in front of the text may be largely intended by the author, or, one might say, the text, but in most cases when there is historical distance involved, it goes beyond such intentions. Usually, there is then a critical appropriation or fusion of horizons that again involves the creative imagination. Numerous contemporaries appropriate in largely positive terms Augustine's political theology in *The City of God*, but one still would say that it is a creative application to a much different context. Calvin is sometimes fairly literally appropriated in terms of his view of providence but at other times is quite creatively appropriated, yet with justification appealing to a Reformed sensibility. Moltmann as a Reformed theologian would be a significant example here as would the "feminist Calvinists" in the American Academy of Religion.[13]

Focus on narrative and systematic theology also enriches the hermeneutical arc. As we saw earlier, the second moment focused on analytical criticism, but one could ask about the constructive or synthetic dimension of criticism. Specifically, if one is testing one's first, naïve reading of a text with a critical reading, even in terms of various analytical methodologies, is there not a place where one critically—and imaginatively—"configures" the world of the text and even the possible refigurations of the text? At this point, one might feel that the arcs may be morphing into a simple blur. I think, however, that they can mutually support one another. The dimension of configuration can fruitfully be considered in critical reflection. One can think of a creative film review, which breaks down the film, to be sure, but also creatively recasts—reconfigures—the way one sees the film. I will suggest in the latter part of this chapter the way that systematic theology itself, surely a basically configurative activity, can function as critical reflection upon the primary sources of religious faith such as prayer, worship, the Scripture, and acts of service and justice. Systematic theology's relation to its sources in this sense is something like a film review to the film. Adding Ricoeur's notion of utopia as critical imagination to the notion of theology, we can see here also the way theology is not just a configurative activity but an imaginative one, deeply drawing on root metaphors and underlying key narratives. For example, Reformed theologians usually draw on the Reformation narrative involving Calvin in particular that is quite distinct from the larger presupposed narratives of the Roman Catholic and Eastern Orthodox churches that presume an origin and validity in the early church.

Conversely, the hermeneutical arc can enrich the narrative arc. This is a bit complex, but one could apply the hermeneutical arc to each stage of the narrative arc. If one analyzes one's prefiguration, one begins obviously with a first or naïve grasp. Then one critically reflects on it, perhaps with methods such as ideology critique. One can then move to a postcritical assessment and grasp of one's preunderstanding and its influence. At the stage of configuration, likewise, one has an initial grasp, as a reader in this case, of the world of the text. Then one can critically reflect on it and break it down and finally move to a postcritical, holistic understanding of it. This dynamic is perhaps most helpful at the point of refiguration. One's initial grasp of the import of a text or a movie or an event for one's life is often powerful but still relatively uncritical. I think here of the first impact of reading in theology a Karl Barth, a Langdon Gilkey, or Karl Rahner, even of Ricoeur. Consider the impact of books and then movies of *The Lord of the Rings* and *Harry Potter*. Almost naturally, one turns to critical reflection. Have I understood aright the import? Should it have this effect or that? I remember the impact of the movie *Dead Poets Society* (1989), starring Robin Williams, that stirred my deep American and Baptist affirmations of individual freedom. After reading Stanley Hauerwas' critique, however, I reassessed the way it fed my hyper-individualistic culture of prefiguration (Hauerwas 1991). Finally, I have appropriated that movie—and Hauerwas' critique—in a critical way, neither fully embracing nor fully dismissing it.

The last point reminds us that appropriation can involve degrees of positive or negative response. For example, I happened to be in a class with Langdon Gilkey while he was involved in the Arkansas Creationist Trial in the early 1980s, a trial that involved an attempt to require a literal interpretation of Genesis 1 such that the universe is only 6000 years old.[14] I listened to and read his account and accepted it quite positively. This meant, however, that my reading of creationist literature was quite negative. When I read or discussed the issue with creationists, I was influenced in a certain way to think about the world differently, namely, to be more sensitive to the way many people read the Scripture and to the pervasive influence of such readings on the preunderstandings of many others in the church. I thus "appropriated" them, too, albeit through rejecting their standpoint.

Yet one more permutation is helpful. Ricoeur generally spoke of appropriation as the one evaluation that the reader makes. It represents the wager and testimony that one takes from a text. One can think, however, of multiple refigurations. Before I move to my "ownmost" reconfiguration, I likely will consider other possible refigurations. They are not yet appropriated but are possibilities. For example, I considered my initial positive appropriation of Robin Williams' movie, but then I considered Hauerwas' very negative one. I concluded, however, with an appropriation different from either of those. So we might add another moment on the arcs, which is that of possible appropriations or possible refigurations before the distinctive personal one. This multiplication of possibilities is quite appropriate, when we think of the general surplus of meaning that Ricoeur emphasizes. In fact, we might consider various possibilities of meanings of the configuration of a text as well as refigurations, some of which are almost equally plausible to us. This happens frequently in commentaries on the Bible. The commentators see various possibilities in the meaning of a word, a phrase, or a larger passage and are often not decisive about which is best. They give the evidence to the reader to decide. Systematic theologies typically are more determinative but still may leave open, for example, the value of the social and individual analogies of the Trinity, various models of the Atonement, and certainly eschatological visions.[15]

A framework for theology

There is much then in the hermeneutical arc that is relevant to the theological task, whether one is considering the interpretation of the Scripture, of tradition, of experiences, or of events. But what of the role and place of systematic theology itself? To reiterate briefly what we saw in the last chapter, systematic theology has been caught in a vortex of change in the late twentieth century and has struggled to find its footing. Earlier in the century, even with the challenge of neo-Orthodoxy both to liberal theology and to conservative systems of theology, systematic theology had a prominent and respected place. There was a sense in which one could write a universal systematic theology for the church. Those days are largely gone and are often identified as part of the passing of modernity. In its place are a plethora of types of theology and sometimes outright rejection of theology as too rationalistic, foundationalist, and nonnarrative. In reaction, some still claim systematic theology as a kind of timeless, propositional truth. In light of these swirling currents of change both from within and without the church, I suggest that Ricoeur's hermeneutical arc can provide a helpful framework for systematic theology in a postmodern context. Even though Ricoeur himself does not engage directly the implications of his thought for systematic theology, the hermeneutical arc does provide a context for this kind of systematic reflection in the critical moment.

Ricoeur's emphasis that reflection always starts too late, so to speak, is significant in light of the critiques of foundationalism.[16] The idea that one can somewhat neutrally reflect on theology and detachedly consider experience, tradition, and the Scripture is challenged by the emphasis that humans emerge in tradition and experience that is already shaped in deep and pervasive ways that can hardly ever be brought to conscious reflection.

In this sense, one can think of theology especially as a dimension of the second stage of the hermeneutical arc that reflects critically on primary sources of faith such as the Scripture, experience, and tradition. Systematic theology then is a second-order discourse reflecting on the first-order experience and discourse. When

Ricoeur spoke of Christian faith, he typically saw it as refracted through interpretation—but not of theology as much as the texts of Scripture and its many genres. As he said, "This world [of the text] is not presented immediately through psychological intentions but mediately through the structures of the work" (Ricoeur 1991e: 96). He is thinking here of the various biblical genres such as narrative, prophesy, hymns, and wisdom. "The referent 'God,'" he subsequently pointed out, "is at once the coordinator of these diverse discourses and the vanishing point" (97). And then he was quick to add, "In this sense, the word *God* does not function as a philosophical concept, not even that of being" (97). Theology moves, however, to conceptual reflection on this name of God.

This relationship of theology to more primary experiences of faith works against two problematic tendencies related to theology. On the one hand, in the Christian tradition, theology has sometimes taken pride of place where faith is understood largely in terms of belief. Theology becomes then the privileged expression of faith itself, often making both the Scripture and religious experience secondary. The movement is seen as one toward theology from the Scripture and experience. Practice may then be inferred from theology, but the relationship is only one way and sometimes is ignored or neglected. In classical biblical interpretation, there are three aspects: exegesis, which interprets what the text meant; hermeneutics per se, which interprets what it means—the theological task proper; and application. Often the third stage is left out, or those disciplines of practical or applied theology fall prey to the traditional privileging of theory over practice. From another perspective, Hans Frei, as we saw, pointed out that "across the board," from conservatives to liberals in the modern period, the biblical narrative had been eclipsed, largely in favor of what one would call a theological (perhaps philosophical) replacement. This was often true not just of liberals who restated faith in terms of a philosophical system but also of conservatives who created a world behind the text from which they developed their system of belief. This Ricoeurian conception of theology would see systematic theology neither as foundational nor as the culmination of development. In Barthian terms, theology can be seen as subordinate to the life of the church and lives only in a dependent way upon the fuller life of the church. In more liberal terms, theology here is secondary to the primary experiences of the church, human experience, and culture.

Having relativized theology on the one hand, this approach also works against the denigration of theology on the other hand. In reaction to the overemphasis of theology, some see little value for it, preferring emphasis on the life of the church, spirituality, or participation in social action. The systematic, prosaic nature of systematic theology can also be diminished through an extreme emphasis on narrative or metaphorical theology. The implication here is that systematic, propositional language distorts the primary forms of faith and should be left behind, even if there is a kind of theological renarrating or re-parabling of the religious story. The value of Ricoeur's arc seen as a framework for theology is that one can avoid overemphasizing systematic theology and also underemphasizing it. Few have done more to highlight the primary nature of narrative and figurative language, yet he also thought that there is a place for conceptual reflection (explanation) that is more prosaic and systematic. While he placed limits on explanation, his conviction was that we understand more by explaining more. The important thing to realize is that such reflection cannot exhaustively "translate" primary religious faith nor its primary expressions. Explanation is always subordinate, partial, and incomplete. Systematic theology in this sense does not have pride of place—but it does have a place. It does serve to explain and elucidate.

This contribution of systematic theology can be seen in the aphorism that Ricoeur takes up from Kant, "the symbol gives rise to thought" (Ricoeur 1967: 347–57). Ricoeur saw that figurative language is a rich resource for reflection—not that it takes the place of reflection. As we shall see, he perhaps did not do enough justice to the way that such figurative language pervades even the language of critical reflection, but his main point is that reflection and explanation do contribute, as he argued for the value of "method" over against Gadamer. In fact, in reflecting on the theological hermeneutics, he connected it with the moment of criticism or distantiation that is an aspect of hermeneutics in general. In the unique case of theological hermeneutics, it contributes to "the de-construction of the illusions of the subject" (Ricoeur 1991e: 100).

We may return here to the analogy of a film critic to a film or to the analysis of a performer analyzing his or her performance, often in terms of larger theories or methodologies. Such critical reflection can point out blindspots and distortions in the life of faith, as Karl Barth did to the state church in Germany during World War II and as Stanley Hauerwas has done to the civil religion in the United States after World War II. Both they and Ricoeur would point to the biblical predecessors of such ideology critique or a hermeneutic of suspicion to the biblical prophets and to Jesus himself. Part of the role of systematic theology in interpreting the faith is to critique its distortions. The creative or configurative side of critique, however, is to point to a more effective and transforming interpretation. In Ricoeur's work on the parables, he understood them as reorienting through disorienting. This aptly describes much of the work of systematic theology in its contemporary setting. Ricoeur thought that the deconstruction of the subject's illusions is "the negative aspect" of a positive turn to the way the new being of faith is formed through the imagination. Systematic theology is not just critique; it points toward transformation, the third moment of the hermeneutical arc.

The role of systematic theology, therefore, is further relativized by seeing it only as the second moment in the hermeneutical arc. It points beyond itself to appropriation. Instead of the third stage of application being a mere optional inference, it is the completion of interpretation. Far from being the acme of interpretation, systematic theology is subordinate both to the first and third stages. To think of a film critic again, one would not want to replace a film with the film review. Often the effect of a review is to make one want to see the film again—but now with the benefit of added insight and understanding. One could make a stronger case that systematic theology has failed if it does not return one invigorated to the life of faith with the proviso that the return may be a critical one that is in some tension with common practice. In terms of a postcritical naïveté, this can be as in the words of Marcus Borg, reading the Bible again as if for the first time (Borg 2002). It is a reading with faith, but a critically chastened faith, which can cover the gamut from conservative to liberal. Conservatives, too, despite the name, are often full of criticism of traditional practices; they often reject current practices, which may have been around for some time, in light of a renewal of what they see as earlier practices. Theology helps to make such a critical case.

Beyond the role of prophetic criticism, however, is the constructive role for theology, which may appear to be much more prominent. Allowing a role for "configuration" even in critical reflection opens up the door for such a role for theology, even if positive configuration itself nevertheless points to more existential appropriation in the third moment of the arc. The constructive role remains critical in the sense that it draws on the plethora of sources of theology, including the diversity within the Scripture itself, to point in a more comprehensive, systematic direction. The role of a film review is to help one see things one has not considered and to make connections that one has not noticed. In a positive review, it helps one to appreciate the film in a deeper way. At the same time, it may be quite critical of certain kinds of interpretations of the film. The constructive task of theology does all of these things with the diversity of resources of faith that go far beyond that of a single film. To refer to Moltmann again, he is an example of how theology can be "game-changers" in his landmark works "resurrecting" eschatology, so to speak, in *The Theology of Hope* and in bringing about a sea change in theology in conceiving of the suffering of God in *The Crucified God*.[17] How does one interpret atonement throughout the Scripture and church tradition? How does one interpret sin and evil in the Scripture, a matter which Ricoeur addressed in *The Symbolism of Evil* in light of other religious and philosophical approaches? How does one interpret eschatology, which shifts dramatically from the Old Testament to the New Testament, and then again in various epochs of church history? In response to such questions, systematic theology cannot help but be critical and configurative as it attempts to pull together various trajectories and to point in an advisable, coherent, and believable direction.

While some push the comprehensiveness and coherence very far in terms of a full-blown "worldview," one can still allow for the helpfulness of systematic reflection without going so far. Ricoeur's philosophy of limits, especially of the limits of rational reflection in light of the surplus of meaning in figurative language, implied more of an allowance for a variety of systematic theologies that draw on different perspectives and traditions—which is actually the reality in the history of the church. Rather than conceiving of a one-size-fits-all theology, every theology can be seen to reflect a perspective, valuable but ultimately partial. This conception of a more limited ambition for theology is itself a major shift from the traditional desire for finding one universal perspective for everyone. The truth is not found so much in one system but in the more partial grasp of a larger reality through various theologies.

This point helps one to see that even this appropriation of Ricoeur in terms of a general framework for doing theology does not support every approach to theology. As we have seen, it does not mesh with attempts from either liberals or conservatives to make theology the centerpiece of faith. Nor does it sit well with the relinquishment of systematic theology. It is critical of modernity in that it rejects a privileging of theory over practice, of propositional language over figurative language, and modern reason over tradition and faith. At the same time, it is not a return to a form of premodernity that rejects a larger historical-critical approach to the Scripture and faith. Its hermeneutical turn resists certain strands in both premodernity and modernity. It is in tension with some forms of postmodernity, the deconstructive forms, in that it attempts to combine both critique *and* conviction, a challenging and ever ongoing task. It does not yield finally to critique or despair but summons to an affirmation of faith that can be compelling but not coercive. As we shall, the nature of theology fits Ricoeur's emphasis on testimony as befitting the nature of both truth and faith claims. Such a "confessional" approach, though, does not mitigate the need and allowance for multiple testimonies.

With this emphasis again on a surplus of meaning, we now turn from the basic hermeneutical arc to Ricoeur's emphasis on a surplus of meaning in the very forms of faith that also represent aspects of a critique of modernity.

4

Figuration and theology

Ricoeur pressed beyond the limits of his basically phenomenological approach, he attested, when it came to evil acts (Ricoeur 1995a: 16–17). *Freedom and Nature* was a largely phenomenological account of the will or of action. The second volume of his projected philosophy of the will was published in 1960 in two parts, *Fallible Man* and *The Symbolism of Evil*. *Fallible Man* already stretched beyond phenomenology toward an ontology of the self; the bounds were completely broken in *The Symbolism of Evil*. The reason: he did not believe that phenomenology as a description of the essences of actions could capture an essentially irrational action. At best, such mysterious actions could only be gestured at or indicated indirectly through symbols and myths; hence began the hermeneutical turn per se, more specifically, a figurative turn that carried through the rest of his career.

This figurative turn had enormous implications for religious language and theology, especially rooted in the fact that he particularly explored the symbolism of evil in the Hebrew Bible. The turn to symbols led to his immersion in the interpretation of symbols in Freud, then to metaphor, and finally to narrative. As such, he participated in and in many ways sparked a major, paradigmatic reconsideration of the nature of language in the Scripture and in theology over the last half of the twentieth century. We will examine these moves in turn after first setting the stage for the significance of this paradigm shift.

Setting the stage

For over a millennium, the dominant approach to religious language
in the church was largely symbolic, more specifically allegorical.
This developed at times into virtually a formula of four senses of
the Scripture, often expressed in terms of the example of Jerusalem
being seen literally as the earthly city, allegorically as the Christian
church, tropologically (a moral sense) as the soul, and anagogically
(the future, eschatological sense) as the future heavenly city of God
(Froehlich 1984: 28). Rooted especially in Christian communities
such as in Alexandria, such a basically figurative approach was
quite common and often led to excesses that resulted by the time of
the Reformation into a revolt away from allegory and toward the
literal sense of the Scripture. Augustine, for example, indicated in
The Confessions that he was repelled by the crudity of the literal
sense of the Scripture, and it was in part due to being introduced
to an allegorical approach by Ambrose that he became open to the
Christian faith (Augustine 1952: 3.5, 5.14). He could, for example,
interpret the days of Genesis 1 in this light as symbolic of ages of
history. This view was countered at the time by another approach
represented by some in Antioch that emphasized the literal sense,
being influenced more by Aristotle than by Plato.[1] While the
Alexandrian tradition had great influence, both Augustine and
Aquinas emphasized that the meanings of the other senses needed to
be rooted in a literal sense elsewhere in the Scripture (Aquinas 1952:
1.1.10). It is also important to realize that a degree of hermeneutical
control was provided by the guidance of what was called the rule
of faith, major creeds, and the teaching authority of the church.
Sometimes the control was also enforced, to be sure, by the sword
and later by the Inquisition.

After the Reformation, Protestants especially emphasized the
literal sense. Martin Luther is an example:

> No violence is to be done to the words of God, whether by man
> or angel; but they are to be retained in their simplest meaning
> wherever possible, and to be understood in their grammatical
> and literal sense unless the context plainly forbids, lest we give
> our adversaries occasion to make a mockery of all the Scriptures.
> Thus Origen was repudiated, in olden times, because he despised

the grammatical sense and turned the trees, and all else written concerning Paradise, into allegories; for it might therefrom be concluded that God did not create trees.[2]

This significant shift was tied to the revolution in the source of authority in the Reformation, which moved from tradition and church authorities to the Scripture itself, captured in the slogan *sola scriptura*. It is not difficult to see that if Scripture is the authority, it is much more attractive for a clearer literal sense to be the basis of interpretation than multiple figurative senses with a much greater range of meaning. Many Protestants in fact emphasized what they called the "perspicuity" of the Scripture to indicate the clarity of at least the basic meaning of the Bible (Marsden 2006: 16, 210–11). Later conservative Protestants extended this emphasis further in developing a doctrine of inerrancy to include virtually all of the Bible as having straightforward clarity.

In the meantime, many have pointed out that the Reformers' turn to the Scripture as an authority combined with emphasis on its clarity and, very important, its greater accessibility due to the recent invention of the printing press used to great effect by Luther had repercussions far beyond what they could have imagined. Luther contributed by highlighting the "priesthood of all believers," but such an emphasis was carried much further by the Radical Reformers who opened interpretation up to everyone, so to speak. These are the groups who proliferated in the nineteenth and twentieth centuries and continue unabated in the global south today. While many of these groups were themselves quite conservative, the turn to an accessible literal meaning also opened up in unforeseen ways the application of individual reason to the Scripture and to faith in the seventeenth century. In Descartes, for instance, as one who is often seen as the father of modernity, an individual's reason and clarity became the lynchpin of modernity. Many Christians in later centuries across the spectrum from liberal to conservative ratcheted higher the claims for the clarity and rationality of the Scripture.

With the rise of a greater historical sense in modernity and along with it historical criticism of the Bible, the Bible came to be seen as subject to critical scrutiny just as any other book. While this move opened up the Bible to a much greater historical and contextual meaning, Hans Frei, as we have seen, indicated how this shift to historical examination of the Bible also led to the narrative shape of the Scripture being lost across the theological spectrum (Frei 1974). His student Charles Wood then portrayed how this move to a focus on the meaning of the Scripture in terms of a prosaic sense continued unabated into the twentieth century (Wood 1981). Specifically, the attempt to render the meaning of the Scripture in historical language was a move to literal, propositional language, whether one affirmed the historicity of the Scripture or not. In other words, the preoccupation of historical-critical methodology on the "world behind the text" led to revision on the part of more liberal Christians and defense by more conservatives. In either case, the "figurative" shape of the Bible was "eclipsed," in Frei's terms.

Another significant aspect of the shift for more conservative theology in the United States was the influence of Francis Bacon and Scottish Common Sense Realism, as briefly mentioned in Chapter 2. This and other influences such as the desire at that time to ally biblical knowledge with scientific knowledge led to an emphasis on the Bible as an encyclopedia of facts that are quite evident and uninterpreted. The understanding of science at the time saw it in a similar way as dealing with uninterpreted facts that led inductively to secure inferences. Theology then was seen as compiling such inferences in a systematic way. As George Marsden, a major historian of this period, indicates:

> When it came to identifying their philosophical stance, until after the Civil War American evangelicals overwhelmingly preferred the method of Francis Bacon·to "metaphysical speculations." Common Sense philosophy affirmed their ability to know "the facts" directly. With the Scriptures at hand as a compendium of facts, there was no need to go further. They needed only to classify the facts, and follow wherever they might lead. (Marsden 2006: 56)

In this way, the Reformation ideal of the perspicuity of the Scripture and the plain or literal sense was extended into an approach to the Scripture and theology that prized transparent facts with little allowance for interpretation. One can connect such an emphasis to a larger, "modern" Cartesian emphasis on "clarity and distinctness." As well, Marsden points out that this view drew on a Puritan emphasis that "[b]iblical interpretation was an exact science with precise conclusions" (Marsden 2006: 60). This view saw only one meaning for any biblical passage. It is obviously difficult to deal in this approach with what Ricoeur would call the conflict of interpretations and the surplus of meaning. In fact, they struggled with the fact that there were many differing interpretations because their approach did not really allow for or "predict" that there should be a disagreement. At one point, an esteemed president of a prominent evangelical college in frustration blamed such disagreements on professors who are influenced by "high pay and extended vacations" as well as tobacco and alcohol![3]

While the large consensus around this approach was shattered in the United States, among other things, by the Scopes Monkey trial of 1925 that brought about tension and even divorce in the alliance of evangelicals and science, one cannot underestimate the continuing pervasiveness of this model among evangelicals.[4] For example, Stanley Grenz and John Franke commented in 2001 on what they saw as a "rationalist approach" still common among evangelicals:

> The rationalist approach that typifies evangelical theology is characterized by a commitment to the Bible as the source book of information for systematic theology. As such, it is viewed as a rather loose and disorganized collection of factual, propositional statements. The task of theology in turn becomes that of collecting and arranging these varied statements in such a way as to bring their underlying unity into relief and reveal the eternal system of timeless truths to which they point. (Grenz and Franke 2001: 13f.)

After 1925, there was a tendency for evangelicals to go in two directions that worked against any hermeneutical emphasis such as Ricoeur's. One was to take the bull by the horns and maintain that their approach to the Bible was truly scientific and factual, which was manifested in the massive popular movements around the beginning and end of the Bible, creationism, and dispensationalism. The other was to retreat into an appeal to fideism.

George Lindbeck argued that liberals avoided the problem of interpretation by letting the modern world, as in philosophy, absorb the biblical world and by theology playing the role of expressing a common inner experience in various ways (G. Lindbeck 1984: 31–2; Murphy 1996: 46–51). However adequate such generalizations are in particular, they represent a common perception of broad tendencies in the twentieth century as Ricoeur was coming onto the scene.

Symbols

Ricoeur turned to symbols especially in *The Symbolism of Evil* but already related them to myth (a certain kind of narrative that portrays meaning through a story of origins) and reflection in philosophy. It is significant that he stresses here a paradigmatic shift on figurative language from earlier modern philosophy that was accentuated only later, namely, that symbols are irreducible to prosaic thought. They cannot by fully translated or transposed into systematic conceptual thought—a move with great ramifications for systematic theology. He nevertheless stressed that they fund such systematic thought without ever being exhausted by it. Here in nascent form one has the themes of his later hermeneutical arc with the emphasis that thought cannot have an absolute beginning, *pace* Descartes, and actually is often sparked by the more primordial language of symbol, that the symbol can enrich thought, that thought can criticize and elaborate the symbol but in the end thought must return to the symbol.

In this book, Ricoeur examined what he saw as more basic and physical symbols for evil such as "stain" and "defilement," noting how these were taken initially in an almost literal way. He then traced how they became more internalized and moralized in terms of concepts such as "sin" and "guilt" (Ricoeur 1967: 1). He thought, though, that the earlier, more graphic meanings were never left behind but continued as a kind of penumbra in the later, more developed symbols. An important insight here is that the range of symbols complement one another, not in a literal way but as figurative, pointing to the way that sometimes symbols are explained not just by literal language but by other symbols—again an idea with significant implications for systematic theology, liturgy, and homiletics.

At this point, Ricoeur explored how these symbols are taken up into myths. In an exercise of comparative religion, he looked at the biblical myth of the fall, the Babylonian myth of chaos and creation, the Greek myth of tragedy, and the Orphic myth of the exiled soul in the body (which influenced Plato) (Ricoeur 1967: 171–4). On the one hand, there is a sense of fate as most of the myths suggest: evil befalls us. On the other hand, evil is a choice: we choose it. He thought the Adam and Eve account in Genesis 3 contains this tension. The serpent and the forbidden tree represent temptation and evil already present, from the beginning until now. Adam's and Eve's actions represent deliberate choice. In this drama, the precarious fallibility of *Fallible Man* erupts into actual fault, which Ricoeur terms the "servile will." He explains:

> The concept toward which the whole series of the primary symbols of evil tends may be called the *servile will*. But that concept is not directly accessible; if one tries to give it an object, the object destroys itself, for it short-circuits the idea of will, which can only signify free choice, and so free will, always intact and young, always available—and the idea of servitude, that is to say, the unavailability of freedom to itself. The concept of the servile will, then, cannot be represented as the concept of fallibility, ... That is why the concept of the servile will must remain an indirect concept, which gets all its meaning from the symbolism that we have run through which tries to raise that symbolism to the level of speculation. (Ricoeur 1967: 151)

Ricoeur offers here a philosophical analysis funded by symbol and myth. He stresses at the end of the book a saying of Kant's that he repeats throughout his work, "The symbol gives rise to thought" (Ricoeur 1967: 347–57). Here is a striking example. In reflection that is consonant with much Christian theology, he stresses over against Martin Heidegger, for example, that fallibility is not yet a fault. He also indicates over against his popular existentialist contemporary at that time, Jean-Paul Sartre, the limitations of freedom. He stressed the reality of freedom and responsibility, yet also its frail and tragic limitations. Like Kant, he pointed to the radicality of evil, its irrationality (Kant 1960). Unlike Kant, he looked to irreducible symbols for illumination. It is a distinctive philosophical position and a defensible one, but one developed as much on the basis of symbolic as conceptual thought.

The kind of theological position to which his reflections have affinity is strikingly in contrast to traditional Augustinian/Calvinist views of the myth of the fall as a literal account. More particularly,

Ricoeur is critical of the way the multivalence of the myth is collapsed in the way that the former theological tradition places all of the weight upon the first couple as the only humans who were ever "free not to sin." Unlike them, all others are "not free not to sin." For this tradition, this meant that only those predestined by God would experience the effectual grace to turn to God. All others would be left in their bondage to sin or their predestination to damnation. Ricoeur, as much contemporary Christian theology, sees this kind of reading as actually a misreading of both the genre and the message of the myth, which is intended to represent an insight into the dynamics of all human fault, from the first to the last.

In Ricoeur's later *Interpretation Theory* (1976), Ricoeur distinguished between symbols and metaphors. While similar in many ways, he saw symbols as hovering closer to nonlinguistic, physical representations such as a tree, a stone, and a star. He noted, "Metaphor occurs in the already purified universe of the logos, while the symbol hesistates [*sic*] on the dividing line between *bios* and *logos*. It testifies to the primordial rootedness of Discourse in Life. It is born where force and form coincide" (Ricoeur 1976a: 59). Earlier he had pointed to the earthy dimension of symbols in Freud's "archaeological" interpretation of dream images (Ricoeur 1970). Both symbols and metaphors, however, are irreducible and rich in meaning. In dreams, sacred spaces, and the density of meaning in many objects, symbols point to the limitations of conceptual prose. As such, they are religiously rich as sources for theological reflection. Symbols are ubiquitous in religion, but Ricoeur is well aware with the rise of modern historical criticism that the symbols are experienced more often as broken, often rejected altogether. Ricoeur expressed a postcritical interactive relationship in this way:

> But if we can no longer live the great symbolisms of the sacred in accordance with the original belief in them, we can, we modern men, aim at a second naivete in and through criticism. In short, it is by *interpreting* that we can *hear* again. Thus it is in hermeneutics that the symbol's gift of meaning and the endeavor to understand by deciphering are knotted together. (Ricoeur 1967: 351)

Hence, a hermeneutical turn that does not displace but spirals around the symbol and figurative language in general is a central feature of Ricoeur's thought from this point.

Metaphor

Ricoeur worked out the dynamics of figurative language more fully, however, when he turned to a philosophy of metaphor. Ricoeur's work is best seen in light of the paradigmatic shift that was occurring about this time, expressed dramatically by Mark Johnson in 1981:

> In the last decade or so the study of metaphor has become, for an ever-increasing number of philosophers, a way of approaching some of the most fundamental traditional concerns of philosophy. Metaphor is no longer confined to the realm of aesthetics narrowly conceived; it is now coming to be recognized as central to any adequate account of language and has been seen by some to play a central role in epistemology and even metaphysics. This burgeoning of interest is a curious phenomenon. Why is it that as recently as twenty years ago (and for centuries before that) it was imprudent to say nice things about metaphor in respectable philosophical circles? And why is it now an embarrassment to be caught without an account of the nature, function, and proper role of metaphor? (Johnson 1981: 3)

Behind Johnson's remarks are two dramatic changes from the Western philosophical tradition on metaphor, which Ricoeur treated in his history of metaphor, *The Rule of Metaphor*, especially going back to Aristotle (Ricoeur 1977). The first idea that is rejected is to think that metaphors are "substitutions" of literal terms and thus are replaceable with literal terms. The second is that the tendency of philosophers to denigrate rhetoric led to metaphor, especially in the modern period, to be regarded with suspicion. In a time when Cartesian clarity and precision were prized, the recognized vagueness (which could on the other hand be seen as richness) of metaphor was often a thing to avoid. For example, Thomas Hobbes (1588–1679) strongly said that people abuse speech "when they use words metaphorically; that is, in other sense than that they are ordained for; and thereby deceive others" (Hobbes 1947: 1, Ch. 4). John Locke (1632–1704) was no kinder:

> Since wit and fancy find easier entertainment in the world than dry truth and real knowledge, figurative speeches and allusion in language will hardly be admitted as an imperfection or abuse

of it. . . . But yet if we would speak of things as they are, we
allow that all the art of rhetoric, besides order and clearness; all
the artificial and figurative application of words eloquence hath
invented, are for nothing else but to insinuate wrong ideas, move
the passions, and thereby mislead the judgment; and so indeed
are perfect cheats. (Locke 1952: 3.10.34)

Certainly such viewpoints, as one can see in Locke, could coexist
with the use of figurative language in literature or rhetoric—or
in sermons. It was allowable but was seen as a concession to
human weakness, an aspect of ornamentation, not of substance.
In preaching, the heart of the sermon was seen as the more prosaic
exposition, and literary ornamentation was used for subjective
reasons. One could sense that there is an implicit wish, as in Locke,
that the whole sorry business of metaphor could be avoided but for
human frailty.

It is quite a sea-change, therefore, to see metaphor, as in Johnson,
as philosophically and cognitively significant. Ricoeur was already
moving in this direction in the *Symbolism of Evil* with the idea
that the symbol gives rise to thought. His hermeneutical arc was
actually worked out in relation to his reflections on metaphor. He
had come to see that not only was criticism subject to hermeneutical
understanding but it was also subject to figuration and the
imagination.

At this time, Ricoeur and others such as I. A. Richards (in 1936)
and Max Black (in 1954) were developing an "interaction" theory
of metaphor over against the substitution theory. Instead of dealing
with replacement of a word, they saw metaphors arising at least
at the level of a sentence where there is a clash between two
semantic frames at the literal level. Ricoeur spoke of a "predicative
impertinence, as the appropriate means of producing a shock
between semantic fields" (Ricoeur 1991c: 172). Ricoeur called this
also a "split reference" where the literal reference had to be denied
that in turn generated a "semantic innovation."[5] Metaphor involves
an "is" and "is not" to which one always must attend (Ricoeur
1975: 88)—an insight that Sallie McFague developed in her project
of "metaphorical theology," which we will explore below. This is
an act of the imagination that often results in new meaning and
new insights, as Ricoeur said, "Imagining is above all restructuring
semantic fields" (Ricoeur 1991c: 173). In this way, Ricoeur purported

that metaphor "redescribes" reality. Richards had suggested that one can indicate things with metaphor that cannot be said in any other way (Richards 1981). Black had shockingly suggested that metaphor not only helps to describe reality but also creates reality (Black 1981). Both views implied that metaphor is cognitive, not just instrumental. Ricoeur later wished to speak of "reshaping" rather than redescribing to avoid the sense that language, even metaphor, simply represents or mirrors nature.[6] Rather, it is always a human, perspectival grasp of reality that does not represent, say, a God's-eye-point-of-view. Nevertheless, metaphor still refers but possesses a "creative referentiality" (Reagan 1996: 107). Ricoeur's special interest was in such creative metaphor expressed in the French title of *The Rule of Metaphor*, *La metaphore vive* (live metaphor). Metaphors are thus irreplaceable and creative. Of course, metaphor may lose its metaphorical punch, or its "ontological vehemence," and become domesticated as literal language. One may think of a space "ship." Rather than metaphor being subordinate to univocal language, metaphor may be the genesis of the latter. Consider the way first-order religious language (which tends to be figurative) and experience generate the second-order language of systematic theology, as we discussed earlier (Ch. 3). Rather than figurative language being replaced by systematic theology, it is a source and also a limit. As we shall see, it may even be an aspect of theology, an implication that Ricoeur himself did not particularly develop.

Out of this "semantic shock" of bringing together two disparate frames of reference, a new meaning is created in a mysterious, elusive way that is difficult to pin down, which is frustrating for philosophers, and theologians, attuned to making everything thoroughly clear—a characteristic of both the Cartesian impulse on the Continent and Anglo-American analytic philosophy. It is interesting to note, as Ricoeur does, that Aristotle himself, while seen as the source of the substitution theory, also could say, "But the greatest thing by far is to be a master of metaphor" (Aristotle 1952: 22). Aristotle added, "It is the one thing that cannot be learnt from others; and it also a sign of genius, since a good metaphor implies an intuitive perception of the similarity in dissimilars" (22). This is a direction in Aristotle that was not taken up in philosophy until recently, but his notion of something that cannot be taught perhaps points to the later understanding of metaphor as irreducible to univocal language, that is, to step-by-step prosaic explanation. Such inexactness can undermine the very notion of metaphor, but it also opens up the semantic richness of metaphor, namely, its fecundity of meaning, its inexhaustibility. If the goal of hermeneutics is to explicate one clear meaning, a view often prized in biblical hermeneutics, this view of metaphor undermines it at the outset. It is frustrating because neither the metaphorical act nor its meaning can be fully explained. Aristotle may reflect this nervousness by attributing it to genius.

On the other hand, from a view of ordinary language analysis, we see that metaphors are widely present in ordinary language and widely understood in the sense that people use them. Not all may be geniuses at metaphors, but the capacity to create, use, and comprehend metaphors is commonplace. In fact, Mark Johnson and his cognitive scientist colleague George Lakoff argue that most common language that one may think of as univocal is actually more deeply structured by metaphor. Root metaphors can help to connect areas of language that otherwise are difficult to relate such as their example:

> ARGUMENT IS WAR
> Your claims are *indefensible.*
> He attacked every weak point in my argument.
> His criticisms were *right on target.*
> I *demolished* his argument.
> I've never *won* an argument with him.
> You disagree? Okay, *shoot!*
> If you use that strategy, he'll wipe you out.
> He *shot down* all of my arguments. (Lakoff and Johnson 1980: 4)

More recently, they have shown how the metaphor, "The Nation Is a Family," structures discourse in US politics (Lakoff and Johnson 1999; Lakoff 2008). As they point out, understanding these deep metaphors helps explain new inferences that we make on their basis. One may think here of biblical language such as the Kingdom of God or the body of Christ.

The wider point is that the process does not have to be fully explicated to be recognized and affirmed. Eva Feder Kittay says of metaphor on this point, "To say a thing is not subject to a given set of rules is not to say that it is subject to no rules" (Kittay 1987: 68). Language familiarity and context usually provide sufficient clues for this area where finding the meaning is neither reckless nor precise. Kittay adds more detail that actually aids Ricoeur's formulation:

> Metaphor breaks certain rules of language, rules governing the literal and conventional senses of the terms. The rule-breaking takes place not in any arbitrary way but in certain specifiable ways. Hence we can tell the difference between metaphors and mistakes, and the difference between metaphors and new, technical uses. (Kittay 1987: 24)

Metaphors can be judged as apt or not apt, fitting or not fitting. Metaphors are not as precise as univocal language, but neither are they chaotic nor anarchic. One may say of a situation that it is a "train wreck" or "work of art." One likely applies and the other does not. People in general, and not just geniuses, are actually fairly adept at such judgments, even if they cannot fully be explained. Yet Ricoeur's idea of "explaining more to understand better" applies here in the sense of not setting the metaphor to the side but of using the metaphor better. A similar dynamic is at work in hermeneutical "understanding" in the hermeneutical arc. It is a holistic grasp of meaning that is augmented by, but is not exhausted by, "explanation." In fact, Ricoeur brought these together with his philosophy of metaphor providing a basis for his wider hermeneutics (Ricoeur 1981c). This dynamic also relates to the way Gadamer appropriates the significance of Aristotle's practical wisdom (*phronesis*) as understanding that which cannot be fully explicated. Ricoeur then developed such a notion as a basis for the understanding of narrative and the self in terms of attestation. Metaphor became at this time a kind of hermeneutical key, so to speak, for hermeneutics itself.

Despite these key insights, Ricoeur did not spell them out as others have done on this philosophical basis. Ricoeur at one point mentioned the concept of "root metaphors" in terms of religious language but did not emphasize their pervasiveness as did Lakoff and Johnson (Ricoeur 1976a: 33). Moreover, he tended, especially early, to see figurative language as contributing to conceptual thought but not being a part of it, for example, the last chapter of *The Symbolism of Evil*. Interestingly, this move has been well developed in the philosophy of science in seeing science itself as deeply involving and even shaped by metaphors, especial in terms of extended metaphorical models.[7] Ricoeur sometimes attributed to scientific language a univocity and precision that does not fit such developments or the more recent philosophy of science of Michael Polanyi, Thomas Kuhn, Thomas Feyerabend, or Imre Lakatos, but at times he also could recognize that there is not a sharp line between the natural and human sciences.[8] He did not particularly treat how the language of philosophy itself is irreducibly metaphorical and is often shaped as much by the illumination of key metaphors as by the elucidation of its prose.[9] He perhaps implied or hinted at such a role for figurative language more in his development of narrative that became then the basis for historiography and for human identity. As we shall see, narrative, as a type of figurative language, shares much of the paradigmatic change that Ricoeur's philosophy of metaphor reveals.

One other aspect of metaphor should be mentioned before turning to narrative, namely, its embodied and emotional nature. Ricoeur brought this out in a provocative essay connecting the metaphor, the emotions, and the imagination.[10] In one of his few published, extended treatments of the imagination, Ricoeur related the schematism of images, which he elaborated from Kant, to the role of the body and the emotions. In Kant, the mysterious schema enables the way in which one can relate a concept to an image. Ricoeur took the schematizing power of the imagination, this enigmatic power of the soul, to be the way that metaphor conveys rich meaning by drawing on the background of the body and the emotions as well as the many connotations of words. Part of the ambiguity and the power of metaphor is its ability to focus on an image, like a picture, the power of a thousand words. Its portrayal is not so piecemeal as the univocal language, but is holistic, which involves a significant felt dimension. This is an aspect of its imprecision but also its depth and breadth. Janet Soskice suggests that the very looseness and fluidity of metaphor is a key to its cognitive power, all the more significant in that she is relating it to science (Soskice 1985: 133). The significance of Ricoeur's essay in the 1970s is related to the way that the body and the emotions are now seen as much more integrally related to cognition than the philosophical tradition has been wont to believe.[11] This connection is prescient in the way that it integrates these heretofore disparate themes of emotions, metaphor, imagination, and cognition. This development is one that is ongoing and has yet to be fully developed, but it is one that has rich implications for theology in terms of

new emphases on embodied practices and the cognitive power of
the emotions. Ricoeur never published an extended work on the
imagination, but he pulled various aspects together in unpublished
lectures that may soon be available.[12] This aspect of Ricoeur's work
has been noticed, some seeing him especially as a philosopher of the
imagination (Evans 1995; Lawlor 1992), but its full extent and its
relation to theology is one of the more promising but undeveloped
features of his thought.

As mentioned, Sallie McFague especially draws upon Ricoeur's
work on metaphor in developing an extended project of a
"metaphorical theology."[13] This means understanding God-talk
and its role in theology as having an essential "is" and "is not"
quality. As such, her work ties in with the rich analogical and even
mystical Christian tradition of beginning with the *via negativa*,
that is, first to deny all language about God being univocal. She
herself sees the analogical tradition as too wedded to the univocal,
too capable of being collapsed into literal language, so she prefers
metaphor.[14] Her viewpoint underscores a point of caution to the
reader in many of these debates. McFague obviously envisages
metaphor as a rich category that allows for irreducible creativity
and a surplus of meaning. In the Catholic tradition, however,
some speak of analogy in this way, such as David Tracy in *The
Analogical Imagination*, following Aquinas who elevated analogy
above metaphor—which Aquinas thought was not as disclosive.[15]
In the Paul Tillich tradition, "symbol" often represents the category
of being able to open up "levels of reality that are otherwise closed
to us."[16] McFague, however, takes metaphor to be, in a sense, a
metaphor for theology. She thus extends Ricoeur's philosophical
reflections on metaphor into the realm of conceptual thought per
se, again, a move that Ricoeur did not fully develop in philosophy
or theology. Theological statements, she maintains, must always
be affirmed and denied. She further elaborates key metaphors to
augment or replace less traditional and suitable metaphors, such
as God as Mother. The warrant for her move is that "Father"
language is already a metaphor that always has to be denied as well
as affirmed. She, of course, says the same about her metaphors of
God as a trinity of Mother, Lover, and Friend as well as the world
as God's body (McFague 1987, 1993). Her approach to theology
allows for conceptual thought but sees its limitation as well as the
limitation of any metaphor. Rather than just explaining metaphor

by prose, metaphors are often best "explained" by other metaphors, which in turn must be denied as well as affirmed. Her approach highlights the way that virtually any theology is influenced by key metaphors.

Narrative

Ricoeur further developed his reflections on metaphor in a rich dialogue with a philosophy of narrative, relating both to his developing conception of hermeneutics and his general discourse theory.[17] He had come to see that his earlier focus on figurative language as dealing with symbols with a double meaning, as in metaphor, was too narrow; rather, hermeneutics opens up the entire range of issues of interpretation, including the unique dynamics of various kinds of narrative (Ricoeur 1995a: 19). He came to see that narrative was the larger umbrella in which symbols and even metaphors largely occurred, which differed from the *Symbolism of Evil* where he had made the symbols primary over the myths. Ricoeur's work with narrative shared in a burgeoning interest in both metaphor and narrative as philosophically significant and also related to an especially strong development of narrative theology.[18] The same paradigmatic shift lies behind virtually all of these developments. As he said of metaphor and narrative, "[b]oth indeed have to do with the phenomenon of *semantic innovation*" (Ricoeur 1991d: 8). Narrative or story is not merely an ornament to straightforward prosaic language nor can it be wholly reduced or explained by univocal language. Some things are said better through story than through prose. In fact, the narrative backdrop may be fundamental and even necessary for the thick description of the univocal.[19]

In the 1970s, Ricoeur first elaborated the way narrative "refers" in relation to the way metaphor makes "sense," each providing a clue to the other (Ricoeur 1981e). He thought that narrative more obviously can be seen to project a world that shapes our self-understanding in relation to reality. He thought that metaphor in its relation to the immanent interplay between words and sentences indicates the way they make sense. It calls in a way then for "explanation," reflecting the basis of this discussion at the time in his development of a hermeneutical arc. At the time, he was much preoccupied, as was the French philosophical world, with structuralism, and he desired to show how one could legitimately appropriate structuralism's intricate analysis. He was also in a complex way drawing upon the philosophical distinction between sense and reference in analytical philosophy. The explanation of a metaphor belongs to the sense. Ricoeur expressed the way he was taking cues from one in relation to the other in this way:

> From one point of view, the understanding of metaphor can serve as a guide to the understanding of longer texts, such as a literary work. This point of view is that of explanation; it concerns only that aspect of meaning which we have called the "sense", that is, the immanent pattern of discourse. From another point of view, the understanding of a work taken as a whole gives the key to metaphor. This other point of view is that of interpretation proper; it develops the aspect of meaning which we have called "reference", that is, the intentional orientation towards a world and the reflexive orientation towards a self. So if we apply explanation to "sense", as the immanent pattern of the work, then we can reserve interpretation for the sort of inquiry concerned with the *power of a work* to project a world of its own and to set in motion the hermeneutical circle, which encompasses in its spiral both the apprehension of projected worlds and the advance of self-understanding in the presence of these new worlds. Our working hypothesis thus invites us to proceed from metaphor to text at the level of "sense" and the explanation of "sense", then from text to metaphor at the level of the reference of a work to a world and to a self, that is, at the level of interpretation proper. (Ricoeur 1981c: 171)

It could be seen the other way. One can perhaps more easily grasp how narratives make "sense" in manifold ways in terms of genre, characterization, emplotment, and so on. Even though it takes "understanding" to follow a story, one can "explain" or analyze a story, especially a fictive story, by breaking it down, so to speak, in order to understand it better. And his emphasis on the "ontological vehemence" of metaphor suggests that its power of redescribing reality is strongly referential, not to mention the idea of a "split reference" for metaphor. As we saw in the last chapter concerning his later work on narrative, he refrained from these analytic categories of sense and reference because of their awkward fit with narrative (in that their home is more in the realm of propositions). The use of "sense" and focus on structuralism also leaves the reader with some question at this time of how such analysis deals not just with deep structures but with the surface structures of say a novel, and how they are not just analyzed but synthesized into a whole to construct a fictional world. It is notable that he largely left both the terms behind in his later work on narrative (Ricoeur 1988: 158).

Concerning narrative, he focused upon the way it refers indirectly. The main point he made over against structuralism is that, however indirectly, such texts do refer. In metaphor, the reference is denied at the literal level only to be reinstated at a second, indirect level. Since it is metaphorical, it is not a precise reference but, as we saw earlier, precise "enough" for common use. Narrative also refers, as mentioned, in projecting a world, a possible world in which one might live. To reiterate, Ricoeur says of structuralism's denial of reference, "I really believe that if such [i.e. reference] were not the function of structural analysis, it would be reduced to a sterile game, a divisive algebra, and even the myth would be bereaved of the function . . . of making men aware of certain oppositions and of tending towards their progressive mediation" (Ricoeur 1981f: 217–18). We will deal more with the vexed issue of reference later, but it is important to see again Ricoeur's insistence upon reference.

Ricoeur's treatment of narrative became much more nuanced in his three-volume treatment entitled *Time and Narrative* (published in English between 1984 and 1988), as we saw in the last chapter. The title implies, however, that he was not just treating narrative, as extensive as the treatment was. He was concerned with how human time is experienced and offered that the quintessential way in which tensions between the modern chronological time of clocks and experiential, existential time are mediated is above all by narrative, which he explored both as fiction and as history (historiography). He posed this issue in dialectical fashion in terms of Augustine's wrestling with time and Aristotle's capturing of time in terms of plot or emplotment. Augustine famously noted, "What then is time? If no one asks me, I know; if I wish to explain it to one that asketh, I know not" (Augustine 1952: 11.14.17). Ricoeur placed against this sense of "discordance" that Augustine could not overcome in this life Aristotle's greater sense of "concordance" in his *Poetics*. In the third volume, Ricoeur pitted against each other the way that Heidegger took up Augustine's brilliant analysis of lived time and Kant's approach of chronological time. "Human time," Ricoeur thought, is grasped, or better lived, through the relation of these two in the interweaving of narrative as history and fiction. In the end, though, Ricoeur never thought that we transcend the aporia that Augustine saw; it is mediated but not dismissed. He thought, "Speculation on time is an inconclusive rumination to which narrative activity alone can respond" (Ricoeur 1984: 6). He thus came to the conclusion that humans are deeply and inherently storied or story-shaped in their self-understanding by way of this reflection on time. This conclusion, which he apparently developed through the course of writing *Time and Narrative*, is at the basis of the contemporary emphasis on narrative in theology and philosophy. It renders narrative, like metaphor, deeply philosophical in such a way that the philosophical tradition has not widely recognized.

More specifically, Ricoeur noted how narrative is able to harness the heterogeneity of life in time, especially through emplotment (Aristotle's *mythos*) by means of the imagination. This does not mean, he thought, that the narrator imposes a story upon something that is chaotic; rather, the narrativist takes up the nascent stories by which people construct their identities and live their lives and develop them more fully. As he indicated, if there were not already a developing story, then the narrativist could not continue. At the same time, he reminded us that this distance between life and narrative is never closed, despite the narrative quality of a life. He said, "Between living and recounting, a gap—however small it may be—is opened up. Life is lived, history is recounted" (Ricoeur 1991d: 5). Here, Ricoeur was giving a more nuanced response to the "shattered *cogito*" at the end of modernity and saw that it cannot be answered by systematic prose but ultimately only by figurative narrative.

As stressed in the last chapter, a major emphasis of Ricoeur is that not only fiction but also historiography is also emplotted or configured. Rather than seeing these as quite different as has sometimes been the case in positivist history, Ricoeur saw them both as works of the imagination, although he did not, on the other hand, collapse them into one another as some do. To continue the above discussion of reference, he still maintained that historiography, as he put it, maintains a debt to the past, even if it is highly creative, fictive-like, in constructing a narrative out of discordant events.

Historiography deals with archives, documents, and traces as well as previous narrative accounts to be faithful to what happened, without assuming that it has recounted the past, in Ranke's famous words, "as it actually happened." Here, Ricoeur is navigating treacherous shoals of controversy and searching for a middle ground. In particular, these controversies about the relationship of history and fiction have played themselves out in biblical studies and theology.

Ricoeur does not see fiction, conversely, as having no reference. Rather, like Aristotle, he understands it to be more "philosophical" than historiography in its indirect way because it deals more with the general or universal (Aristotle 1952: 3.9). Another way of putting it is that the meaning of history rather than the chronicle of history may be better portrayed in fiction than in historiography. Fiction also often projects into the future what *could* be the case or *could have been* the case, whereas historiography focuses on what *was* the case.

Both fiction and history, however, are works of the productive imagination that involve the basic dynamics of storytelling. Both produce a synthesis out of the heterogeneous, a degree of concordance out of discordance. Neither are replicas; neither are wholly subjective constructions of reality without wider relations to reality. It is the "interweaving" of the two that Ricoeur finds productive in dealing with the meaning of time. Ricoeur can even speak of "an interpenetration of history and fiction, stemming from the criss-crossing processes of a fictionalization of history and historization of fiction" (Ricoeur 1988: 246). The tacking back and forth between their two related but distinct imaginative functions further clarifies how human identity is not a given but a continuing task. Our identity is the result of all the things we have read, as he said later, "The story of a life continues to be refigured by all the truthful or fictive stories a subject tells about himself or herself. This refiguration makes this life itself a cloth woven of stories told" (246).

Ricoeur especially developed this "figurative" dimension in the narrative or mimetic arc, as I have called it, around which he structured *Time and Narrative*. As we saw in the extensive discussion in the previous chapter, the narrative arc is a key complement to the earlier hermeneutical arc, extending it in some helpful ways. For our purposes here, the narrative arc underscores the figurative and configurative elements in any narrative, including historiography.

It also helps us see in the movement from prefiguration, then configuration, to refiguration the dynamic process involved in human identity, which Ricoeur explored further in *Oneself as Another*. In the latter, humans are narratively shaped, much as Heidegger had argued that humans are hermeneutical beings all the way down. Such an ongoing dynamic, perhaps better captured also in the idea of a narrative spiral as much as an arc, again underscores Ricoeur's earlier critique of the transparent self in modernity in favor of selfhood as an ongoing project. It also develops the pervasive role of the imagination, captured in Ricoeur's favored term of *mimesis*; through all aspects of *mimesis*, one through three, the imagination is crucial.

In terms of hermeneutics, and we may say theology, an implication is one of Gadamer's favorite emphases, namely, that interpretation is not an exact reproduction. As Gadamer puts it, "It is enough to say that we understand in a *different* way, *if we understand at all*" (Gadamer 1991: 297). The fusion of horizons that is involved in any act of understanding can be seen more fully developed here as an activity of the figurative imagination.[20] Ricoeur develops this notion more explicitly in terms of "translation" in his late work on that issue. Translation is always more or less adequate, an "equivalence without adequacy," even when it involves understanding someone in oral discourse in one's own language (Ricoeur 2006: 10, 24). Such an approach works against the idea that a text, for example, has a single reproducible clear meaning but points toward the surplus of meaning. As Ricoeur expressed it in a rich aphorism, "A text means all that it can mean" (Ricoeur 1981c: 176).

This surplus of meaning, as we saw in the case of metaphor, does not imply chaos or hermeneutical anarchy. Ricoeur was quite clear that one can rule out some meanings; a text does not mean everything. As he wrote, "The text is a limited field of possible constructions. The logic of validation allows us to move between the two limits of dogmatism and scepticism. It is always possible to argue for or against an interpretation, to confront interpretations, to arbitrate between them, and to seek for an agreement, even if this agreement remains beyond our reach" (Ricoeur 1981f: 213). There is no uncontrolled free play of the imagination in the way that some have appropriated the Derridean deconstruction—although it is unlikely that Derrida himself meant anything like that. Ricoeur in any case seemed to think in terms of a *directed* meaning but not a *precise* meaning. One may imagine a vector, which begins at a point but moves toward infinity, yet a vector does not include all of a circle, perhaps only a small part. It is what one may call, somewhat paradoxically, a "limited infinity." Texts, especially rich ones such as metaphors and narratives—but also systematic theologies—have a surplus of meaning that is inexhaustible yet not necessarily out of control.[21] Ricoeur's philosophy of narrative illuminated this general hermeneutical point.

Ricoeur especially emphasized the role of the imagination and its power of projecting possibilities through texts when it came to religion and faith, which can be seen in a key text "Philosophical Hermeneutics and Biblical Hermeneutics" (Ricoeur 1991e). He argued especially that Christian faith is mediated hermeneutically through texts because of the centrality of the Scripture. In this sense, it displays an incarnational nature in being an instance of a general hermeneutics. The expressions of faith in the Scripture are first inseparable from their forms of discourse, whether symbol, metaphor, narrative, legal, prophetic, and so on.[22] The canon becomes in a sense "a structural act that demarcates the space within which the forms of discourse enter into play with one another" (90). Thus, one cannot treat the meaning of the Scripture apart from its form. Ricoeur warns here of the temptation of a theology of the Word of God that ignores this move from speech to writing. Especially because of this inscripturation, "Christianity is, from the start, an exegesis" (94). The consequent inherent distantiation situates the message of faith between introducing "prematurely existential . . . categories' apart from such hermeneutical mediation (taking the short route, so to speak) and between structural categories that never reach existence" (95). Although he was sometimes identified in the context of existentialist hermeneutics and as placing the reader above the text, Ricoeur actually warned, "The primary task of a hermeneutics is not to bring about a decision in the reader but first to allow the world of being that is the 'thing' of the biblical text to unfold" (96). Moreover, because it is a matter of the "world" of the text, Ricoeur, for all of his emphasis upon personal appropriation, stressed that the scriptural message is not just a personal one, an I-Thou relationship, but has many other dimensions such as the social, political, and even cosmological. Also because it is a projected world, it becomes "one that is poetically distanced from everyday reality" (96). This poetic dimension through the imagination opens up faith as a world in one which one might dwell. It is personally appropriated, but it is not something that is simply self-generated; it is a "kingdom that does not come from us" (97). Yet "it is in the imagination that this new being is first formed in me" (101). Such formation is not, however, uncritical. The dynamics of interpretation and the inherent distantiation also bring in an element of critique that he conjoined to the immanent prophetic critique within the Scripture. Ricoeur saw in this moment of criticism another displacement of the subject being in control (100).

At this point, Ricoeur saw a turn from the Scripture as a regional instance of general hermeneutics as potentially inverting the relationship where the Scripture becomes a unique case. Why? Because the referent of this poetic world and all of the figures of the Scripture is God, who is "at once the coordinator of these diverse discourses and the vanishing point, the index of incompletion, of these partial discourses" (97). For a hermeneutical philosopher, Ricoeur then surprisingly stressed the limits of language to capture the referent at both ends, that of God and that of the act of faith. He concluded, "The thematics of faith eludes hermeneutics and attests to the fact that the latter has neither the first nor the last word" (99). Nevertheless, there is a dialectical relationship, where "a poetics of existence responds to the poetics of discourse" (101). Faith is mediated through figurative language but is not reducible to language or human subjectivity. Understanding Ricoeur's careful threading between the subject and the object, experience and text, faith and expression is central for seeing how he fits into the different types of narrative theology.

Narrative theology

Metaphorical theology was discussed in connection with metaphor. Narrative theology has been a more extensive development, including its great influence on homiletics, that is, narrative preaching, from the 1970s forward. The themes of narrative theology generally resonate with, and in some cases spring from, Ricoeur's emphases on narrative. Broadly, narrative is not seen as subordinate or ornamental to conceptual thought but as distinctive, even primary. It is not seen as reducible to or substitutable by systematic theology but as a continual source of insight and evaluation. Distinctions do exist, however, between broad types of narrative theology, where sometimes Ricoeur is narrowly placed within one type, the so-called Chicago School, which became of inordinate importance in the way Ricoeur has been seen in North America (Comstock 1986). While we saw that Ricoeur's narrative arc has some weaknesses and areas to be developed, we shall see that such a positioning has reflected, ironically, a major misinterpretation that continues to influence the perception of Ricoeur in North America especially in connection with theology. Its correction, which is ongoing, gradually has allowed Ricoeur's thought to be a leavening factor in the discussions of the various types of narrative.

At one point in the last two decades of the twentieth century in North America, as indicated in Chapter 2, much debate centered around a type of narrative theology centered in the University of Chicago Divinity School and a type in the Yale Divinity School, even though narrative per se was only one aspect of the debate. At this point, when such debate and distinctions have abated, it is possible to relate Ricoeur more constructively to the issue of narrative theology. In general, much narrative theology has focused on the central role of narrative in human life and in particular as an essential aspect of human identity. Such a focus was reflected especially in the philosophical interests at Chicago, which was influenced by Tillich, Gadamer, and Ricoeur mediated especially through David Tracy. Ricoeur fit in with this emphasis in the sense that he developed a narrative approach to human identity especially in *Time and Narrative* and *Oneself as Another*.

The central Yale theologians Frei and Lindbeck also emphasized the narrative shape of the Scripture in their own ways. Frei dealt especially with the loss of appreciation of narrative in the modern period and how it caused both liberal and conservative to look for the world behind the text rather than the world of the text (Frei 1974). This loss also meant that theologians failed to see how the Scripture rendered a specific character such as Jesus Christ in narrative form (Frei 1967). Lindbeck's postliberal approach dealt with the intratextual nature of the Scripture and also the way that, sociologically, the Scripture and its communal tradition shape adherents more than does experience. In terms of the latter, he criticized the way that liberals begin from experience, often thinking of a common, universal experience, and move to interpretation, rather than seeing how interpretation shapes experience. Calling this the "experiential-expressive" approach to religion, this approach makes interpretation seem secondary, as various ways in which one's common experience is "expressed." In its place, Lindbeck offered a "cultural-linguistic" approach, drawing especially on the later Wittgenstein and the anthropologist Clifford Geertz, focused on the role of language and especially narrative. Lindbeck also referred to what he saw as the more conservative "cognitive-propositional" approach that did not do justice to narrative or identity formation, much as Frei (G. Lindbeck 1984: Chs. 1–2). Lindbeck at times did indicate, though, that there should be a place for a propositional element of reference that is mediated by the larger cultural form of life that is seen as much in practices as in propositions (G. Lindbeck 1984: 66).

Initially, one could see how Ricoeur's hermeneutical, textual, and narrative approach would fit in well. He did not think of a common, universal experience, certainly not one that was unmediated by language and tradition (nor did Gadamer). He would emphasize also that narratives shape identity in ongoing ways through a tradition (as would Gadamer in his own way). The emphasis on culture and language was a common theme in hermeneutical philosophy in Gadamer and Ricoeur. Ricoeur especially emphasized how one could not impose a general hermeneutical approach on specific areas or traditions, but did insist that there is a dialectic between one's generalities and the uniqueness of particular regional hermeneutics (Laughery 2002: 156). Ricoeur also in his religious writings indicated the identity-forming nature of the Scripture and actually went much further than either Frei or Lindbeck in dealing specifically with the way different genres in the Scripture affected identity. Gadamer and Ricoeur both emphasized how hermeneutics is embodied in practices in terms of appropriation.

So far so good, but a seemingly natural alliance was not to be. As we saw earlier, Frei and Lindbeck both as theologians were quite suspicious of what they perceived as philosophers imposing a general, modern schema upon theology. This was despite the fact that both drew on literary theorists, Wittgenstein, and anthropologists to buttress their approaches. They cautioned, though, that such usages should be "ad hoc" and not be allowed to dominate distinctive subject matter—an emphasis that Lindbeck saw in Wittgenstein and, as we have seen, a point explicitly made by Ricoeur. They were familiar, though, with Tracy, whose earlier work, *Blessed Rage for*

Order, seemed to match all their worst Barthian fears of theology trimming its sails to the tide of modern culture and seemed to interpret Ricoeur through Tracy.[23] Lindbeck said that theology should let the biblical world absorb the modern world and not the modern world absorb the biblical world (G. Lindbeck 1984: 117–18). The latter is exactly what they saw in Tracy's *Blessed Rage for Order* and to some extent in his later *The Analogical Imagination* (1981), with some justice. Tracy proposed that hermeneutics, drawing on the Gadamer-Ricoeur tradition, is the discipline for explicating the "meaning" of the Scripture and the Christian tradition for the theologian. In terms of evaluating the "truth" of these "classic texts," however, one must turn to contemporary philosophy such as process philosophy for adjudication. Then these two can be "correlated" in a "mutually critical" correlation. The latter already suggests that a simple collapse of truth into the "modern world," in Frei's and Lindbeck's terms, is not what Tracy had in mind, especially as he moved forward to *Plurality and Ambiguity* (1987). And one should note also that the limited role of hermeneutics in this account of Tracy in *Blessed Rage for Order*, which is quite different than the idea of "the universality of hermeneutics" in Gadamer and Ricoeur, which applies to truth as well as meaning. Nevertheless, it is not difficult to see in the early Tracy's approach the kind of modern liberal approach disavowed by the postliberals Frei and Lindbeck, as they came to be called.

It took some heated exchanges in publications, often by students of these protagonists, before calmer encounters, "dialogue" in the best hermeneutical tradition, muted the tension. First, Tracy pointed out the oversimplicity and perhaps caricature of the initial claims by Frei and Lindbeck (Tracy 1985). He stressed that the collapse of the hermeneutical tradition of Gadamer and Ricoeur (and himself) into Lindbeck's reading of Schleiermacher did not do justice to the major criticisms of Schleiermacher by hermeneutical philosophy. The idea of a common universal religious experience that preceded interpretation had long ago been left behind by hermeneutical philosophy as well as the later Wittgenstein. In fact, as Tracy pointed out, such an interpretation likely does not even do justice to Schleiermacher himself. It must also be pointed out that caricatures of Lindbeck and Frei also occurred from Chicago representatives, charging them with relativism and sectarianism.[24] Moreover, those sympathetic to Frei and Lindbeck have also pointed out that the understanding of both of them in terms of a school distorted their thought.[25] Making all allowances for the use of such "ideal types," which are often almost by definition distorting, the rather simplistic notion of the types as applied to these thinkers was taken up and passed on, ironically, as a tradition or preunderstanding that has often been brought to these texts of Ricoeur in particular without much recourse to the primary texts (Blundell 2010: 46). For example, Paul DeHart's otherwise helpful account of the conflict and concern about caricatures of the Yale thinkers continues without qualification Frei's view of Ricoeur as offering an apologetic or global hermeneutical theory that collapses the particularity of Christian theology (DeHart 2006: 134, 199, 200). George Hunsinger's insightful account of the difference between Lindbeck and Frei does the same (Hunsinger 2003: 52).

In the other direction, other scholars began to see more congruence. Frei himself in posthumously published papers surprisingly placed what seemed to be his own view quite close to Schleiermacher. His description of the Barthian view could fit Ricoeur himself.[26] He allowed for significant dialogue with other disciplines in shaping theology as long as the integrity of theology itself was not threatened or subsumed. William Placher, a student of Frei, and a noted scholar, indicated that Ricoeur was closer than had been thought of to the concerns of the Yale School (Placher 1987). Another graduate of the Yale Divinity School, Charles Scalise, saw much similarity between their concerns (Scalise 1994). Both Mark Wallace and Boyd Blundell have shown that Ricoeur was quite compatible with Barth, who was so emphasized in the Yale thinkers (Wallace 1990; Blundell 2010). In fact, Blundell argues extensively that Barth and Ricoeur make highly compatible dialogue partners between theology and philosophy and that "productive appropriation of Ricoeur's hermeneutics into theology may actually be in the hands of those whose theological sympathies lay with Frei and Lindbeck" (Blundell 2010: 52).

In the final analysis, it is true that Ricoeur is a philosopher and not a theologian, whereas Frei and Lindbeck are theologians, which accounts for different emphases.[27] In addition, sometimes Ricoeur's comments on theological views have led some to place him as a subjectivist, even a noncognitivist in theology, that is, that religious language is about private human experiences and has no external reference, even though, as we have seen, he rejects this position.

A view I recommend with Blundell is that Ricoeur's philosophical position should be taken as the primary guide, which was Ricoeur's own wish, especially as compared to his ad hoc, unsystematic comments on theology.[28] In this sense, Ricoeur's philosophy is open to a variety of critical theological appropriations across the theological spectrum from liberal to conservative. Ricoeur himself, however, argued in a way similar to Frei that philosophy should not dictate the specific nuances of a "regional hermeneutic" such as theology. While theology is textual and cannot avoid common dynamics of textuality, it is in turn unique and reacts back upon and subordinates philosophical hermeneutics.[29] Ricoeur's "philosophy" is that philosophy is more open-ended and cannot be monolithic or imperialistic.

Not every theology or every narrative theology in particular, however, would be compatible. On the conservative side, postmodern "post" conservative theologies such as those of Stanley Grenz, Roger Olson, and Kevin Vanhoozer would be quite compatible. Ricoeur himself saw his work as compatible with Barth and Moltmann. More hermeneutical, mainline theologians such as Tracy, Mark Wallace, William Schweiker, and John Hick would also be compatible. Ironically, Ricoeur's approach would be incompatible with the same types to which Lindbeck opposes his postliberal cultural-linguistic model, namely, the experiential-expressive and propositional models.

In terms of narrative theology per se, one can think of approaches with different emphases, if we are careful not to push the typology too far.[30] The Yale thinkers emphasized THE story, that is, the biblical narratives; the Chicago thinkers emphasized OUR story, that is, the narrative- and tradition-shaped nature of human experience; and there was a third emphasis on biography or autobiography, MY story. The latter could be seen as a California school since it is influenced especially by James McClendon, who was in California in various institutions, and by his students such as Terrence Tilley and Michael Goldberg. Although Ricoeur did not particularly develop a biographical approach to narrative, his work on the narrative shape of human experience and especially of human identity makes him a potent dialogue partner.

A more recent emphasis on narrative comes from the Radical Orthodoxy movement. The principal figure, John Milbank, in his major work notably stressed that one cannot out-argue opponents but must "out-narrate" them (Milbank 1993: 330). He accepts the basic postmodern rejection of classical foundationalism and a nonhermeneutical vantage point, while still arguing for robust knowledge claims that are narratively based. One could take this approach as well as the emphasis on narrative or "tradition-constituted enquiry" of Alasdair MacIntyre and their influence on theology to represent another fruitful dialogue yet to be had with Ricoeur's hermeneutical emphasis on narrative and tradition. Their traditions in turn flesh out in more detail, for theology especially, implications of Ricoeur's thought. For example, MacIntyre came to develop a notion of how rival traditions could argue with one another in a way that avoids relativism, where one tradition is able to answer the other traditions questions on its own terms (MacIntyre 1988, 1989). Such an approach to the vexed issue of relativism is one way of concretizing Ricoeur's general emphasis on a nonfoundational approach that is both referential and nonrelativistic.

Ricoeur contributes to these approaches, besides his general philosophy, more attention to the detail of the Scripture and to the nuances of genre. Even in comparison to the Yale theologians, he is careful to point out that there are many genres in Scripture, not just narrative, and that "the medium is the message" in each genre. They all have complementary emphases and cannot be reduced just to one. This is an emphasis that Vanhoozer, drawing on Ricoeur, especially makes in elaborating the significant advance on the nature of biblical authority by Yale theologian David Kelsey (Kelsey 1999). Kelsey had argued that many theological debates were unfruitful in that they questioned whether the other truly affirmed the Scripture. Rather, he argued that many if not most views presupposed the authority of the Scripture; Scriptural authority is almost a tautology among theologians. They differed, however, in their construal of the Scripture. He pointed out that most theologians construed the Scripture's meaning in a certain way that shaped their theologies, whether it was based on propositions, story, or metaphor. Vanhoozer agreed with Kelsey's main point but extended it in noting that the Scripture has multiple genres; thus, theologians need to attend to the diversity of genres in the Scripture, not just to one way of construing it (Vanhoozer 2002).

One of the often-cited challenges for narrative theology is how to be critical of narratives. Goldberg as a Jewish theologian has been helpful in cautioning about the way the Bible is assumed to be easily or only readable in a Christian way (Goldberg 1989). Besides his caution about narrowing the surplus of meaning, Ricoeur could be quite helpful here in his work on ideology and a hermeneutics of suspicion, which we will treat in Chapter 6. His last major work, *Memory, Forgetting, History*, especially deals with issues of ideology when it comes to the narrative shape of memory. We will deal more with this aspect of Ricoeur's thought in relation to truth claims after examining more closely his emphasis on an "incarnational" approach to the self, a major emphasis in contemporary philosophy and theology.

5

The capable self and theology

In the last decades of Paul Ricoeur's life, following his major work, *Oneself as Another*, he emphasized the "capable human being" (*homo capax*).[1] He expressed a desire to write a book on that subject, but, perhaps ironically, his increasing age and limitations did not allow it. Nevertheless, it represented a continuation and enrichment of what was perhaps the central theme running throughout his work, namely, the self, and enhances what is, alongside his hermeneutics, the richest resonance for contemporary theology. I say contemporary theology because Ricoeur's emphasis is on the holistic and situated self, while much of Christian theology in the past has been dualistic and somewhat other-worldly in relation to the self and the "soul." Ricoeur's approach, however, represents a turn to a more integrated view of the self in the twentieth century in a striking convergence between biblical studies, philosophy, psychology, and biology—all of which point toward a holistic view of the self and the soul. In fact, as biblical scholars now commonly attest, the Hebraic view of the self is holistic and embodied, not pointing to the more traditional view of a person as a "soul who *has* a body" but a person who "*is* an embodied soul."[2]

This relatively recent dramatic shift in theology is not ploughing old ground but new ground, and in the grander scheme of two millennia of Christian theology, it will take some time for its cracks and crevices to be explored and traversed. We are currently in the midst of that project, and Ricoeur's philosophical project, grounded in central Christian convictions, is, to stay with the agrarian metaphor, a useful means of cultivating this field. The balance, or better, tension, that he maintained between polar positions provides a distinctive path into, and perhaps out of, the current travails in this area.

On the one hand, there is a long Christian tradition of pessimism about human nature and its bondage that hovers over, if not falls into, determinism. One can argue that an affirmation of predestination is the major theological position in Western Christianity, stemming from Augustine and running through Aquinas, Luther, and Calvin, all deeply influenced by Augustine. This position in philosophy approaches a compatibilism where freedom and determinism or necessity are compatible, a view that has also a strong presence in contemporary biology and psychology. While not going so far, the Heideggerian position that equates human finitude with a kind of fallenness and inauthenticity and the Foucaldian pronouncement of the "end of man" who is a cipher in the nodes of many entangled webs of power both also represent pessimism concerning human capabilities (Foucault 2001: 386; Heidegger 1962: sec. 38). One could add the radical emphasis on the empty self in Jacques Lacan and Slavoj Zizek.[3]

On the other side is the transparent, unitary self of the Enlightenment reflected in classical Protestant liberalism, where the self is primarily rational, self-possessed, and little afflicted by sin. Christ becomes largely in this view a moral guide. As mentioned, there is a conservative side of this trajectory as well where the biblical text is transparent and, surprisingly, reason is little affected by fallenness. This optimistic tradition is the one against which Karl Barth, Reinhold Niebuhr, and Paul Tillich reacted so sharply, feeling that it was woefully inadequate on human enmeshment in evil, especially in light of the woes of the early twentieth century. Stanley Hauerwas represents a continuation of this critique on the current scene with his blistering criticism of the Enlightenment, even as he deepens the critique of a Niebuhr or Tillich (Hauerwas 1991, 2001).

Ricoeur responded to both of these polarities in his affirmation of a situated, fragile, but capable self that actually runs throughout his work. Against the more "pessimistic side," he affirmed human capability and a situated freedom in spite of the wounded cogito and a will that does find itself in bondage. Against the more "optimistic side," he clearly affirmed the postmodern and neo-orthodox critique of the disembedded, unitary self, with an emphasis on the fragility and discordance of human life and the need for an ever-present hermeneutics of suspicion. We will pursue the thick description of his complex notion of a capable self as these themes are sounded throughout Ricoeur's work.

The embodied self

An important place to begin is with Ricoeur's first major work, *Freedom and Nature: The Voluntary and the Involuntary* (1960). In writing that book, he explicitly mentioned the background that he had with both Gabriel Marcel and the inspiration of Maurice Merleau-Ponty's *Phenomenology of Perception* in terms of embodiment. Because Ricoeur has not particularly focused on embodiment since that time, it is an important dimension of his overall thought as it also does not appear that he rejected it or left it behind. Rather, he seems to have assumed it. Sometimes Ricoeur's later works are seen as his principal ones, for example, Anthony Thiselton in a recent introduction to hermeneutics naming *Time and Narrative* and *Oneself as Another* as Ricoeur's major works (Thiselton 2009: Ch. 12). The danger in that approach is that it omits the central aspects of Ricoeur's thought that he more assumes than abandons. By all accounts, his early two-volume project of a philosophy of the will is a major bookend to his later thought.[4] With the contemporary emphasis on embodiment, especially, it repays attention.

Ricoeur envisaged a phenomenology of the will as a sequel to Merleau-Ponty's phenomenology of perception. In terms of embodiment, it thus represents a significant contribution beyond Merleau-Ponty's landmark work. Both are inspired by Edmund Husserl's phenomenological approach, but both go beyond it in major ways, in actuality along the lines of Heidegger's revision of Husserl's phenomenology in *Being and Time*.[5] Heidegger moved to a more holistic view of an embodied self in tantalizing ways that he did not flesh out, such as his emphasis on Dasein as being-in-the-world. Both Merleau-Ponty and Ricoeur do flesh this out in their works. As such, they represent a vein of French phenomenology that has been called an incarnational philosophy, including Marcel, Merleau-Ponty, Mounier, and Ricoeur.[6] In this sense, it is a rejection of the Cartesian dualistic and highly intellectualist tradition in France, ironically represented in significant ways by Jean-Paul

Sartre, Merleau-Ponty's sometime collaborator. This incarnational emphasis is not as such a religious notion, especially with Merleau-Ponty, but it has resonance with contemporary emphasis on the significance of incarnation in Christology, which attempts to do much more justice to the embodied humanity of Jesus and then also to the embodiment of humans.

Ricoeur moved beyond Husserl and a strict phenomenological method in seeing that one needs a mixed or "diagnostic" approach in dealing with embodiment. In other words, like Heidegger, Marcel, and Merleau-Ponty, he thought that phenomenology includes and even results in a rich understanding of embodiment. On the other hand, there is also a place to include scientific or physical understandings of the body, mixed in with phenomenological description of experience of the body. Ricoeur compared this to the way a medical doctor draws upon the patient's description of symptoms (as well as his or her own experience) as well as medical knowledge of the workings of the body. While Ricoeur thematizes this, in some ways Merleau-Ponty exemplifies it more. It is an aspect of understanding the human that Ricoeur does not particularly draw out beyond this book until later in his dialogue with the neuroscientist Pierre Changeux in *What Makes Us Think?*, in the last section of *Oneself as Another*, and his last major work, *Memory, History, Forgetting*, where he deals to some extent with the biological basis of memory and forgetting.[7]

An important aspect of his approach in his philosophy of the will is that he concluded that phenomenology's description of essences cannot capture the inscrutability of evil or fallenness, which is not essential but a kind of rupture of freedom. His diagnostic phenomenology, however, provides a basis for approaching—but not capturing—this moment of freedom, much in the way that he later thinks of a philosophy of religion approximating—but not capturing—the moment of testimony of the sacred or Absolute. And even later, it points to the way that "forgiveness" as an aspect of a rupture on the positive side responds to the irruption of evil (Ricoeur 2004: 459–70).

The central thesis of *Freedom and Nature* is that there is a complex dialectic between the two, or the voluntary and involuntary as he alternatively puts it, without separating them. He captures this subtle interplay in this way, "The involuntary is *for* the will and the will is *by reason* of the involuntary" (Ricoeur 1966: 86). The voluntary and the involuntary cannot be understood apart from each other. This is very similar to the way biblical scholars attempt to convey the holistic conception of the "soul" in terms of the inherent intermingling of the physical and the mental or spiritual. Ricoeur laid this out in terms of his phenomenology of willing as involving a tripartite form: I decide, I move my body, I consent (Ricoeur 1966: 6). This way of putting it appears as if rational choice is the beginning point, but Ricoeur includes the involuntary at each point. In deciding, needs and pleasures influence motivation for a decision. Movement involves instincts (which he calls "preformed skills"), emotions, and habits. Consent involves character traits, the unconscious, and the influence of biological and psychological development.[8] Ricoeur treated Freud in this book but expanded upon him in his later *Freud and Philosophy* (originally 1965). While focusing thereupon what one may call "Freudian hermeneutics," which decenters the unitary self of the Enlightenment, he developed of course the emphasis on the unconscious that is not easily accessible to consciousness and the "hermeneutics of suspicion" to what does appear to consciousness.

In contrast to Heidegger's emphasis on our constant awareness of death, Ricoeur emphasized throughout his work how birth and our early years influence us beyond our conscious memory or awareness—an emphasis shared by Hannah Arendt.[9] The conclusion in "consent" is already a pointer to his move beyond Descartes in terms of a "wounded cogito," a fragile self that is not transparent or in control. Although Ricoeur did not bring it out explicitly here, one can see consent also underscoring the many ways in which the will has to come to grips with blocks and limitations. Ricoeur began this book during his years in the prison camp, and here one can easily think of the way in which choice was severely limited—but not demolished—in such straits. His later emphasis on the way the self's agency is always constrained, often by suffering, even as it attempts to act extends what might seem at first an odd emphasis. At the time, he was also likely thinking of the "limit situations" that Karl Jaspers underscored that emphasize human boundaries as well as possibilities. One can also see here a way in which Heidegger's notion of "thrownness" is taken up with Heidegger's parallel emphasis on Dasein's projection into the future. Ricoeur pointed out that these three dynamics occur together and not necessarily in strict serial fashion, which helps in that one could easily see the limitation of consent coming into play virtually before the "I will."

Ricoeur's treatment of the emotions in terms of movement, drawing particularly on Spinoza, is of continuing significance due to the recent awareness of the inherent role of emotions in cognition, going against the rationalist tendency of the West to see emotions as somewhat inferior, related more to the body than the mind, and even being a threat to rationality. This tendency can be seen in both Plato and Descartes and in the long-held assumption in theology that God, as divine, must be "impassible," not having experiences or emotions.[10] Ricoeur on the contrary, while not seeing emotions at this time as positive as some more recent thinkers such as the brain scientist Damasio Antonio or the philosopher Martha Nussbaum did, similarly, however, sees them as inherent to the self and to the self's actions.[11] This is consistent with Ricoeur's fundamental orientation to the self not so much as a knower but as a doer or, perhaps more accurately, one who desires, again following Spinoza and Jean Nabert. Ricoeur developed these themes of the affective and conative (desire) further in *Fallible Man*, which we will explore next.

The analysis that Ricoeur carried out over several hundred pages cannot be dealt with sufficiently here, but his "mixed phenomenology" can be seen in two illustrative issues. One is freedom. Discussions of freedom have oscillated between a determinism and denial of genuine freedom often found in science (and in some philosophy and theology) on the one hand and an emphasis of radical freedom on the other; for example, Sartre's unbridled emphasis on freedom that means that a person must take full responsibility for everything that happens to one. Often defenses of compatibilist freedom are posed in terms of a rejection of a libertarian freedom that is seen as unrealistically unaware of all of the limitations upon human consciousness, such as physical and unconscious impediments. Ricoeur asked, "Can we speak of a free act in an isolated instant? Is it not the case, rather, that the degree of a man's freedom can be calculated or imputed only on the basis of the quality or the flow of his whole life, or at least of a period of life that is viewed against the background of an unfolding destiny" (Ricoeur 1974c: 36). Ricoeur's treatment is helpful here in offering a middle ground of a "situated freedom," which may be, and in fact, needs to be limited in significant ways. In other words, even genuine libertarian freedom does not occur apart from conditions that limit it but also in a sense make it possible. Freedom apart from a situation virtually makes no sense. Ricoeur thus envisaged a dialectic in this way: "the naturalizing of freedom and the interiorizing of nature" (38). Here, one can compare the careful discussions of the relation of chance and necessity in chaos theory where chance can only occur in relation to conditions of necessity.[12] In an essay published in 1962, Ricoeur lamented the Sartrean type of ontological dichotomy between freedom and nature.[13] He alluded to the "mistaken" fight over essence and existence and the parallel equation of essence with being. Rather, Ricoeur saw being as primarily act and for humans' effort or desire. "Being is act before it is essence, because it is effort before it is representation or idea" (Ricoeur 1974: 32). This power, he urged, "is not the 'other' of freedom but the mediation which its becoming-real demands" (35). In this way, freedom is rooted in being or nature and arises inherently within nature. He concluded thus, "Nature is not in the first instance a resistance to be overcome, but a tendency to be taken up" (38). Ricoeur in fact further constrained the phenomenological conditions of freedom in *Freedom and Nature* and *The Symbolism of Evil*, where he saw the will as not only conditioned but also "servile," in bondage to some extent and enmeshed in radical evil. Nevertheless, freedom remains and is the foundation of responsibility, which he later developed in terms of a basis for ascription of acts to a responsible agent in *Oneself as Another* and in his late writings on justice. Such a conception of a situated freedom for a "capable self," despite all of the limitations maintaining a sense of genuine agency and selfhood, remains a via media between various polarized positions. It is of continuing significance in debates about freedom, determinism, and mind and body in both philosophy and theology.

This conception of freedom points also toward a more recent discussion about studies of the evolutionary, neurobiological basis of spirituality or religion. There is no doubt, contradicting deeply held assumptions, that there is a strong biological basis and correlate for spiritual experiences.[14] A holistic view like Ricoeur's and one now widely held in theology, however, would predict nothing else. Yet such findings continue to raise questions about whether there is anything but biological in such experiences. In other words, if spiritual experiences relate strongly to neurobiological activity, can they "just" be neurobiological activity? This reductionist approach, common again in much scientific discussion, is similar to the "freedom" issue in that a similar assumption implies that if willing is strongly correlated with such neurobiological activity, then there is nothing left over, so to speak, for freedom or spirituality. At this point, Ricoeur's diagnostic phenomenological approach could be helpful in pointing not only to a holistic self that assumes a biological basis for every human activity but also allows for a phenomenological description of genuine freedom that is consistent with, but not reducible to, deterministic biology. Situatedness, therefore, does not in and of itself imply the absence of freedom. Similarly, brain activity, in and of itself, does not deny experience of something outside the brain, any more than the thought of a tree or food being in fact brain activity rules out trees or food. The question of a spiritual reality transcendent to the individual self is clarified by brain studies but is not answered by them. The issues of freedom and spiritual reality are complex questions that admit of no easy answer and probably will represent ongoing philosophical and scientific debates, just as the corresponding Calvinist and Arminian debates in theology over freedom are ongoing and probably undecidable in terms of external evidence. Ricoeur's discussion and often debate with the neurobiologist Jean-Pierre Changeux is instructive at this point where Ricoeur both admits and appreciates all of the brain studies to which Changeux refers but doggedly insists on a phenomenological basis for an experience of consciousness and freedom that is not clearly reducible to the "brain"—and likely never will be. Rather than an ontological dualism, Ricoeur posits a "semantic" dualism, a Spinozist point where the two languages of science and phenomenology cannot be collapsed into one another (Changeux and Ricoeur 2002: 14). Perhaps where he goes beyond *Freedom and Nature* in this later book is his appeal to a "third language" that traverses the other two without abolishing the integrity of either.[15]

Semantic dualism (margin annotation)

The hermeneutical self

The complex phenomenological approach to the self already seen in *Freedom and Nature* is the basis for further development of a hermeneutical self, one might say, rooted in Heidegger's turn to ontological hermeneutics that sees the self as hermeneutical through and through. As we have seen in Ricoeur's hermeneutics thus far, his hermeneutics arises out of his phenomenological description of the self as dispossessed, as not transparent to itself (giving rise to a phenomenological hermeneutics). The self is consequently always an interpreting self, all the more so, as we have just seen, because of the self's embodiment and "diagnostic" nature of being an unsteady, holistic synthesis of freedom and nature. Ricoeur went on to elaborate this sense of the self's very being as a catalyst for interpretation in widening spirals, one might say, of a hermeneutical arc, from *Freedom and Nature* to an even greater sense of disproportion of human fallibility in *Fallible Man*, to an unavoidable recourse to symbol and metaphor in dealing with the movement from fallibility to fault in *The Symbolism of Evil*, to deceptions of the self in ideology, and then to a deeper conception of how the self in all respects is story-shaped.

In *Fallible Man*, Ricoeur elaborated a fragile disproportion of the self in thought, action, and feeling. In doing so, he pursued a path of the self's fragility based not on actual fault but on a polar tension between finite and infinite dimensions of the self. As Ricoeur expresses the move beyond *Freedom and Nature*, "I sketched [in *Freedom and Nature*] the neutral sphere of man's most fundamental possibilities, or, as it were, the undifferentiated keyboard upon which the guilty and the innocent man might play" (Ricoeur 1986: xli). *Fallible Man* expresses further "the constitutional weakness which makes evil possible" beyond the basic phenomenological or ontological understanding of an embodied self (xliii).

In each arena of thought, action, and feeling, Ricoeur indicated the disproportion between a finite and an infinite dimension in an unsteady mediation. For thought, which Ricoeur takes as focusing upon the conscious understanding of objects in the world, the relationship is between a finite perspective and a universalizing capacity of language that moves beyond the moment and the situation, which is then related in imagination. Here Ricoeur referred to the way in which language "precedes me and envelops me. . . . This ability to express sense is a continual transcendence, at least in intention, of the perspectival aspect of the perceived here and now" (Ricoeur 1986a: 27). The imagination's resolution, however, of the particular and the universal is not itself fully understood and gives rise to endless philosophical speculation about how they are related. Short of efforts to reconcile them on the side of the concept in absolute idealism or the object in radical empiricism (41), we are left with something of a mystery, a "marvel," in Kantian terms, "an art concealed in the depths of nature."[16]

In an intricate pattern, Ricoeur moves from such a "transcendental synthesis" to the "practical synthesis" of action that involves self-consciousness relating to persons. He moves from one's own human desire and character that opens up a finite perspective on life with others to the infinite and total desire for happiness that involves the good for others as well as the self, moving in a sense from the human to humanity (Ricoeur 1986a: 70). Their synthesis lies in what Kant called "respect," which attempts to combine the universal with the concrete individual in complex situations.

It is in the arena of feeling, however, that Ricoeur finds the greatest sense of fallibility, as an affective fragility (Ricoeur 1986a: 82). One does not just know or experience this disproportion; here one "feels" it. Along with the finite focus on the pleasure of vital bodily feelings (*epithumia*), one also experiences infinite desire (*eros*). Their "restless" synthesis is found in the "heart" (*thumos*), which is "the fragile moment *par excellence*" (82).

In this compact, dense work, Ricoeur reveals that disproportion is found everywhere. The human is thus at best a fragile equilibrium that easily falls apart. It is the delicacy of this knife edge of balance that represents the fallibility, virtual inevitability, of the human propensity toward fault—an in-depth philosophical analysis that corresponds to theological analyses by theologians such as Reinhold Niebuhr and Paul Tillich of the meaning of "original sin" and the "Fall" (Niebuhr 1949: 228–40; Tillich 1957: 29–44).

Ricoeur argued at some length that although we always begin too late, starting from fault, the very awareness of fault points back to a fallibility preceding fault. He said that we would not be cognizant of the fault if we did not have some sense of what precedes fault. When he said "precedes," he is not of course referring to a temporal precedence but a logical or ontological priority. In this, he follows the mainstream of theological reinterpretation of the Adam and Eve fall account in Genesis 3, where the account is seen as not the unique story of the first man and woman (who in the Augustinian and Calvinist accounts are the only ones who are free) but the story of every man and every woman, from the first onward.[17]

It is at this point that Ricoeur turned in the *Symbolism of Evil* to the symbols and myths of human frailty and brokenness. As mentioned, Ricoeur did not think that a conceptual account could do justice to the rupture or break that is represented by the free and irrational move from fallibility to fault. As we saw in the earlier chapter on symbols, he looked not only at the Judeo-Christian tradition but also at other ancient cultural approaches to the phenomenon of human evil. Ricoeur noted that symbols or metaphors,[18] such as of stain and defilement, are a primary way of approaching this phenomenon. These then yield to less physical and more moral symbols of sin and guilt (Ricoeur 1967: 1).

Finally, though, the symbols are taken up into myths, such as the Greek myth of tragedy, the Babylonian myth of creation out of chaos, the Orphic myth of the exiled soul in the body that one discerns in Plato's philosophy, and the biblical myth of Genesis 3 (Ricoeur 1967: 171–4). Ricoeur argued that the biblical myth in a certain way includes the emphases of the others. As with the earlier symbols, Ricoeur saw these myths as of continuing importance to attain a fuller view of the panorama of evil. In fact, he says, "The pre-eminence of the Adamic myth does not imply that the other myths are purely and simply abolished; rather, life, or new life, is given to them by the privileged myth" (Ricoeur 1967: 309). Evil is something people choose, yet it is somehow already present as a lure and temptation, symbolized by the serpent in the Garden of Eden. It is a choice and a break but also something we slip into gradually. Freedom and destiny are combined in a fateful brew.

The upshot is that critical reflection on such figurative language, where the "symbol gives rise to thought," leads to a deeper awareness, if not understanding, of the dynamics of fault. In light of the hermeneutical circle, it is not the first understanding alone but the second, postcritical understanding that is enriched by critical explanation that opens up a fuller grasp. Ricoeur warns in this light against a theological explanation that evacuates the symbol of its tensive nature and explains too much, which he saw the Augustinian theology doing with the fall myth.[19] In terms of the narrative arc, we should note here already that the symbols can hardly be understood apart from a larger narrative (mythical) context, pointing to the way that Ricoeur later placed metaphors in the context of larger narratives. At this point, though, he privileged the symbol over the myth. It is thus only a fuller hermeneutical approach that includes figurative and conceptual language that can do justice to actual human experience of frailty and fallenness.

One should add that Ricoeur's careful separation here of figurative language from the prose of philosophy cannot be sustained. While he never fully rejects this position, it is softened by his later emphasis on the narrative shape of human identity. We have already seen, in fact, the recourse to metaphors in *Freedom and Nature* and *Fallible Man*. In light of the insight that even science itself can hardly do without figurative language, one can conclude that the symbol gives rise to thought—and in part constitutes it. This does not deny the distinction between genres where some are distinctly fiction and others more prosaic philosophy, which is Ricoeur's main point. It does relativize their distinctiveness, however, just as Ricoeur later relativized the distinction between history and fiction—and allows the richness and pervasiveness of figurative language to enter into the explicatory power of philosophy itself, and of theology.[20] With this aid, Ricoeur elaborated how human beings are not just interpretive beings but require the full range of interpretive genres to be interpreted. Hermeneutics is required to capture humans not just as knowers but as embodied fragile and fallen creatures. It is striking that Ricoeur develops such a view so consonant with twentieth-century theological views in his *philosophy*, a view that was recognized as such and became widely influential and taken up in religious studies and in theology in the 1960s.

Ricoeur's turn to myth, as indicated, points ahead to his understanding of human identity as story-shaped. In dealing with the enigmas of personal identity much contested in Anglo-American analytical philosophy, Ricoeur especially in *Oneself as Another* developed a dynamic interplay between two aspects of identity, one of his singular contributions.[21] One he termed *idem* identity that refers to the way that human identity involves a strong element of sameness, much in the way that the identity of physical objects is seen. In order to deal with the vexed way in which humans are however also quite changeable, he termed *ipse* identity the way that humans bear a similarity-in-difference over time (Ricoeur 1992: 116). It is narrative, he thought, that enables us to bring these two together in a continuity through time that undergirds human identity. In joining identity to narrative and time, he moved beyond analytical philosophy's tendency to conflate humans with objects and the temporal moment. He thus rejoined Heidegger again who saw that temporality was crucial to human identity but went beyond him in providing fine-grained detail of how this works— and does not work. As in his earlier work, Ricoeur saw in character and also in continuity of the physical body the side that pertains more to sameness, to *idem* identity. In contrast, he saw in the dynamic capacity to make promises and projects and to attempt to remain true to them the side of self-sameness or self-constancy, *ipse* identity. In promising, humans project themselves into the future. The latter represents a more fragile yet nevertheless real dimension of identification, a particularly human one. As Ricoeur said, "Unlike the abstract identity of the Same, this narrative identity, constitutive of self-constancy, can include change, mutability, within the cohesion of one lifetime" (Ricoeur 1988: 246).

Where Ricoeur oddly left the discussion here is without much mention of another striking human dimension, namely, the failure of people to keep their promises, a place where the earlier attention to fallibility and fault helps. In the end, though, Ricoeur retains the Marcellian mystery of the self in seeing that there is in all concordance a discordance to the self's identity, wherein one can discern traces of his earlier emphasis on human disproportion. Humans are a narrative in progress—with full awareness of fallibility and fault, it is a broken narrative. Until death, we are not finished works but are continually writing and rewriting our stories, stories that we have both constructed and deconstructed. The difference in narratives of our lives and fictional narratives is that we do not control the contingencies of nature and other people that constantly impinge upon us. We are being written as well as writing—which makes rewriting a necessity. Our failures to keep even our own promises often catch us up short, as if this happens to us, drawing on a theme in *The Symbolism of Evil*. Consequently, our identities are not just unfinished but irrational and sometimes tragic.

Ricoeur perhaps comes at this issue indirectly by bringing in also the tragic in *Oneself as Another*, a section he poignantly dedicated to his son who committed suicide (Ricoeur 1992: 241). He emphasized the way that history happens to us as well as being shaped by our personal initiative. Our identities come from what we *suffer* as much as what we *do*. He noted that in his later years, "I never forget to speak of humans as acting and suffering" (145). To bring forward *Fallible Man* and *Time and Narrative* into this conversation, the unfinished discordant concordance that we all are stems from our fallible embodiment that makes us vulnerable both to external and internal assaults that threaten to decompose a genuine but quite fragile narrative identity.

The social self

All of the foregoing assumes Ricoeur's early rejection of the autonomous self of the Enlightenment. Rather, the self cannot be understood apart from its interlocking as an embodied being in the world with other people and with institutions. Merleau-Ponty saw the self as "inextricably entangled in the world." Ricoeur developed this insight to see how humans are "inextricably entangled" with other people in all sorts of ways, including the ethical and political as aspects of identity. These relations in turn, much like the hermeneutic spiral, rebound on previous discussions both to illuminate and also to complicate them.

It is interesting that Ricoeur was quite active politically and in writing on ethical and political philosophy in his early period, but after the disaster of 1968 he did not seem to focus particularly on the subject until *Oneself as Another*—and then the floodgates were opened.[22] His ethical philosophy has been seen as a unique contribution to contemporary ethics and politics. Bernard Dauenhauer, for example, argues that the combination of Ricoeur's political philosophy and his action theory means that "Ricoeur's third way between liberalism and communitarianism is a substantial contribution to the theoretical debates about democracy" (Dauenhauer 1998: 319). This later emphasis in Ricoeur was worked out in terms of a social phenomenology whose implications are only now being appropriated to any great extent in terms of political philosophy.[23]

The preeminent focus on the social self is in *Oneself as Another* and *The Course of Recognition*. Ricoeur pointed out as others have done that we are birthed into a social world, and the language and culture and tradition that shapes us comes from others. He is fond of saying that identity also comes from all the books that we have read, meaning that our story is influenced and intermingled with other stories—which we could add that also stem from film, poetry, and oral story-telling. Ricoeur's later *The Course of Recognition* depicted the way in which recognition involves recognition of objects, recognition of others, and a receptive being-recognized by others, which points toward a society, perhaps a utopian regulative ideal, where all are validly recognized. These are based on actions and gestures, such as surprising forgiveness, which, Ricoeur said, "cannot become an institution, yet by bringing to light the limits of the justice of equivalence, and opening space for hope at the horizon of politics and of law on the postnational and international level, they unleash an irradiating and irrigating wave that, secretly and indirectly, contributes to the advance of history towards states of peace."[24] This passage exemplifies the movement from the interpersonal to the political—and perhaps ecclesial—that we will explore next.

Ricoeur has drawn deeply on Emmanuel Levinas to agree that personal identity is shaped by encounter with the face of the other, although he does not root it so starkly and perhaps one-sidedly in obligation. Ricoeur said of Levinas' *Otherwise than Being* that its use of hyperbole, "to the point of paroxysm," does not sufficiently deal with the ability of the self to respond to the Other, which involves "a capacity of discernment and recognition" (Ricoeur 1992: 338, 339). In a question that Richard Kearney develops much further in *Strangers, Monsters, and Gods*, Ricoeur wondered whether Levinas' stress on passivity before the accusation of the Other allows one to distinguish "the master from the executioner, the master who calls for a disciple from the master who requires a slave?" (Ricoeur 1992: 339; Kearney 2002: 67, 79–82). Ricoeur also added the sympathy that stems from solicitude for the other person, which includes also the esteem and companionship of friendship. We come to understand ourselves, insofar as we are always a "discordant concordance," in and through others. Ricoeur spoke of this interweaving in terms of the loss of a loved one that touches the self at a deep affective level:

> It is in experiencing the irreparable loss of the loved other that we learn, through the transfer of the other onto ourselves, the irreplaceable character of our own life. It is first for the other that I am irreplaceable. In this sense, solicitude responds to the other's esteem for me. But if this response were not in a certain manner spontaneous, how could solicitude not be reduced to dreary duty? (Ricoeur 1992: 193)

In his preoccupation with human evil that runs from his philosophy of the will to his late *Memory, History, Forgetting*, Ricoeur was also well aware of the negative dimension of otherness, in other words, the way that we ourselves suffer from others and relate to the suffering of others. The Other breaks in upon us both in solicitude and in sorrow. As a French European who experienced quite directly the tragedy of the two world wars, the specter of personal and institutional evil is always present as a backdrop. The striking thing is that with this shadow and almost obsession with evil, Ricoeur maintains, unlike many existentialists but like his mentor Marcel, a positive dimension of human life that always stands in tension with threat. Even in the weakness of suffering, he reflected:

> For from the suffering other there comes a giving that is no longer drawn from the power of acting and existing but precisely from weakness itself. This is perhaps the supreme test of solicitude, when unequal power finds compensation in an authentic reciprocity in exchange, which, in the hour of agony, finds refuge in the shared whisper of voice or the feeble embrace of clasped hands. (Ricoeur 1992: 191)

He broke here thus with the Cartesian tradition of an isolated self and the idealist tradition that tended to reduce the Other to the Same and concluded, as a hermeneutical philosopher, with ongoing dialogue with irreducible Others. As he concluded concerning his reflection on Levinas, "Is it not necessary that a dialogue superpose a relation on the supposedly absolute distance between the separate I and the teaching Other?" (Ricoeur 1992: 339). The Other is thus ineradicably Other; yet it is also a co-shaper of our identities. We see ourselves "as" another, not totally different or the same.

He has been charged, however, with collapsing the Other into the Same. It is true that Ricoeur rejected an utter foreignness of others and strove for a balance between an emphasis such as Levinas and Derrida and an assimilation of the other. In a certain way, he pointed to the narrow balance that feminist philosophers often strive to find between criticism of an essential self that is not open to genuine otherness and a converse dissolution of the self that does not provide a basis for a empowered self.[25] The frustration that feminists see in some postmodernists is that "we should not abandon subjectivity just as we are beginning to define ourselves as agents."[26] Pamela Sue Anderson queries, "How could it make sense for feminists to seek the power to act for their own needs and interests if rational agency is given up?" (Anderson 1998: 55). Concerning Ricoeur, Louise Derksen and Annemie Halsema point out that on the one hand, Ricoeur's concern for similitude from a feminist perspective does not do justice to the otherness of gender, but they also think his view of the self "as ethical and ontologically open to otherness" is a balanced one that "can enrich feminist notions of identity."[27] Ricoeur did not focus on the issue of gender in personal identity, which can be seen as a weakness, but he did provide a model, especially through the dynamic interplay of *idem* and *ipse* identity, that lies between the liberal Enlightenment self and the death of the self, the kind of position that Susan Hekman, for example, sees that Julia Kristeva provides.[28] Anderson finds in Ricoeur's affirmation of life and capable self "great potential for feminist theory."[29]

The dimensions of solicitude, suffering, and evil also bring up the way that the self as social is inherently an ethical self, for ethics is itself not private but social. Ricoeur in fact conceived the ethical arising when one moves beyond the two of friendship to the "three" of others, often unknown others, that give rise to institutions. In Ricoeur's so-called little ethics in *Oneself as Another*, he creatively integrates the Aristotelian teleological tradition with the Kantian deontological tradition. Despite his great appreciation for Kant, he thought that the Kantian deontological "right" is rooted in the Aristotelian teleological "good" (Ricoeur 1992: 170). He nevertheless argued for a moral "ought" that arises out of the teleological ethical aim. He conceived this aim as wider than that of the individual and commonly, if not universally, one of *"aiming at the 'good life' with and for others, in just institutions."*[30] Ricoeur added, "The other is also other than the 'you.' Correlatively, justice extends further than face-to-face encounters" (Ricoeur 1992: 194). The Golden Rule, which is at the heart of Kant's categorical imperative and most world religions, is also inherently social. Ricoeur showed here the transition from esteem in the ethical aim to respect in the moral norm. The indignation felt at injustice undergirds the absolute prohibition, "Thou shalt not." The interpersonal solicitude of the ethical aim, however, adds depth to the impersonality of the Kantian anonymity of the other where one cannot do justice to the thick texture of ethical decisions, such as the Kantian example of always telling the truth, even when—to update to the twentieth century—the Gestapo is knocking at the door and asking about the Jew whom one is hiding. Ricoeur had great "respect" for the power of the justice of Kantian universalization of the norm that counters tendencies to favoritism and partiality. On the other hand, he desired to add to the complexity and depth of moral decisions the kind of social depth seen in Aristotle and Hegel, which he sometimes referred to as his "post-Hegelian Kantianism."[31]

In fact, Ricoeur, like Alasdair MacIntyre, moved from just decisions—or quandary ethics—to the practices and character of the self and connects with the emphasis in philosophy and theology on virtue and character ethics (MacIntyre 1984, 1988; Murphy, Kallenberg and Nation 1997; Volf and Bass 2002). Any complex human practice, such as science, involves practice and thus excellence that mark its success. More specifically, norms and precepts then arise out of them. Ricoeur did not develop as much as MacIntyre the way that character embodies these practice and excellence, but the latter's approach would be a significant integration with what Ricoeur says elsewhere of character. The life plan or project of a person thus involves such practices and precepts, but how are they integrated? Ricoeur turned to narrative as the way to bridge the "is" and the "ought" (Ricoeur 1992: 170). Narrative, in the way that it synthesizes the heterogeneous, spells out, so to speak, the way that the "ought" is inscribed with the "should." The abstract formalism of the moral needs ethical substance. The ethical, however, is refined and extended by passing through "the sieve of the norm" (170). Even with the discordance that remains in any person's life, perhaps because of it, narrative is the preeminent way in which these aspects are integrated. The puzzles of analytical philosophy's treatment of the self, treated in the beginning of *Oneself as Another*, are here transcended. What cannot be resolved *speculatively*, Ricoeur argued, can be made productive *practically* (147). To add to the way that here in the ethical Ricoeur brought together significant dimensions of his thought, the metaphorical leap or productive imagination is what enables one to integrate other narratives creatively into one's own life plan. Although it is not immediately transparent, one can see how in the way that so many of Ricoeur's themes are taken up in *Oneself as Another*; it attains the status, if any work does, of being Ricoeur's *magnum opus*.

Another significant dimension of this narrative basis of the ethical self is that the kind of knowing and self-understanding involved is one he calls "attestation," related to his earlier treatment of a "hermeneutics of testimony" in his philosophy of religion. We will treat this issue more in the next chapter, but he connected attestation with Aristotle's practical wisdom (*phronesis*) that represents conviction about self-identity between the poles, one might say, of modern certainty and postmodern skepticism. Self-awareness and the conviction of conscience then are situated between modern transparence and postmodern dissolution.[32] Ricoeur consistently spoke of this in terms of a wager or risk, "We cannot eliminate from a social ethics the element of risk. We wager on a certain set of values and then try to be consistent with them; verification is therefore a question of our whole life. No one can escape this" (Ricoeur 1986b: 312).

Ricoeur further connected attestation with conscience, wherein is situated an understanding and call to identity (Ricoeur 1992: 309). With Freud in the background, Ricoeur saw this more in the Heideggerian sense of a call to authenticity but highlights suspicion in conscience as "that place par excellence in which illusions about oneself are intimately bound up with the veracity of attestation" (341). Ricoeur added in *Memory, History, Forgetting* the way that memory is itself ethical and social. It can be almost prophetic in remembering what others around one are trying to forget, and yet it can be complicit in societal denial of the unpleasant past. Ricoeur's narrative approach to conscience, therefore, adds a thicker ethical dimension to Heidegger that helps deal with the enigma of how someone like Heidegger, who could emphasize authenticity, could leave it nevertheless so faceless—and perhaps partially account for Heidegger's Nazi complicity.[33] Another dimension is forgiveness that goes beyond simple justice, transforming it and also the conscience. Conscience, therefore, as well as narrative, integrates the dispersal of the self into a conviction, "Here I stand! *I cannot do otherwise*" (Ricoeur 1992: 352). It can accuse, call, but it can also receive forgiveness. Ricoeur consequently has added, however, to Aristotle a dimension of tragic wisdom that is not yet a despairing wisdom.

Ricoeur increasingly turned to the issue of living the good life "in just institutions." In doing so, he picked up themes in political philosophy that had preoccupied him in the 1950s. His argument in *Oneself as Another* is that when one moves beyond acquaintances to seek justice with many others who are unknown, the ethic of distributive justice becomes more important. He finds John Rawls' intuitions helpful here for democratic societies, but, as one might suppose, rejected the hermeneutical neutrality in the early Rawls' idea of an "original position" where one can evaluate a society without any biases concerning what kind of gifts one might have or opportunities of family or chance.

From Ricoeur's wartime experiences, he was understandably wary of the exercise of State power. What is more unexpected is that even in the 1950s, he could balance the dangers of such power with the necessity and advantages of such power, even while being arrested for protesting against State policies toward Algeria. In an early essay, "The Political Paradox," he argued that the State will always have and exercise power (Ricoeur 1965e: 255). This actually provides the basis for a society and for its stability and protection, staving off the chaos of a lack of government. The paradox is that with the good always comes the bad, namely, the tendency of the State to overreach. What is needed, he thought, is not pessimism or optimism in light of this fact but "lucidity" and "vigilance" (260, 261). In an essay published in 1958 that explicitly deals with the tension in the New Testament between the suspicion of the State in Revelation 13 and its affirmation in Romans 14, Ricoeur said, "The State *is* this dual-natured reality, simultaneously instituted and fallen" (Ricoeur 1974a: 203).

Also in the 1950s, Ricoeur argued that society is more complex than the Marxists saw, having a political as well as an economic function (Ricoeur 1965: 251). While Ricoeur advocated socialism, he warned presciently that because the governmental role is higher in socialism, the political power probably needs to be curtailed even more by democratic processes than in capitalist societies due to the tendency of government to overreach in its use of political power (Ricoeur 1965: 262, 264 1974a: 214). In other words, the political could subsume the economic.

Ricoeur returned to the issue of State power in his treatment of ideology and utopia in the 1970s, which will be treated more fully in the next chapter (Ricoeur 1986b). At this point, it is enough to realize that he understood both a positive and negative view of ideology (as narrative) as well as utopia. He saw in them a dialectical relationship where the abuses of ideology can be criticized by the hopes of utopia, and the fantasies of utopia can be corrected by the constitutive power of ideology. In an earlier, religious work, he noted, "The same phenomena that we have reviewed under the sign of rationality can also be reviewed under the sign of demonism" (Ricoeur 1974a: 207). This is an institutional correlation to the way that human fallibility inevitably leads to fault. Ricoeur proposed, however, that utopia can provide a source of ideology critique. Interestingly, Ricoeur noted that every ideology virtually begins as a utopia, so one can in the end have the nascent utopia in an ideology critiquing a burgeoning new utopia.

In an interesting way, Ricoeur connected love with justice especially in terms of institutions. As we have seen, justice is essential to human relations. As such, it is not counter to love and in fact, as an appeal to equity, as in the Golden Rule, is an expression of love. As he put it once, "Love cannot replace justice; even less can it dispense with justice. Love requires more than justice; it asks that justice be at once even more universal and even more singular" (Ricoeur 2010b: 31). On the other hand, justice without love, even the Golden Rule without love, falls into a dreary economy of exchange. Ricoeur asked, "If such is the spontaneous tendency of our sense of justice, must we not admit that if it were not touched and secretly guarded by the poetics of love, even up to its most abstract formulation, it would become merely a subtly sublimated variety of utilitarianism?" (Ricoeur 1995b: 328). The relationship between the two, perhaps we can call it an "interweaving" between the two, however, cannot be legislated, so to speak. They can only be practically mediated, "mediations, let us quickly say, that are always fragile and provisory" (315). Their disproportion is that in part justice can be commanded but love cannot. As Ricoeur said, "Love does not argue . . . . Justice does argue" (321). The genres are also not the same; the rhetoric of justice is met by the poetics of love. The challenge is "to build a bridge between the poetics of love and . . . the prose of justice, between the hymn and the formal rule" (324). Love expresses an "economy of the gift," perhaps an odd expression, which brings a "logic of superabundance" to justice's "logic of equivalence" (325). "Economy of the gift" is odd in light of the lively discussion in Continental philosophy, sparked especially by Jacques Derrida, on the "gift." For Derrida, the gift escapes logic, which applies to the economy of exchange. In fact, a gift is impossible in a certain sense because if one is aware of a gift, it lapses into reciprocity. A gift must, in a sense, be anonymous, even to the giver. The challenge of the gift is a kind of impossible demand that nevertheless motivates.[34] Ricoeur had already worked out in many ways the backdrop for his basic ideas in connection with the parables in the mid-1970s in a slightly different way (Ricoeur 1975). While agreeing with the challenge of the gift in many ways, he saw it as nevertheless practicable, fragile but possible. In his essay, "Love and Justice," Ricoeur urged that "this economy of the gift touches every part of ethics" (Ricoeur 1995b: 328). The relationship of love and justice is an "unstable equilibrium" but one that in the particular situation is feasible. He added, "I would even say that the tenacious incorporation, step by step, of a supplementary degree of compassion and generosity in all our codes—including our penal codes and our codes of social justice—constitutes a perfectly reasonable task, however difficult and interminable it may be" (329).

Perhaps this position reflects Ricoeur's basic optimism and even hope, but, as we have seen, it is at best a kind of tragic hope. Ricoeur turned his attention to the difficult issue of forgiveness in the context of the horrors of the twentieth century such as war, the Holocaust, and Apartheid in South Africa in the epilogue to *Memory, History, Forgetting*, also joining a significant and related Continental discussion led by Derrida. Ricoeur highlighted Derrida's affirmation that only the unforgivable can be forgiven, something that is an impossibility, yet a stimulus for Derrida (Derrida 2001: 32). Yet Ricoeur relates this to the "capable being" where "forgiveness exists" (Ricoeur 2004: 457). "The proclamation summed up in the simple phrase: 'There is forgiveness' resonates like an opposing challenge" (Ricoeur 2004: 466). Ricoeur sets what he termed the "height" of forgiveness against the "depth" of fault. Similar to his treatment of love and justice, he contrasted the two genres: "below, the avowal of fault; above, the hymn to forgiveness" (457). Again, in a surprising way, he called this the "forgiveness equation" that is nevertheless a tension that is carried "almost to a breaking point"; it is a "torment" (458, 468). The forgiveness equation lies in the economy of the gift as set out above: it is a "logic" of superabundance. Forgiveness cannot be required. As he noted, "There is no politics of forgiveness" (488). Forgiveness, however, is needed just as love is needed to watch over justice. Forgiveness gives hope for personal relations and relations among and within nations, perhaps best described as "eschatological," a hope for a "happy memory," perhaps better, "peaceful memory, reconciled memory" (457, 496). Ultimately, Ricoeur saw, hoped, that forgiveness is "difficult: not easy but not impossible" (457). Actually, there is at best an "odyssey of the spirit of forgiveness."[35] It involves forgiving without forgetting—and yet forgetting and remembering in the right way. This is perhaps a practical wisdom (*phronesis*) saturated with grace. It is an odyssey that involves a work of memory, a work of forgetting, and a work of mourning that is guided by a spirit of forgiveness (456, 504). In a hymnic tone, remarkable for the context of the sorrows and "concerned memory" of the twentieth century, personal and social, he appealed to a note of superabundance, "[c]arefree memory on the horizon of concerned memory; the soul common to memory that forgets and does not forget" (505).

One can see how this very complex approach to the problems of personal and social relations can open up also fresh a perspective on the church as an institution that exhibits all of these dimensions. As is increasingly realized, the Christian is essentially ecclesial, just as the self is essentially social and political.[36] The self must live its life and write its narrative in the midst of the "adventures of the state"—and the Christian lives amidst the adventures of the church. The tensions between the uses and abuses of power in both State and church call for "a vigilance which excludes sterile criticism as much as millenarian utopianism."[37] In theology, this is a way of extending fallenness to institutions, of moving from individual to corporate evil. Conversely, one can appeal to the Kingdom of God as a utopian critique of such fallenness. This is surprising in that the Marxist tradition has underscored only the escapist dimension of utopia. The critique of escapist utopianism, however, does not militate against the positive critical power of the utopian imagination to renew ideology and offer transforming alternatives. It is here that the "passion for the possible" combined with the creative, productive imagination is a continual source of renewal for the church (Ricoeur 1980b: 160). This application of the tradition of utopian thinking in Ricoeur to ecclesiology has surprisingly hardly been made.

Ricoeur's reflections on the State in political philosophy typically assume a citizen in a stable nation, but for issues of identity, it is not as clear how his thought applies to people in anarchic or chaotic states, or especially refugees or others who do not find themselves at home in any State but are strangers. What does it mean in these cases to aim for the good life in just institutions? Ricoeur did write on the issue of the stranger in the 1990s but focused more on how a state like France and her citizens should treat the stranger (Ricoeur 2000: 133–45). And in his development of the concept of recognition, one can discern a point of contact for a concern for the stranger and the displaced in both society and church when he observed, "The idea of a struggle for recognition is at the heart of modern social relations" (Ricoeur 2010a: 24). One can assume that the narrative approach to the self still holds in such a chaotic situation, with much less emphasis on the ethical aim in just institutions of a stable State. For example, Kwok Pui-Lan in relating feminist and postcolonial theology speaks of the "diasporic female subject" who is "multiply located" and thus needs a diasporic imagination (Pui-lan 2005: 46–7). She says, "I want to conjure a female diasporic subject as multiply located, always doubly displaced, and having to negotiate an ambivalent past, while holding on to fragments of memories, cultures, and histories in order to dream of a different future" (2005: 46). It is not as though the need for a narrative imagination that helps to synthesize the heterogeneous is lacking, even though the limits, as Ricoeur indicated, are always there. The ethical aim for the good life with and for others in just institutions may be as strong or stronger than ever. The human productive imagination cannot be minimized as diasporic people continue to seek and even find their own identity. Perhaps their ethical aim often remains more of a utopian gesture than an integrative myth or ideology.[38] Discordance sometimes comes to the fore and thus calls for utopian critique and alternatives.

The theological self

The longing for something more as well as the mention of the call of conscience points to a religious consciousness to which Ricoeur adverts throughout his work—but in occasional essays and never in a sustained way. His care to keep philosophy accessible to the nonreligious is valuable, but it is clear in these essays that he desired his philosophy to be open to the religious direction, thus making it also quite accessible to theology. Ricoeur developed a self that is like one of Karl Rahner's early works, as a "hearer of the word" (Rahner 1969). In other words, humans have a capacity to encounter God or at least to be open to a religious and theological experience. As Rahner the theologian saw it, humans have been created in the image of God already with an openness, even directedness, toward hearing the word of God. This is a "point of contact," if you will, of the human with grace.[39]

For Ricoeur, this openness is seen especially in an essay that was a part of his Gifford Lectures but was published separately from

Oneself as Another. Here the call of conscience is the call of God (Ricoeur 1995c: 262–75). He also adumbrated this openness in his recourse to the idea of "primary affirmation" in Spinoza and Nabert.[40] This is not per se a specific theological affirmation and could belong as well to an atheist or naturalist, but it is an affirmation of the meaningfulness of life. One could point here to similar ideas in theologians who passed through the Chicago Divinity School such as the idea of "basic faith" in David Tracy, Schubert Ogden, and Hans Küng, or a dimension of ultimacy in Langdon Gilkey, all of whom saw faith as its "re-presentation" or fulfillment (Tracy 1979; Ogden 1977; Küng 1976; Gilkey 1969). Such primary affirmation is an opening to transcendence or to the Absolute, whose fulfillment can at best only be a "testimony," as Ricoeur calls it in "A Hermeneutics of Testimony" in the 1970s but which he calls "attestation" in *Oneself as Another* (Ricoeur 1980c). Such a witness can be contested, but it cannot be transcended. It could appear to be fideistic, but he rejected that appellation since he saw that it was rational in being tested. It is nevertheless a "summoned self" at this point who receives a call from beyond that from a theological perspective is not reducible to the self.[41]

The capable and suffering self

We draw together these multiple dimensions of Ricoeur's philosophy of the self with implications for his late emphasis on the capable self. In Ricoeur's address to special conferences in France in 2000, he spoke on the "capable man" or the capable self. He said simply, "It is in my desire to be, in my capacity to exist, that the arrow of the religious comes to hit me" (Ricoeur 2010b: 27). Hence, the religious self and the capable self are "interwoven," to use one of his favorite terms. His characterization of the capable self summarizes what we have related in this chapter. They in turn undergird a religious perspective on selfhood.

Ricoeur spread out human capability in four areas: the capacity of speech, the capacity of "an incarnated agent" to act, the capacity for recounting history and time, and the capacity for imputation of responsibility. As he succinctly puts it, these relate to the ability "to speak, to do, to tell, and to impute" (Ricoeur 2010a: 28). Interestingly, in light of the prominence of "capability," he pondered that these capacities reveals themselves most clearly through their counterparts, their impotence, particularly in the experience of evil. Here he returned to his favored approach, a quite Kantian one in relation to the phenomenon of evil, seen in his early philosophy of the will. He acknowledged that one could approach them through "experiences of abundance," but considering them in light of evil "has the advantage of making the religious appear from the direction of a fault, of a defect, of a break, beyond which the happy continuity between the new capacities engendered by the religious and more fundamental capacities constitutive of the human being could be restored" (28).

Despite his attention here to the experience of evil, Ricoeur also turned in his later thought to a renewed emphasis on primary affirmation related to the doctrine of creation. He said, "I now think that there is a philosophical side of creation that allows us . . . to help the theologian not to cover over too quickly a theology of creation by a theology and Christology of redemption. This reminds us that creativeness comes before law, guilt, and even redemption" (Ricoeur 2002: 283). Ricoeur's emphasis here chimes in with the renewed theological attention to creation, seeing that it has often languished or even been denigrated in the light of sin and redemption. Ricoeur added, "As radical as evil may be, it will never be more originary than goodness, which is the *Ursprung* in the field of ethics, the orientation to the good as being rooted in the structure of the human being, or in biblical terms: creation, created."[42]

Ricoeur expressed that in his later life he came to see not so much evil but suffering as the focus, which includes but is broader than wrongdoing. The limit of capable effectiveness is suffering. "Fallible Man" moves to the "fragile self." Early in *Freedom and Nature*, Ricoeur already stressed that "consent" is an aspect of action, that is, recognition of the limits of action. An aging Ricoeur later saw that the limits of action involve the constraints that come from economic, social, and even physical barriers, leading up to silence and death. To tie to his work on narrative, Ricoeur ended an address he gave at the conference "Haunted Memories? History in Europe after Authoritarianism," which was held at the Central European University of Budapest, Hungary, in March 2003, entitled "Memory, History, Oblivion," with a quotation by Isak Dineson, "All sorrows can be borne if you put them into a story."[43] Ricoeur hinted at this potential when he said, "The story of a life continues to be refigured by all the truthful or fictive stories a subject tells about himself or herself. This refiguration makes this life itself a cloth woven of stories told" (Ricoeur 1988: 246). Such redemptive story-telling requires deployment of all the resources of the productive, metaphorical, even utopian imagination, often in situations of great deprivation and desolation. Perhaps Dineson's "if" recognizes that in tragedy there can even be an end to story-telling, that suffering cannot be taken up. These limit-situations require the concept that Ricoeur took up from Freud of "working through" sorrow, yet with greater resources of the imagination. An aspect of the self as a task is experiencing and responding to the suffering through imaginative configurations that lead to practical refigurations of life, both of one's own and one's capable intersection with one's social milieu. In speaking of the creativity of ethics, Ricoeur later said at one point, "In the moral order, the past leaves not only inert traces, or residues, but also dormant energies, unexplored sources which we might assimilate to something like unkept promises . . . . This dormant character of as-yet-unfolded potentialities is what allows for resumptions, rebirths, reawakenings, through which the new gets connected with the old. . . . It is always after the fact that one discerns in the past what did not reach maturity in its own time" (Ricoeur 2007: 181–2). Ricoeur thus walked a narrow line between the limitations encountered in life that render human life so fragile and between openness to the continuing springing up of possibility. His last ruminations in the fading years of his life were a desire to "live up to death" (Ricoeur 2009). Ricoeur's "passion for the possible" through the creative imagination in the midst of fragility and suffering is hence a thread that ties together many aspects of his thought—with obvious theological implications.

Redemption in this life hence occurs in the context of continuing capability, fallibility, and fault, a situation which Tillich called ambiguity (Tillich 1963: Part IV; Gilkey 1979: Part IV). Ricoeur always saw here both capability and fragility. The massive evil experienced in the twentieth century, focused in Ricoeur's life in his almost five-year wartime imprisonment, is a reminder of fragility; resistance, survival, productivity, and utopian hope beyond it attest to capability. Ricoeur was more interested in relating this view of the capable and fragile self to political issues; it is the theologian's task to work it out more deeply and critically in relation to the church and society.

6

Thought and theology

Descartes began the modern period with a dream—in fact, several dreams—and ended with a method that would ensure certainty.[1] Thus, he instigated for a variety of reasons a "quest for certainty," as John Dewey put it, that would drive philosophy for several centuries (Dewey 1929). Perhaps the early Wittgenstein and logical positivism in analytical philosophy and Husserl's phenomenology in Continental philosophy—as well as structuralism at times—were the last great gasps of this movement. All of these came under intense scrutiny and critique in the late twentieth century, resulting in a shaking of the foundations, even a rejection of all foundations, whose aftershocks continue to reverberate throughout philosophy and contemporary culture. The passion of modern philosophy was epistemology, inspired by the Cartesian quest that focused on how one can know with certainty. While in some sense, the postmodern move questions this focus on epistemology, it cannot avoid its own genealogy. Some of the most important aspects of a paradigm change, if there is a genuine one, thus have to do with a reworking of epistemology.

Ricoeur is someone who straddles this shift, beginning with Husserl but already questioning the objectivist assumptions behind Husserlian phenomenology. His Marcellian background pushed him to question the absolutist pretensions of epistemology, as we have seen, through his emphasis on the "wounded cogito" and the knowledge of reality as hermeneutical "all the way down." Yet he does not follow skepticism and suspicion all the way to abandonment of any grasp of truth or rationality altogether. As such, Ricoeur represents a significant model for a transformed epistemology that, as he himself puts it, avoids "the epistemic exaltation of the cogito in Descartes" and "its humiliation in Nietzsche" (Ricoeur 1992: 21). Ricoeur's reworking of an epistemology that has made the interpretive turn joins the ferment in theology that is also coming to grips with much more communitarian and hermeneutical approaches to the issue of faith and reason at the same time that they hold on to the meaning of a confession of faith in the reality of God.

In exploring the significance of Ricoeur's work on epistemology for theology, we will first recapitulate the implications of previous chapters, look more closely at the issues of objectivity and attestation in relation to the complex relation of philosophy of religion to religion in Ricoeur, and then at the role of a hermeneutics of suspicion or ideology critique for theology.

Hermeneutical epistemology

As we have seen, Ricoeur has consistently questioned the ideal of absolute knowledge and set it under limits, which, in light of our theological concerns, he saw as eschatological limits. It is not until the "Last Day" that one might have a chance at such knowledge. In this life, he would agree with the Apostle Paul, "We know in part" (1 Cor. 13:9).

This non-Cartesian view of epistemology is rooted in the wider spirals of this thought. It is based on his denial of the transparent self and thus the "wounded cogito." It also rejects the uninterpreted object, set over against the self, knowledge of which is guaranteed by rigorous methods. He agreed with Heidegger and Gadamer that at the bottom all knowledge is set within hermeneutics, however much within hermeneutics one can use methods and attain a high degree of certainty, as in some scientific endeavors and in mathematics. The object is always entangled in the world of the self, of tradition, of culture and language, and is thus always hermeneutical. With Hegel, he affirmed that knowledge always begins too late to avoid presuppositions and thus rejects classical foundationalism. As he expressed it, perhaps thinking of his own fascination with Husserl, he said:

> Perhaps one must have experienced the deception that accompanies the idea of a presuppositionless philosophy to enter sympathetically into the problematic we are going to evoke.

In contrast to philosophies concerned with starting points, a meditation on symbols starts from the fullness of language and of meaning already there; it begins from within language which has already taken place and in which everything in a certain sense has already been said; it wants to be thought, not presuppositionless, but in and with all its presuppositions. Its first problem is not how to get started but, from the midst of speech, to recollect itself. (Ricoeur 1974g: 287f)

Against Hegel and with Kant, however, he believed that knowledge is thus a process within the hermeneutical spiral that never attains absolute knowledge, hence his "post-Hegelian Kantianism." Like Kant, he affirmed a reference, a postulate, in the arena of faith but one that is always partial. We will deal later with whether such grasp of transcendence in faith can be considered as only regulative or also as a form of knowledge.

In epistemology, therefore, Ricoeur followed the hermeneutical line that runs through Marcel, Heidegger, Nabert, and Merleau-Ponty. Especially with regard to the social sciences, humanities, and religion as they involve self-knowledge, they are based on self-knowledge as a project, a task, and not an achievement. His language earlier is somewhat inconsistent in the area of the natural sciences, but the logic of his position, following Gadamer, is that even they are ultimately not foundational and are hermeneutical. In fact, in a later interview (1982), he pointed this out:

We are now no longer so sure about this deep gap [referring to Dilthey] between the so-called science of the spirit and the so-called science of nature. The notion of fact in the natural sciences is strongly put in doubt and criticized. There is also interpretation in the field of the natural sciences. (Reagan 1996: 102)

His view then was that selves are based on continual interaction "with all the books they have read" and all other encounters, especially with people. Hence his conclusion was that self-identity is "oneself as another," which ultimately impinges on all other knowledge.

Ricoeur placed himself within what he calls the tradition of "reflexive philosophy" that is still rational but opposed to Cartesian certainty. Despite the focus on the self, which it shares with traditional Continental philosophy, it is based, in Heideggerian terms, on one's being-in-the-world, including a "with-world." Ricoeur of course greatly fleshed out this perspective beyond Heidegger with the help of others such as Marcel and Merleau-Ponty. Ricoeur points to Baruch Spinoza, Gottlob Fichte, and Jean Nabert as indicative of the self as a project that roots epistemology not so much in knowing but in acting, more precisely, in desiring, desiring to be. In this basic affirmation of being, Ricoeur saw a hint toward the support of the "Absolute" and ultimately God but only a partially grasped reality, based on testimony. It is a fragile hint that makes its affirmation one of risk, of a wager, and ultimately of faith. It is here that the dividing line between faith and reason became quite blurred in his thought.

While some have regarded this focus on the self as preventing Ricoeur from breaking out of the subjectivistic problems of modern philosophy, he saw it as moving beyond subjectivism and toward the self-in-the-world, indeed, a social self. The irony is that Ricoeur went to great pains not to deny a reference to reality or the self altogether, as, for example, some postmodern thinkers do in seeing the self as a social construction, virtually a fiction. As we saw in the last chapter, Ricoeur's position here, as typical, is mediating. And its veracity depends on where one is in evaluating that position. As Ricoeur puts it, he stakes out a position between Descartes and Nietzsche, Kant and Hegel. In terms of a position that is conducive to the relationship between philosophy and theology, it is quite promising. It rejects the hegemony of absolutist reason that eliminates the mystery and transcendence of religion from one perspective and a skeptical, even nihilist position, from another perspective that also eliminates transcendence. In his reflection on the Marxist tradition, Ricoeur gave voice to his analysis of the present time, "This process of suspicion which started several centuries ago has already changed us. We are more cautious about our beliefs, sometimes even to the point of lacking courage; we profess to be only critical and not committed. I would say that people are now more paralyzed than blind" (Ricoeur 1986b: 313). At the same time, he rejected the alternative of returning to a precritical, premodern past or yielding to such paralysis. In pointing toward a *postcritical conviction*, he rejected the alternatives of objectivism and relativism, as Richard Bernstein described them, as part of the false dilemma of modernity but pointed to a genuine, albeit hermeneutical, knowledge (Bernstein 1985).

Objectivity

Ricoeur's mediating but genuinely postmodern stance can be seen and illuminated in his early treatment of objectivity in the 1950s. From early on, Ricoeur tended to separate what one can "know" or substantiate more easily from what one cannot. At the same time, however, he would indicate the virtual inseparability of the two, leading to a degree of ambiguity about what he regarded as within the ambit of philosophy per se and what was not.

In an article originally published in 1952, entitled "Objectivity and Subjectivity in History," many of the themes of Ricoeur's later works appear in incipient form as well as the tension with which we are concerned (Ricoeur 1965c). Here, Ricoeur treated the problem of whether there is a proper objectivity in history, despite the attention to the subjectivity of any historian. Since positivistic history seemed untenable to him already at this time, he wondered whether we are left with a polar relativism on the other side. Are we caught within the dilemma of modernity between objectivism and relativism? This is especially acute in a discipline such as history, even more when Ricoeur moves to the discussion of whether there can be a *philosophy* of history.

Ricoeur first accepted an unavoidable subjectivity for several reasons. There are the issues of the historian's choices and perspective, the historian's own historical context, and the fact that the historian is dealing inevitably with the role of human beings in the causation of history (Ricoeur 1965c: 26–31). These factors remind one of Ricoeur's later emphasis on the inherent role of imagination and configuration, closely related to fiction, in historiography in *Time and Narrative* in the 1980s. Second, he argued, calling especially upon Marc Bloch, that there is a difference in historiography between "good and bad subjectivity and we expect the very exercise of the historian's craft to decide between them" (22). He pointed out that there are "levels of objectivity" in various fields, so one should not expect historiography to be physics (21). The historian does not deal with brute facts (any more than the physicist, in actuality), so, third, the issue is one of making integrated judgments that are based *on* analysis, not *in spite of* analysis. He used the hermeneutical word "understanding" for these kinds of judgments, which he argued are not opposed to "explanation," to anticipate the way he integrated them in his hermeneutical arc of the 1970s (24). Fourth, such use of the understanding and of making syntheses does not take history out of the realm of reason or knowledge. He called it a "near rationalism" at one point but also pointed out that it is like modern physics in this respect, so "there is no reason for history to have an inferiority complex" (25). Significantly, at another point, he said, "Feeling and imagination used to be opposed to reason; today we put them back, in a certain way, into rationality" (31). On the other hand, he later contrasted historiography with the way that mathematics may "denominate" its object thus leaving historiography as "inexact and non-rigorous" (27). In the tradition of Dilthey and Collingwood, he spoke of the way that the historian must have not only careful analysis of documents but also a sympathy for human beings in order to understand them in their historical exigencies. "Reasoned analysis," he said, "is a kind of methodical step between an uncultivated and an educated sympathy" (29). Such a need for intuitive sympathy, however, does not mean a collapse into relativism; rather, he concluded, "We have only specified the kind of objectivity that arises from the historian's craft" (29).

When he turned to the issue of a philosophy of history, he recognized and valued the suspicion that a historian might harbor toward it, but he still argued for its viability and its own level of objectivity. In an article published in 1953, "The History of Philosophy and the Unity of Truth," he accepted, however, the historian's suspicion against a Hegelian closure of history. He returned to this theme in the third volume of *Time and Narrative* in saying, "The leaving behind of Hegelianism signifies renouncing the attempt to decipher the supreme plot" (Ricoeur 1988: 206). Despite the threat of skepticism and relativism, he pointed toward the unity of truth as a regulative idea in the Kantian sense, one that could never be attained in history (Ricoeur 1965d: 53). He used the language in the earlier article of such a unity being at best a matter of hope, even eschatological hope (55). He emphasized a phrase that he often repeated later, namely, "I hope I am within the bounds of truth."[2] The implication is that one makes fallible truth claims within history that one hopes can hold up. It is important to highlight here Ricoeur's use of holistic judgments in historiography and in the philosophy of history that are rational, defensible, and objective but not in an objectivist sense, involving feeling and imagination in holistic ways that are not opposed to reason or knowledge but are integrated within it.

One more dimension of his thought can be added from essays within this time to the eschatological hope of truth, namely, the "primary affirmation," drawn from Jean Nabert, that is also based on hope. The failure of Hegelian idealism raises the question of the meaninglessness of history, of any hope for meaning at the end of history. Ricoeur is concerned here in dealing with this failure to differentiate between true and false anguish (Ricoeur 1965f: 294). He argued in dialogue with Jean-Paul Sartre that only by moving through the depths of existential negation can one "reachieve" primary affirmation, reminiscent of his later language of a postcritical naïveté or a second understanding in his hermeneutical arc (288). Even in dealing with Kant's radical evil or the Jobian threat of an evil God, there is a possibility of an affirmation or upsurge of being that never leaves the question behind of what he calls a "timid hope" or a "tragic optimism."[3] Ricoeur said, "Thus, although hope is the true contrary of anguish, I *hardly* differ from my friend who is in despair; I am riveted with silence, *like him*, before the mystery of iniquity. Nothing is closer to the anguish of nonsense than timid hope" (303). Is this a matter of faith outside of reason? Ricoeur rather says, "Hope therefore enters into the scope of reflection, as reflection of reflection and through the regulative idea of the totality of the goodness of being. But unlike absolute knowledge, primary affirmation, secretly armed with hope, brings about no reassuring *Aufhebung*; it does not 'surmount,' but 'affronts'; it does not 'reconcile' but 'consoles'; this is why anguish will accompany hope until the last day" (304).

What is difficult at this point is to determine whether such a hope or primary affirmation and the judgments made in light of it are in the realm of knowledge, reason, and philosophy or in the realm of faith. On the one hand, he seems to think that the judgments one makes in history in light of one's hope for truth are clearly philosophical and rational, belonging to the proper objectivity of a philosophy of history. In the way that Ricoeur develops the centrality of primary affirmation, it is difficult to see how it is clearly outside of philosophy. On the other hand, the language of hope as regulative at least puts it in Kantian terms as a matter of faith, even if a rational and moral faith.[4] In an essay from 1951 explicitly addressing a Christian theology of history, Ricoeur identified the meaning of history in terms of hope as "an object of faith" (Ricoeur 1965a: 94). He said of the Christian that he or she "hopes that the oneness of meaning will become clear on the 'last day,' that he will understand how everything is 'in Christ'" (94). Such language certainly seems to place a view of history in this light as a *theology* of history and not as he otherwise termed it as a *philosophy* of history, although in terms of their finitude, openness, and allowance for ambiguity, they seem to be quite similar.

Attestation

In the development of a hermeneutical arc, Ricoeur similarly pointed toward a postcritical naïveté that involved an "appropriation" of the world in front of the text that, as we saw, operated in terms of its own kind of logic, a logic of probability in interpretation that was a risk. It is something that was backed by life as much as by a method or logical arguments, even though those could be included and even central as an aspect of explanation. As such, these appropriations functioned as knowledge claims and a conviction about reference.

It is interesting that at this time Ricoeur also gave lectures on ideology and utopia where he dealt with the imprecision of noetic judgments (Ricoeur 1986b). In this context of politics and culture, he again argued clearly against any kind of Hegelian absolute knowledge. In dealing with the Marxist tradition, in fact, he pointed out that Karl Mannheim had dealt with the issue of whether one could ever be free from ideology as Marx had desired. In other words, in criticizing an ideology, is one not instituting another ideology? Ricoeur concluded, "I consider Mannheim's attempt to overcome this paradox one of the most honest and perhaps *the* most honest failure in theory" (166). He goes on to say:

My own conviction is that we are always caught in this oscillation between ideology and utopia. There is no answer to Mannheim's paradox except to say that we must try to cure the illnesses of utopia by what is wholesome in ideology . . . and try to cure the rigidity, the petrification, of ideologies by the utopian element. It is too simple a response, though, to say that we must keep the dialectic running. My more ultimate answer is that we must let

Spiral

ourselves be drawn into the circle and then must try to make the circle a spiral. We cannot eliminate from a social ethics the element of risk. We wager on a certain set of values and then try to be consistent with them; verification is therefore a question of our whole life. No one can escape this. (312)

Such a conclusion may raise, Ricoeur thought at one point, the specter of fideism (Ricoeur 1986b: 312). In another essay on ideology about the same time, however, Ricoeur dismissed fideism. In light of the ubiquity of ideology, he asked, "How can we take a decision which is not a mere toss of the dice, a logical bid for power, a movement of pure fideism?" (Ricoeur 1981d: 241). In answer, he appealed to "a viable solution" that he saw in his "hermeneutics of historical understanding" (242–3). He then added, "This knowledge cannot become total. It is condemned to remain partial, fragmentary, insular knowledge" (245). In dealing with such political and historical judgments, even existential judgments that relate to larger meaning, Ricoeur implied that these limitations of reasoning do not expel them from the realm of knowledge and philosophy. They are reminiscent of his earlier account of a certain kind of objectivity in the philosophy of history and in historiography.

His emphasis shifted, however, also about this time when he turned to the issue of philosophy of religion and its claims. Relating to his work on symbol and metaphor at this time, he wanted to move to the more concrete advocacy of a position in terms of testimony. It is perhaps surprising in light of his affirmations of the "ontological vehemence" of symbols and metaphors that he thinks that they lack "historical density" in relation to testimony (Ricoeur 1980c: 122). He placed the content of testimony within the orbit of faith. The account of testimony, however, he thought could be the way philosophy "approximated" faith, that is, it comes right up next to it but cannot cross the divide.

He dealt with this most clearly in the "post-Hegelian Kantianism" that he unfolded in an essay written in 1968 entitled "Freedom in the Light of Hope" (Ricoeur 1980b: 166). He followed Kant in a philosophy of limits that nevertheless allows a "practical demand for totalization" or a regulative idea of hope that Kant called a postulate or faith (167). He did say that this "discourse of religion within the limits of reason alone" is funded by being able to say, "*Spero ut intelligam*, I hope in order to understand" (166). In drawing on Kant's aphorism, "the symbol gives rise to thought," Ricoeur indicated that philosophy is generated by the symbols of religion at times and in turn can speak of the conditions of possibility that can approximate religious faith (Ricoeur 1967: 347–57).

In "The Hermeneutics of Testimony," published in 1972, he developed further the way that not just a symbol but a concrete conviction by someone—perhaps inspired and illuminated by symbols—engenders philosophy and goes beyond philosophy. He began again with Nabert and saw testimony relating to primary (here translated "original") affirmation of the Absolute, which he then conflated with testimony about God as a matter of faith (Ricoeur 1980c: 120, 130). Testimony thus involves a "quasiempirical" claim to have experienced something, a claim which, despite its empirical character, is already a hermeneutical claim. It then involves a "quasijuridical" dimension, which implies the way a claim must be evaluated. The judgment of one's testimony, however, is also a hermeneutical judgment. It concerns, as Ricoeur says of it and hermeneutical judgment in general, "not the necessary but the probable" (126). Third, as an aspect of its uncertain nature, testimony runs the risk of false testimony. This leads to what we might call a "quasimarturial" dimension. Witnesses historically were martyrs, who backed up their testimony with their lives. This backing does not guarantee the veracity of a belief, but lack of commitment undermines it (129). As Ricoeur indicated, "Testimony is also the engagement of a pure heart and an engagement to the death" (130).

Ricoeur then wanted to relate this more secular view of testimony to religious language, but differences arise. Ricoeur stated, "What separates this new meaning of testimony from all its uses in ordinary language is that the testimony does not belong to the witness. It proceeds from an absolute initiative as to its origin and its content" (Ricoeur 1980c: 131). Nevertheless, the same dynamics continues. For instance, "The conjunction of the prophetic moment, 'I am the Lord,' and the historical moment, 'It is I, the Lord your God, who has led you out of the land of Egypt and out of the house of bondage' (Exodus 20:2)—is as fundamental as the conjunction of the prophetic moment and the juridical moment" (133).

Ricoeur noted that the movement from the Old Testament to the New is an intense interiorization. God the Holy Spirit testifies in one's heart, representing the "internal testimony of the Holy Spirit" so important to Calvin and Ricoeur's Reformed tradition.[5] Ricoeur maintained, however, against a subjectivist understanding that exterior history and signs are of continuing importance: "Testimony-confession cannot be separated from testimony-narration without the risk of turning toward gnosticism" (Ricoeur 1980c: 139).

On this basis of examination of the profane and sacred uses of the term, Ricoeur raised the question of how these meanings relate to a philosophical affirmation of the Absolute. Ricoeur pointed to Lessing's "ditch" that posited a disconnection between the contingency of history and absolute truth. As Ricoeur said, "An immense obstacle seems to close off the horizon of the response: do we have the right to invest a moment of history with an absolute character?" (Ricoeur 1980c: 142). In other words, is a "philosophy of testimony" possible? Ricoeur answered that it is but only as a "philosophy of interpretation" or of hermeneutics. An added complication is that the philosopher is often interpreting someone else's testimony. All of the hermeneutical dynamics, however, still apply when one appropriates or believes another's testimony.

The stakes are raised when the testimony is to the philosophical notion of the Absolute, for Being, for ultimate reality, which in a religious context is spoken of as God. This also involves one's judgment of oneself in relation to the Absolute, which Ricoeur, following Nabert, refers to as one's "criteriology of the divine." Ricoeur thus summarizes, "Thus the hermeneutics of testimony arises in the confluence of two exegeses—the exegesis of historic testimony of the Absolute and the self in the criteriology of the divine" (Ricoeur 1980c: 142).

Such an account of the Absolute involves all three facets of evaluating testimony. There is the *empirical* side of manifestation where something is given to be interpreted. In the midst of history, Ricoeur says, "The absolute declares itself here and now" (144). Here is one of his strongest affirmations of a reality reference, even to the Absolute. If not, "a hermeneutics without testimony is condemned to an infinite regress in a perspectivism with neither beginning nor end" (144). This is true even when in the testimony of Christian faith, as Ricoeur put it, "there is no separation between the Jesus of history and the Christ of faith" (145).

Such a testimony as this, however, insistently calls for the *juridical* moment. In assessment, "a split is sketched, a split which is not the ruin of testimony but an endless mediation on the divided immediacy" (Ricoeur 1980c: 145). Ricoeur indicated that the early church already began this chain of interpretation in their proliferation of titles for Christ (145). In this case, an event and its meaning are inseparable. The issue of suspicion must be taken seriously. Ricoeur said, "Hermeneutics arises there a second time: no manifestation of the absolute without the crisis of false testimony, without the decision which distinguishes between sign and idol" (146).

The juridical is followed by the *marturial*. The truth of the Absolute's manifestation is evaluated as an aspect of the disciple's commitment to it. Ricoeur meditated:

> The testimony of Christ is his works, his suffering, and the testimony of the disciple is, analogously, his suffering. A strange hermeneutic circle is set in motion; the circle of Manifestation and of Suffering. The martyr proves nothing, we say, but a truth which is not strong enough to lead a man to sacrifice lacks proof. (Ricoeur 1980c: 146)

Then one still must deal with oneself and one's own stance toward the Absolute. Is there such transcendence? If so, what is its nature? How does one interpret oneself in light of it? The hermeneutics of the self must pass the same tests as the hermeneutics of history. Ricoeur asks, "Is it not the same trial which, little by little, proves to be the trial of testimony and the trial of the predicates of the divine?" (Ricoeur 1980c: 148). At this outermost edge of the capacity to grasp reality, Ricoeur and Nabert speak here of the dynamics of losing one's self in order to find it, "The criteriology of the divine corresponds to the greatest divestment of which human consciousness is capable in order to affirm an order freed from the limitations from which no human existence can deliver itself" (147–8).

This "knowledge" is a chastened knowledge— neither one of Cartesian certainty nor Hegel's absolute knowledge (Ricoeur 1980: 149–50). It is thus characterized by a double hermeneutic humility stemming from the hermeneutics of history and of the self (149). Ricoeur acknowledged that this is a kind of probable knowledge that is nevertheless crucial. He says, "To attest is of a different order than to verify in the sense of logical empiricism" (150).

Ricoeur saw at that time the relation between the testimony to the Absolute and our analysis of it as the relation between religion and philosophy, faith and reason. Philosophy can never be adequate to the testimony. Their difference, he said, "prevents us from subsuming, in Hegelian fashion, religious representations to the concept" (Ricoeur 1980c: 153). Philosophy can approximate but not quite attain such testimony, according to him. This is where he concluded, "The mutual promotion of reason and faith, in their difference, is the last word for a finite consciousness" (153).

The problem is that the stark difference is not so clear in this analysis. It is true that philosophy cannot prove or verify such an experience in a fully empirical way, but this is already recognized in the very nature of testimony to the Absolute. It is not clear why an appraisal of someone's witness cannot be a philosophical appraisal that has to do with knowledge. If so, why is the original claim necessarily in a totally different realm? Ricoeur's distinction is helpful in seeing how philosophy can elucidate dynamics of such a claim and the nature of testimony and its evaluation. As such, it cannot appeal without further ado to a special revelation or to a Holy Book. On the other hand, as an experiential claim, it can be tested by wider experience as well as one's own. In fact, Ricoeur implied that there is no philosophy without original "religious" testimony. Testimony, like symbols, gives rise to thought. Thought has its necessary place, but it cannot supersede the testimony. The modern philosophical ideal is humbled by the inescapability of testimony and its expression in symbol and narrative. As Kevin Vanhoozer puts it, "Indeed, the image of the philosopher with cupped hands—or better, open ears—is especially appropriate for describing the humble spirit of Ricoeur's philosophy that only begins with a revelation from poetic texts" (Vanhoozer 1990: 275).

Philosophy cannot transcend the trial of hermeneutics, because it must attend to the Absolute in its ambiguous manifestation in history and to the self in its dispossession. Philosophy cannot, therefore, transcend the humbled reasoning that Ricoeur calls here testimony or attestation. Yet it is not clear why the original testimony to an experience is set outside of the realm of reason and knowledge altogether.

Many philosophers testify to a particular conception of the Absolute, which is their particular comprehensive construal of reality and the meaning of reality, even atheists in their own way, such as Sartre. In light of this, it seems odd to say of primary affirmations and the philosophical developments of them that they belong to an invincible chasm between reason and faith, that reason or philosophy can only deal with conditions of possibility and not argue for certain construals of possibility, such as those of Descartes, Spinoza, Hegel, Marx, Heidegger, Sartre, and so on. Moreover, there is a difference between an absolute claim about the Absolute and a fallible testimony to the Absolute, both of which remain within the bounds of philosophy. In fact, Ricoeur ended the article on the hermeneutics of testimony not with the sharp contrast between reason and faith that he had just mentioned but with a contrast between two seemingly epistemological philosophies, "We must choose between philosophy of absolute knowledge and the hermeneutics of testimony" (Ricoeur 1980c: 153). This opposition seems to be the more decisive. Ricoeur seemed to conflate these different dynamics in these articles. In his hermeneutical arc and in his treatment of the philosophy of history, he defended the epistemological legitimacy of a second understanding that is irreducible to a scientific knowledge of objects, which is much like the hermeneutics of testimony, but in these articles, as we have seen, he takes that imprecision to mark faith over against reason.

To complicate matters further, in *Oneself as Another*, published in the late 1980s, he placed at the epistemological center of a hermeneutics of the self the concept of "attestation," which was quite close to the earlier category of "testimony." He offered a "hermeneutics of the self" that is positioned between the modernist notion of a transparent, unencumbered self and a skeptical dissolution of the self (Ricoeur 1992: 4). He said further, "To my mind, attestation defines the sort of certainty that hermeneutics may claim, not only with respect to the epistemic exaltation of the cogito in Descartes, but also with respect to its humiliation in Nietzsche and its successors. Attestation may appear to require less than one and more than the other" (Ricoeur 1992: 21).

These judgments about the nature of the self also relate to ethical judgments about the good and the moral that Ricoeur developed in his creative synthesis of Aristotle and Kant.[6] It becomes clear here that he has creatively appropriated Aristotle's *phronesis* or practical wisdom for his broader usage of attestation. This conclusion is confirmed in his similar reference to "phronetic judgment" in his later book on political judgments, *The Just* (Ricoeur 2000: xxii).

As such, these judgments about the self and the affirmations of value by the self seem to fit his appeal to "partial, fragmentary, insulary knowledge" as related to political judgments about ideology and utopia as well as the considered judgments about interpretation in the hermeneutical arc. These would seem to belong to the realm of knowledge, even if partial. However, "attestation" is obviously quite close to his earlier category of "testimony," which relates very much to affirmations of religious meaning for the self. In his acceptance speech for the 2004 Kluge Prize in the Humanities, he clarified in connection with his emphasis on the capable self:

> Capacities can be observed from outside, but they are fundamentally felt, lived in the mode of certainty. The latter is not a belief, considered a lesser degree of knowledge. It is rather a confident assurance, akin to testimony. I am speaking here of attestation: attestation relates to the self as testimony relates to an event, a meeting, an accident. (Ricoeur 2010a: 22)

Even with this distinction, which perhaps does not do justice to the similarity between testimony in the earlier essay and attestation in *Oneself as Another*, testimony, too, seems to belong to a hermeneutics of the self. Yet, as we recall, he saw this kind of judgment earlier as across the divide between reason and faith, philosophy and theology.

These reflections point to a broad category of phronetic judgment or thinking that runs throughout Ricoeur's work and manifests itself in a variety of ways. It is, moreover, similar to the way Gadamer appropriated *phronesis* as an epistemological category. As in Gadamer's idea of "the universality of hermeneutics," which meant the fundamental place of *phronesis* in all thinking, the tenor of Ricoeur's overall work is that basic judgments of philosophy, of meaning, of history, of law, and of self-understanding are phronetic (Gadamer 1991: xxviii–xxix). The fact that these are holistic acts of the understanding that involve tradition and the emotions and are neither wholly objective nor certain does not undermine their genuine epistemic nature, especially when he always saw them as allied with considered "explanation." Yet at other points he took what seems to be the same kind of reasoning and placed it on the side of faith, beyond the capabilities of philosophy. Another instance is the following quotation given in the previous chapter, where he is suggesting that the call of conscience might be from beyond the self:

> Perhaps the philosopher as philosopher has to admit that one does not know and cannot say whether this Other, the source of the injunction, is another person whom I can look in the face or who can stare at me, or my ancestors for whom there is no

representation, to so great extent does my debt to them constitute my very self, or God—living God, absent God—or an empty place. With this aporia of the Other, philosophical discourse comes to an end. (Ricoeur 1992: 355)

Here, the division between the philosopher who cannot say and the believer who testifies is hardly tenable. The point that Alvin Plantinga makes, whose view of the epistemology of faith we will look at more closely in the next chapter, is that it is artificial, in a sense, for such commitments of the believer, which may be claims to knowledge in their own right, to intimate that such convictions are not already effective in their philosophy. It does not take a hermeneutical philosopher to realize that such convictions will have effects, whether conscious or unconscious. Is it better to acknowledge such presuppositions, as always, and then be critical of how they affect one's philosophical judgments?

It is striking, then, that Ricoeur had second thoughts about the sharp distinction that he had earlier drawn between reason and faith. Ricoeur said in a later interview (given apparently in parts in 1995 and 2003):

And I might even concede here a point made recently by my young colleagues Dominico Jervolino and Fabrizio Turoldo that my thought is not so removed from certain religious and biblical issues as my standard policy of "conceptual asceticism" might have been prepared to admit in the past. I am not sure about the absolute irreconcilability between the God of the Bible and the God of Being . . . . The tendency of modern French thought to eclipse the Middle Ages has prevented us from acknowledging certain very rich attempts to think God and being in terms of each other. I no longer consider such conceptual asceticism tenable.[7]

While there are practical, political, and sociological grounds for distinguishing religious truth claims and philosophical truth claims, these reflections suggest that such lines are philosophically blurred. A conviction that there is a larger spiritual or rational reality, as in Whitehead say or even Hegel, is not necessarily that different as a judgment than the conviction that reality is wholly material. Nor is it that different from a metaphysical judgment that reality is deterministic or contains libertarian freedom. As we have seen, these are phronetic judgments similar in many ways to political, historical, and hermeneutical judgments. Some of these are considered philosophical judgments and some religious, but they are similar in striking ways. Perhaps the factor that makes them similar is not that they are partial, holistic, and underdetermined by the evidence but that they have moved through the testing of testimony in a way that many religious claims have not. In others words, these are all aspects of a hermeneutics of testimony that pertain not only to religion but also to interpretive, historical, ethical, and political judgments. As such, the critical issue for philosophy then is that such judgments have undergone a "trial" and have been tested.

A hermeneutics of suspicion

This notion of testing is one that is crucial to either a philosophical or religious epistemology and one that Ricoeur took up especially in his earlier work on Freud and Marx. Despite the rather positive impression that Ricoeur often conveyed in looking for symbols to be recharged with meaning, with a primary affirmation of the value and source of Being, with an appropriation of a possible world from texts, the shadow of criticism haunts all of Ricoeur's work. It is expressed at a basic level in the rejection of absolute knowledge and an absolute standpoint, with the awareness that we are condemned to "partial, fragmentary knowledge." It is reflected in the partial phenomenology in his early philosophy of the will where the voluntary is limited by the involuntary and where evil is accessible only indirectly through the symbol rather than the concept. It is reflected in the eschatological reference to the full knowledge only being possible in the "last day." It is reflected in his hermeneutical arc in the middle moment of "explanation" that is the critical moment par excellence. And it is reflected in the "juridical moment" of a hermeneutics of testimony, as we have just seen, where a witness' claim can be contested and perhaps refuted. In virtually all of his works, he left them open in a kind of continuing discordance that cannot be overcome. Even in his last major work and in its last section of forgiveness, as we have seen, he ended with the word "incompletion" (Ricoeur 2004: 506).

It became a focus for the well-known phrase, a "hermeneutic of suspicion," in his work *Freud and Philosophy*, although he himself used the phrase in a limited way primarily in that work.[8] He was interested in Freud as an interpreter of symbols, as a preeminent hermeneutician, but he did not avoid the question that Freud raises about meaning. As such, he joined the many Continental interpreters of Freud who see in him a basis of ideology critique, where Freud is joined with the Marxist and neo-Marxist traditions. Freud for Ricoeur represents an archeology.[9] It is an explanation, based in part on explanatory mechanisms, a "hydraulics of drives," that accounts for hidden and distorted meaning.

Ricoeur pointed not only to Freud but also to Nietzsche and Marx in this period of the 1960s and 1970s. His engagement with Habermas in the *Hermeneutikstreit* with Gadamer showed much appreciation for Habermas, who was also appropriating Freud as a way to provide an explanatory standpoint in order to reveal a "systematically distorted communication," something which Gadamer's work did not readily address. Ricoeur allowed for such a "method" as an aspect of "explanation" in his hermeneutical arc that can indeed make us aware of the deep distortions of ideology. At that time, he stressed, however, the limits of such ideology as not escaping the hermeneutical dynamics of tradition, pointing out that ideology critique is itself also a tradition (Ricoeur 1981a: 99). As Habermas himself has continued to realize, it is difficult to find a neutral place to stand apart from hermeneutics. Allowing for methods, however, as Ricoeur did, can aid in identifying the subterfuges of communication without rescuing one wholly from the challenges and dangers of such distortion.

In Ricoeur's lectures on ideology in the 1970s, as we saw in the previous chapter, he looked to the utopian imagination as a way of dealing with ideology. Ricoeur began with dissatisfaction with the simple understanding of ideology as distortive. Deconstructing Marx, one might say, he used Marx against Marxism to point to a broader, more humanistic, view of ideology (Ricoeur 1986b: 183). Rather than seeing ideology as something that can be contrasted with a Marxist, scientific view of things, or a Habermasian quasitranscendental viewpoint, he saw that we are inextricably entangled with ideology. Yet he also posited an integrative and legitimative function of ideology along with the distortive. He then argued that the dangers of ideology are best countered by utopia. Utopia's imaginative exploration of promising possibilities calls ideology into question, but ideology in its constructive forms cautions against the destructive delusions of utopia.

To reiterate, he posited three different dimensions of ideology, drawing on the work of Max Weber, Karl Mannheim, and Clifford Geertz. He delineated an *integrative* and *legitimative* along with a *distortive* function of ideology (Ricoeur 1986b: 254–55). Any society, he argued, drawing here on Geertz, has a symbolic, cultural dimension that integrates and legitimates it. It is usually idealistic, or we might say, utopian, to begin with. To anticipate the connection with utopia, there is a dialectical relationship with utopia, where utopia functions as the place of criticism of ideology. A new society or new regime usually begins as a utopian criticism of the old. As it gains power and authority, the utopia falls into ideology. In this sense, ideology has a constitutive and potentially healthy function. In a revealing statement, Ricoeur explained, "Logically if not temporally the constitutive function of ideology must precede its distortive function. We could not understand what distortion meant if there were not something to be distorted, something that was of the same symbolic nature" (182). In an essay on science and ideology, he offered another positive influence of ideology, "Its role is not only to diffuse the conviction beyond the circle of founding fathers, so as to make it the creed of the entire group, but also to perpetuate the initial energy beyond the period of effervescence" (Ricoeur 1981d: 225).

The problem is that ideology always has to simplify, and one could add that its idealistic side also simplifies complex and harsh realities. A gap therefore between reality and the ideology has to be filled in by belief in order to have legitimacy. "My argument," he said, "is that ideology occurs in the gap between a system of authority's claim to legitimacy and our response in terms of belief" (Ricoeur 1986b: 183). In an insightful appropriation of the Marxist idea of "surplus value," he used it as the way that legitimation simplifies and thus goes beyond reality, which is where the destructive side of ideology typically arises (183, 200–2). In order to defend legitimacy against attack, ideology hardens and is used as a weapon by the dominant class to suppress criticism. Ricoeur added, "This feature appears to contradict the first function of ideology, which is to prolong the shock wave of the founding act. But the initial energy has a limited capacity; it obeys the law of attrition" (Ricoeur

1981d: 227). Founding myths have a place, a point that is easy to miss in the context of a solely negative approach to ideology. If one sees them in terms of narrative identity, they are indispensable, but they always call for a degree of demythologization. The modern Marxist suspicion of ideology is the dominant perspective on ideology for a reason; the positive functions of ideology, due to their surplus value, all too easily slide over into negative.

This is where utopia fits in. Ricoeur saw it also as having a threefold structure that correlates with ideology (Ricoeur 1986b: 310). In fact, it is a dialectical correlate to ideology. As mentioned, ideology usually begins with the high hopes of utopia. Utopia usually arises as an alternative to an existing ideology. Ricoeur discusses at some length whether they can be separable and decides that they cannot. Utopia, too, can be *destructive*, and as Marx saw, even serve the ends of ideology, by being wishful and unrealistic thinking. It can be dangerous in the minds and hands of fanatics. Where ideology distorts, utopia can be illusory. Ricoeur said in an essay on this topic, "It is as though we have to call upon the 'healthy' function of ideology to cure the madness of utopia and as though the critique of ideologies can only be carried out by a conscience capable of regarding itself from the point of view of 'nowhere'" (Ricoeur 1991b: 324). At best, however, utopia can provide either a genuine and better alternative to the status quo or serve as continual, constructive criticism. In this positive sense, where ideology legitimates, utopia provides an *alternative*. Its main relationship, as literally the view from nowhere, is to call into question the problems and stress points of ideology. Ricoeur said, "It is always from the point of view of the nascent utopia that we may speak of a dying ideology. It is the conflict and intersection of ideology and utopia that makes sense of each" (Ricoeur 1986b: 181). The third correlate then is that where ideology preserves identity, utopia explores possibilities. Ideology integrates, whereas utopia *subverts* through invention (Ricoeur 1991b: 319–20). Ricoeur stated:

> Whether distorting, legitimating, or constituting, ideology always has the function of preserving an identity, whether of a group or individual. As we shall see, utopia has the opposite function: to open the possible. Even when an ideology is constitutive, when it returns us, for example, to the founding deeds of a community—religious, political, etc.–it acts to make us repeat our identity. Here

the imagination has a mirroring or staging function. Utopia, on the other hand, is always the exterior, the nowhere, the possible. The contrast between ideology and utopia permits us to see the two sides of the imaginative function in social life.[10]

L,U p,182

A significant element of Ricoeur's approach is to note the distinction between ideology and utopia in terms of both being works of the imagination. Utopia is more literary, individual, and related to a particular context, whereas ideology is more anonymous and general. Utopia can represent the productive imagination in a way that transcends the situation, reminiscent of the way Ricoeur saw creative metaphor as involving a semantic shock that reconfigures reality. Narrative also can project an imaginative new world in which we can live. As such, imagination can perform not just a constructive but also a quite critical function. For Ricoeur, one of the best examples is Jesus' parables that reorient by disorientation (Ricoeur 1975). Interestingly, he hardly makes these connections himself in the text.[11] Ideology also in its more integrative sense is a work of the imagination itself but posed in a defensive, legitimizing mode rather than a contrary one.[12] Ricoeur further distinguished between literary utopias and practical utopias, that is, utopias that are exemplified in experimental communities, often communes. Another distinction is between utopias that are so "unreal" that they are virtually impossible of fulfillment, utopia as nowhere, and utopias that are good places, eu-topias, which are perhaps realizable. Interestingly, Ricoeur as a Christian thinker prefers the latter even though the Kingdom of God idea seems much more like the former. The Kingdom of God has indeed functioned in escapist ways, as Marx saw so well, but it has also served to subvert the status quo in terms of an appeal for a basic equality of all people.

Even though Ricoeur's conception of ideology and utopia is like calculus compared to the simple treatments of ideology as invariably harmful and also a negative view of utopia, it can be expanded. It does not do justice to some of the most significant ways in which they interact. Ideology is obviously related to the past, usually an idealized one, and thus involves memory. Ricoeur mentions celebrations such as the Fourth of July in the United States, the fall of the Bastille in France, and Lenin's tomb in the Soviet Union (Ricoeur 1986b: 261). It can be misused, as already noted, in a defensive way to appeal, for example, to the promotion of democracy as a pretext to impose by

force "freedom" on another nation or to appeal to the Revolution
for the workers to keep a small bureaucratic elite in power. Ricoeur
preferred to speak of utopia as the key to criticizing these abuses,
but one can see that sometimes it is "the utopian element," one
might say, in the ideology that can be used against it, for example,
when Abraham Lincoln appealed to the idea of equality in resisting
slavery. One could also easily construe Lincoln's appeal, as one could
later Martin Luther King's "I Have a Dream" speech, as utopian in
bringing criticism of the present. Ricoeur, however, only hinted at
the possibility of a continuing utopian element in the ideological
and, in fact, seemed to rule it out by his larger architectonic.

What is missing from his view in his work in the 1970s, apart
from tantalizing hints, is the possibility of utopian stirrings within
an ideology that disturb the past-oriented, legitimative elements of
ideology. This dimension allows for renewal from within the city,
so to speak, rather than lobbed from outside the walls. In fact,
Ricoeur acknowledged in his discussion of Henri de Saint-Simon
concerning utopia, "The spiritual location of utopia is between
two religions, between an institutionalized religion in decline and a
more fundamental religion that remains to be uncovered" (Ricoeur
1986b: 185). If one can see that the latter is a return or renewal
of the first utopian vision, an even more dialectical relation can
be seen at times, where utopia emerges from within the ideology.
In his later discussion of Charles Fourier and utopia, Ricoeur
even more suggestively commented, "The religious overtone of
Fourier's proclamations raises an issue about utopia as a whole: to
what extent is utopias' futurism fundamentally a return? Fourier
comments quite often that what he advocates is not a reform but
a return, a return to the root. He has many pages on the topic
of forgetfulness" (307). One could easily point here to Ricoeur's
last major work, *Memory, History, Forgetting*, concerning the
significance of the past for moving forward to the future (Ricoeur
2004). It is important what we remember and what we forget. We
often remember the wrong things and do not remember the right
things. Ricoeur speaks here of "the abuses of memory, which are
also abuses of forgetting."[13] He adds, "It is justice that turns memory
into a project" (88). Memory, in a sense, is an ethical duty. When he
turns later in a creative way to root the deontological right in the
teleological good, the appeal to the good is usually to the good in
a tradition. As he puts it in *The Just*, "The deontological intention,

and even the historical dimension, of our sense of justice are not simply intuitive; they result from a long *Bildung* stemming from the Jewish and Christian as well as from the Greek and the Roman traditions."[14] He adds in this context, "In a sense all founders of philosophies, religions, and cultures say that they are bringing forth something that already existed" (Ricoeur 1986b: 307). Although Ricoeur does not develop this direction, these notes open the door to a more nuanced picture of the relation of ideology and utopia. Utopia may not then always be "the exterior, the nowhere." It is not always thus the view from nowhere but the view from somewhere, perhaps the somewhere of a return to an original utopia or ideal of the good buried within an ideology. Like ideology in general, this type of utopia conserves an identity—but only through renewal and hermeneutical transformation (Ricoeur 1991b: 318).

Ricoeur could have seen this point more clearly. After all, he is the one who reminded Habermas that "critique is also a tradition." In other words, the attempt to speak from nowhere always reveals traces to the past. Utopias like Thomas Moore's, Voltaire's, and Edward Bellamy's make sense only in light of contrast with their present realities. As Lewis Mumford said in his classic work on utopia, "Almost every utopia is an implicit criticism of the civilization that served as its background; likewise it is an attempt to uncover potentialities that the existing institutions either ignored or buried beneath an ancient crust of custom and habit" (Mumford 1962: 2).

This is especially significant with respect to the church and theology also. Most criticisms of the church are renewal movements that do not speak from outside but from what is seen as a more genuine place within. Theology itself, while its criticisms can be scathing, speaks almost by definition from within and not without. Yet it is difficult to deny the utopian dimension of such renewal movements and theological critiques.[15]

At one other point, Ricoeur draws on atheism as a fire through which faith must pass.[16] After the horrors of the wars and Holocaust, then encountering atheism and especially Freud, Ricoeur affirmed how atheism is a fire through which any belief must pass. Atheism thus provides a hermeneutics of suspicion for religion, yet opens up a horizon for "a postreligious faith or a faith for a postreligious age" (Ricoeur 1974e: 440). Atheism can help religion deal with infantile, escapist religion that is based more on wish-fulfillment than faith. It alerts one to the way that religion is often used as a weapon, not to love others in their otherness, but to diminish if not destroy them in an attempt to reduce the Other to the Same. Religion can serve in many ways to conceal the shadow within by projecting one's worst side onto others. As Marx saw, religion can function as a distortive ideology to serve vested interests. As Nietzsche saw, it can be an enemy to the joys of the world and the body and undermine genuine humanity by promoting an other-worldly spirituality. It can conceal aggression by a mild exterior, which Nietzsche called a slave mentality. In the modern period, religion can be reactionary in promoting fears of science and change. Its utopian imagination, as we saw, can be illusory rather than transformative. In all of these ways, religion and theology not only can but also need to pass through the sieve of the challenges of modern atheism. In more recent years, as the "new atheism" has become more aggressive in claiming that religion is a dangerous virus, too dangerous to be tolerated, and that it "ruins everything," Ricoeur's approach calls for the hermeneutical approach of listening and heeding these salient and valuable criticisms, even while looking toward a postcritical affirmation of faith.[17]

Ricoeur's dialectical approach, however, is to bring the critical dimension of hermeneutics to bear even upon the critique. As he put it, "Guile will be met by double guile" (Ricoeur 1970: 34). The doubt can itself be doubted. From the reflections on epistemology in this chapter, one can raise questions about the assurance of modern science or philosophy to render religion superfluous or even to question claims to certainty of a rejection of transcendence. One cannot prove transcendence, but neither can one disprove it. Then what? Here one moves, in Ricoeur's perspective, in either case to testimony, to risk, to wager, to a lived life. In the "long detour" that is necessary, the result can be faith, albeit a "tragic faith," which is beyond "nostalgia" for the infantile wish for the father and ontotheology.[18] He concluded, "An idol must die so that a symbol of being may begin to speak" (Ricoeur 1974e: 467).

Religious believers are often resistant to critique, sometimes seeing questions and doubt as the opposite of faith. Here is where a more robust view of faith can actually welcome criticism.[19] Ricoeur himself connected Christian critique not only with atheism but also, indigenously, so to speak, with its biblical roots. The prophets challenge the narrative, and the Wisdom tradition particularly can shake faith to its very foundations (Ricoeur 1980). The reorientation of both Jesus and Paul in the New Testament rest upon radical disorientation that rivals any ideology critique. Faith and reason are thus not so opposed as so often thought. Ricoeur has undermined the notion of a detached reason that is cut off from attestation. He has thrust faith into the hermeneutic spiral where it continually meets the analysis of such a reason. Ideology critique therefore is not a foreign element inserted within theology but an inherent component. The development of a hermeneutics of suspicion in dialogue with the modern masters of suspicion such as Nietzsche, Marx, Freud, and their descendants, does not add to so much as supplement the moment of critique in the hermeneutical arc.[20]

In the end, despite the stress in the *Lectures on Ideology and Utopia*, utopia is not the only way to deal with ideology. There are many ways: metaphors, narratives, utopias, methods, even atheistic philosophy. They do not guarantee the transparence of the distortions of ideology—but they help. From the perspective of Ricoeur's hermeneutical philosophy, hermeneutics can and must become critical hermeneutics, but there is no guaranteed method that assures the truth over against its pretenders. As hermeneutics became critical hermeneutics in Ricoeur, it does reject a modernist desire to find a neutral or transcendent standpoint, to be sure, but it takes up the mantle of critique while being open to orientation on the yon side of disorientation.[21] Here as elsewhere in epistemology, he affirmed that we hope to be within the bounds of truth.

The importance of the stress on a hermeneutics of suspicion is that it addresses one of the common criticisms of hermeneutical philosophy, stemming from Habermas' critique of Gadamer, namely, that it has no place for dealing with the depths of ideology critique. In an introduction to critical theory by Jere Paul Surber, for example, in an otherwise outstanding treatment of a wide range of critical theories, his conclusion is that hermeneutics cannot deal with critique (Surber 1997). As one reads further, though, one finds that no movement can find a sure place to stand, although each supplies insights. In the critical turn that Ricoeur makes in hermeneutics, it embraces critique, such as other methodologies, while recognizing limits even to critique and thus also allowing room for affirmation.

Besides such philosophical methodologies, one can add that not only philosophy but also literature provides some of the best critical insights—an insight congruent with an emphasis on the philosophical importance of narrative.[22] In both philosophy and theology, additionally, cross-cultural discussion opens up new perspectives that can be both critical and enriching, as in Kwok Lui-Pan's postcolonial perspectives. For theology, perhaps more than in philosophy, the center of the church is moving to the southern hemisphere and brings challenges and perspectives that Eurocentric theology of the West will be addressing, probably for centuries (Jenkins 2002). Perhaps this criticism from within the church will be a greater challenge than anything that comes from Western philosophy and atheism. Theology's confessions and affirmations do not escape the hermeneutics of suspicion; in fact, they are a part of it. The utopian imagination that is able to find renewal and transformation from within and without the Christian tradition has always played a significant role in theological development, as it has moved from paradigm to paradigm. In the delicate balance that theology seeks to find between faithfulness to the tradition and prophetic transformation of it, a nuanced epistemology such as Ricoeur's can be a significant resource. It is important to realize that the role of hermeneutic argumentation, one could say, or "phronetic reasoning," will be as important in theology or faith as in philosophy. "No one can escape this."

7

Ricoeur and theology

The focus in previous chapters has been on Ricoeur's philosophy and its implications for theology, not as much on what he specifically says about theology. In this concluding chapter, we will look more closely at some of those instances where he expressed his own tentative theology, one might say, for it will be attractive to some in its own right. First, however, we will recapitulate some previous discussions in which Ricoeur touched on religious questions per se and consider their significance. In the process, we will be able to revisit the significance of Ricoeur for theology, with its possibilities and limitations. We have seen where Ricoeur made forays into explicitly religious reflection in *The Symbolism of Evil*, the interpretation of Jesus' parables, and eschatology. In this chapter, we will look more broadly at Ricoeur's religious reflections for the implications of Ricoeur's work for theology.

Ricoeur and systematic theology

As already indicated, Ricoeur did not say much about systematic theology and seemed generally uninterested. He was primarily a philosopher who dealt with topics that often pertain to theology. While he did address theological issues at times, it was not in major works; it was more often directly related to exegesis of the Scripture or philosophy of religion, and was ad hoc.

In fact, the central proposal made in Chapter 3 that systematic theology can be strategically placed and understood in terms of Ricoeur's hermeneutical arc is an appropriation of Ricoeur and not an application that he himself made. This is an example of Ricoeur's primary value lying in his philosophical work that can be creatively and variously appropriated in theology. Nevertheless, Ricoeur's insistence that a second-order critical dimension is virtually inherent in faith, which arises in reflection on the primary experiences of faith, suggests the indispensable role of theology. My argument has been that Ricoeur's philosophy provides one of the best conversation partners for contemporary Christian theology, in part because Ricoeur's underlying convictions are themselves Christian out of his Reformed tradition, as we will see even more clearly in this chapter. In the hermeneutical parlance, his preunderstanding (prefiguration in Ricoeur's terms) is already oriented toward or at least open to Christian theology, even if the implications of his work are quite open-ended.

To reiterate, situating systematic theology as a dimension of explanation or configuration in light of Ricoeur's hermeneutical and narrative arcs indicates the virtual necessity of theology as a way of explicating the significance of first-order expressions of faith such as religious experience and genres in the Scripture such as poetry, wisdom, and narrative. As Ricoeur said, "To explain more is to understand better." At the same time, the hermeneutical arc pushes beyond the explanation to a second, postcritical understanding, which in effect is a "seasoned" return to the first-order sources of theology. This counters the modern tendency to see the Scripture and experience as subsumed within systematic theology as their true expression. The arc's trajectory toward practice also resists the tendency to understand the significance of religion primarily as a set of beliefs. The limits that Ricoeur set on a hermeneutics of testimony, even explicated as the systematic theology, also caution against overestimating the achievement of a particular systematic theology. Rather, Ricoeur's eschatological reserve when it comes to any kind of truth claim, even the way God may be named through various Scriptural genres, retains a lively sense of mystery that is being reclaimed in theology.

One could also see Ricoeur's work as a kind of Christian philosophy, but that phrase, too, is shot through with tension. Ricoeur himself, as we have noted from his French context, did not want to be seen as a Christian philosopher, which was seen as unduly circumscribing the significance of a thinker's philosophical work.[1] Ricoeur wanted to avoid any sense of a philosophy expressing a dogmatic, unitary Christian worldview that does not do justice to the mystery of God or to the surplus of meaning in the Scripture and tradition. Nor did he want to intimate some kind

of superior vantage point in philosophical discussion stemming
from a special revelation. This is also a valid point in that Ricoeur
was not self-consciously attempting to work out his philosophy in
light of Christian theological perspectives; to the contrary, he was
concerned to be faithful to his philosophical vocation, especially
in the French context of secularization. Perhaps he is best seen as
a philosopher who is a Christian. On the other hand, in another
context not as fraught with objections to a Christian philosophy
taken in a broader sense, perhaps Ricoeur's work could be viewed
positively in this light from a Christian theological perspective.

For instance, if one takes a significant contemporary model of
Christian philosophy in the United States, that of Alvin Plantinga
that has been influential in the Society for Christian Philosophers,
Ricoeur's philosophy fits quite well. Plantinga argues that
philosophers should not bracket their beliefs or refrain from allowing
them to influence their philosophy. Rather, their prephilosophical
beliefs in fact do influence and should be allowed to influence
and be influenced by their philosophies. The realization that one's
explicit philosophical beliefs are shaped and influenced by one's
context and tradition is a realization that Ricoeur as a hermeneutical
philosopher himself makes. Plantinga clarifies:

> Philosophy is in large part a clarification, systematization,
> articulation, relating and deepening of pre-philosophical opinion.
> We come to philosophy with a range of opinions about the world
> and humankind and the place of the latter in the former; and in
> philosophy we think about these matters, systematically articulate
> our views, put together and relate our views on diverse topics,
> and deepen our views by finding unexpected interconnections
> and by discovering and answering unanticipated questions. Of
> course we may come to change our by virtue of philosophical
> endeavor; we may discover incompatibilities or other infelicities.
> But we come to philosophy with pre-philosophical opinions; we
> can do no other. And the point is: the Christian has as much
> right to his pre-philosophical opinions as others have to theirs.
> (Plantinga 1984: 268)

Plantinga goes to some length to indicate how secular philosophers
also draw upon convictions that are not so much argued for as
assumed. They can be developed as arguments but such "framework"

beliefs are notoriously difficult to "prove." Here we can draw on Ricoeur's epistemology to indicate how such beliefs can be attestations that involve evidence and arguments, and are not fideist, but in the end are wagers. It is also not the case that Christians are allowed to do this but not others. Plantinga's point, which is backed by hermeneutical philosophy—and any other postmodern philosophy—is that everyone does this, and everyone has a right to do this. In this sense, the playing field is even. From that point, the needed critical process of argumentation and validation should go on, as it does in philosophy and theology, causing some beliefs to fall by the wayside or to be significantly changed, but in the end such evidence and arguments usually underdetermine the conclusions. What is important, as Gadamer emphasizes, is to try to be aware of and critical of one's "preunderstandings," not to try to rid oneself of them in an Enlightenment quest for a God's-eye-point-of-view. Ricoeur acknowledged later in his life that he could not "maintain this duality in watertight compartments" and, following Charles Taylor, saw his religious beliefs as "sources," which he did not master. Rather, he confessed, "My two allegiances always escape me, even if at times they nod to one another" (Ricoeur 1998: 150). In this sense, Christian philosophy is a philosophy that is realistic and open about its presuppositions. It does not mandate particular conclusions to a great extent due to the great diversity in Christianity, a point that Plantinga himself does not make very well. In fact, to suggest that Ricoeur fits Plantinga's model of a Christian philosopher does not imply that Ricoeur and Plantinga are similar in their specific views. In other words, different Christian philosophers may vary widely in their conclusions just as much as secular philosophers. Perhaps the former are more open to transcendence, but not necessarily more so than a secular philosopher. The former will be open to a divine reality, an Absolute in philosophical terms, but the emphasis on mystery and eschatological, Kantian limits, for instance, in Ricoeur and in many theologians, leaves much open in detail, just as nonreligious philosophers might be open to an Absolute of some kind but differ greatly in detail.[2]

As Ricoeur implied, philosophy is one way, indeed one of the best ways, in which such precritical beliefs and practices can be brought to the fore and examined. Though Ricoeur's hermeneutical arc in fact gives depth to Plantinga's proposal in the way that Ricoeur calls for criticism, it also propels toward a postcritical appropriation in terms of praxis. Especially when it comes to religion, it is important not to overvalue the role of beliefs in relation to practice, an error that is common among Christians perhaps more than in any other religion.

In light of the discussions about the concerns of Frei and Lindbeck, it is important to point out again that Ricoeur's own view of the relation between theology and other disciplines is in fact quite close to theirs. In other words, his is an affirmation of the independence and integrity of theology on its own and represents Ricoeur's rejection of a foundationalist approach to philosophy and theology. Ricoeur also rejected the idea that a general hermeneutical theory colonizes every regional hermeneutics, such as a theological hermeneutics. This is where Ricoeur is situated much closer to Karl Barth than the North American reception recognized. Ricoeur explicitly stated that the theological hermeneutics maintains its own integrity. As a philosopher he moved beyond Barth in seeing that the regional hermeneutics itself contributes to the understanding of hermeneutics in general. His thought is open to a dynamic relationship where the contributions of many regional hermeneutics to a general hermeneutics in turn can spiral back to illuminate the regional hermeneutics. As George Taylor has pointed out, for example, legal hermeneutics, as well as theological hermeneutics, also has distinctives (G. H. Taylor 2010). Here one might also compare the "interweaving" that Ricoeur saw between fiction and history in narrative. They are alike in a broad way as narrative configuration, but they also differ in distinctive ways. Likewise, theology and philosophy differ. Ricoeur's hermeneutical theory thus would be compatible with the way that Frei draws on literary theorists and Lindbeck draws on Ludwig Wittgenstein not as essential foundations to their work but as dialogue partners that help illuminate and elucidate what they are trying to express in theology. Ricoeur's own philosophy, I have argued, can function in similar ways as a particularly fruitful dialogue partner for systematic theology.

Ricoeur's approach is thus opposed to a kind of silo effect of theology that protects it and isolates it from other discourses, and he is likewise opposed to a simple synthesis, a melding of them all, and an assimilation into philosophy. Ricoeur discussed the contemporary critique of the fusion between God and being in the Christian tradition, criticized especially as ontotheology by Martin

Heidegger, which does justice neither to philosophy nor theology. On the one hand, Ricoeur questioned whether Heidegger does justice to the care that theologians often took, such as Aquinas, to preserve the transcendence of God (LaCocque and Ricoeur 1998: 356). On the other hand, Ricoeur agreed that the coincidence of the Greek and Hebrew thought is questionable. He observed:

> Historically contingent, the coincidence of the biblical god and the Being of philosophers also appears to be conceptually fragile. Pascal reminds us: between the God of the philosophers and the God of Abraham, Isaac, and Jacob, the difference remains insurmountable. As for us, after the contemporary critique of metaphysics, we find ourselves confronted with the nonphilosophical origin of God and his nonnecessity for philosophy. God remains someone we can pray to. (354)

Ricoeur also at this point saw Heidegger's turn to the Greeks and Nietzsche as a way of marginalizing "any Christian thought with a Jewish origin" that indeed separated philosophy and theology but at a cost (LaCocque and Ricoeur 1998: 357). Ricoeur applauded fresh ways that the resources of Judeo-Christian thought could give rise to approaching God as in the thought of the Jewish Emmanuel Levinas (an ethics without ontology) who has "found echoes among Christian thinkers" such as the Roman Catholic Jean-Luc Marion (a God without being but not without the gift of love), whom Ricoeur called "the most brilliant of these new philosopher-theologians" (358). Ricoeur nevertheless expressed concern for their effort to dissociate God from being and often with philosophy. He said, "This attempt to think God apart from being poses a problem for theologians concerned to preserve a link with philosophy." Does such a disconnection, he wondered, "contribute to reinforcing the current vogue for irrationalism?" (358–9). Further,

> would a theology of love that sets out to do without ontology be in a better position to conclude a new pact with Western reason, on the level, for example, of the criticism this latter exercises today as regards its own totalizing or foundational claims? This would be the case if, in rejoining philosophy in the midst of its crisis, the theology of love were to invent a new mode of inculturation into the Western sphere of thinking, a new pact capable of supporting

the comparison with the one once formulated in support of the Judeo-Christian conjunction with Hellenistic neo-Platonism and then with medieval neo-Aristotelianism. Without this pact, declaring themselves totally foreign to Greek thought, identified globally with the metaphysics of being, do Jewish and Christian thought not "disenculture" themselves and consent to their marginalization? (359)

Ricoeur's own response was to point to the way that being can be said in many ways, as Aristotle indicated, beyond the limitations of Greek culture. He asked, "Why not say that the Hebrews thought being in a new way?" (360). Ricoeur again is concerned here to find a position beyond theologians who would not be concerned to "preserve a link with philosophy" or to avoid irrationalism. On the other hand, he saw the "contingent and conceptually fragile" relation between theology and philosophy, wanting to preserve their integrity. And, moreover, he saw the way that the tradition of faith can open up philosophy itself in creative and unforeseen ways, again, in the way that a symbol gives rise to thought.

To extend the dialogue with theology further, Ricoeur did not discuss relations among religions at great length, but he offered at one point parameters for discussion between the religious and the nonreligious that are pertinent for theologians in dialogue with philosophy and in general with the public realm. First, he said, we must recognize that "religion is fragmented." For example, "I must be prepared to say that Buddhism, despite its atheism . . . has something that is profoundly religious." Second, he belonged to a culture where "Judeo-Christian culture has always been confronted with its other." This means that he must deal with the nonreligious fellow citizens as they must deal with his belief. Third, politics should then be conceived as a "set of procedural rules for living together in a society where there are religious persons and non-religious persons," realizing that one cannot choose to ignore those around one, however different.[3] This is similar to Charles Taylor's point that the religious imaginary now, compared to 500 years ago, is that no matter how committed one is to one's own faith, one is aware that there are other options (C. Taylor 2007: 3). Ricoeur himself in his later years engaged public issues in France of wearing the burkha, of refugees, and of contamination of blood, issues where religion, philosophy, and politics easily commingle.[4] Ricoeur's philosophy in general is open to a variety of appropriations, theology being one of them, whether or not it is ad hoc or more integrated. And the appropriation by theology itself can go in a number of directions.

On the other hand, as I pointed out in Chapter 3, but which should be reiterated here, Ricoeur's philosophy is open to but is not compatible with any and every theological project. It militates against the earlier tendency to assume one and only one theology for all but rather points to a surplus of theologies that arises out of the surplus of meaning—and also the ongoing hermeneutics of suspicion. It actually undermines not dogmatics per se but a dogmatic theology that purports to rid theology of both risk and mystery. This is true across the board, whether it be a conservative or a liberal theology. It moves away from a "modernist" theology that is foundationalist, propositional, too individualistic, too rationalistic, or too heavily subservient to philosophy, whether conservative or liberal. His emphasis on an eschatological reserve and the hermeneutics of testimony actually points to confessional theology that retains elements of both risk and affirmation. There is nevertheless much room for many types of contemporary theologies to appropriate Ricoeur that could go in various directions. We shall see this illustrated in Ricoeur's own theological explorations.

The eschatological horizon

One of the places where Ricoeur more explicitly spoke in religious terms has to do with eschatology. Early in his work he was comfortable speaking of a Christian view of history, as we saw in the last chapter. From this perspective, he rejected a Hegelian or Marxist teleological or deterministic view of history, which in a sense knows where it is going. Rather, lingering closer to Augustine (and perhaps to the Reformed reticence about eschatology found in John Calvin), Ricoeur saw history as ambiguous and awaiting illumination only in an eschatological beyond. God is too mysterious to grasp in history, and reality as a whole is similarly under the brackets of mystery. Even in a later interview, Ricoeur could say, "If there is an ultimate unity, it resides elsewhere, in a sort of eschatological hope. But this is my 'secret,' if you wish, my personal wager, and not something that can be translated into a centralizing philosophical discourse" (Kearney 1984: 27–8). This is behind Ricoeur's later self-appellation as a post-Hegelian Kantian, being post-Hegelian in that he rejected Hegel's Absolute standpoint at the end of history and retaining a greater sense of Kantian limits. He approached this issue in another way in his reflections at the end of the third volume of *Time and Narrative*, where he took up Augustine's reflections on time where "eternity" is a horizon for this earthly existence (Ricoeur 1988: 264–6).

This eschatological approach has epistemological implications, as one can see in the previous quotation, for it means that knowledge itself in any large-scale perspective is a risk, a wager that has a backing but no proof. It is testimony or attestation, not possession, either of the self or of objects. In this area, we can see where Ricoeur moved rather easily to and fro between his Christian convictions and corresponding philosophical perspectives. In fact, it appears that his Christian perspective on eschatology shapes his philosophical views, although one need not be a Christian to accept the philosophical views, which indeed are shared by many nonreligious philosophers. One should also point out that not all Christian theologians are as reticent when it comes to history and knowledge as Ricoeur, so they are his *particular* Christian convictions (testimony) that relate to his philosophy.

In 1970s when he was more careful in separating his faith and philosophy, he nevertheless affirmed the significance of Jürgen Moltmann's emphasis on resurrection and hope as Ricoeur attempted to work out a philosophical approach to hope that "approximates" religious hope.[5] He was not specific about the nature of resurrection, but he affirmed in a way that is similar to the earlier writing that life is lived under the sign of hope, which cannot be proven or known in a strong sense. Instead of "eschatology," he seemed to use the word "hope" in a similar way. His consistent emphasis on hope is tied in with the way that there is a gift of grace and of superabundance, as seen in the parables of Jesus, that can accompany life just as much as suffering and loss. In fact, the extravagance of hope occurs "in spite of" tragedy in life as the "how much more."[6] He asked the question, "What is freedom in the light of hope?" And his response was, "I will answer in one word: it is the meaning of my existence in the light of the Resurrection" (Ricoeur 1980b: 159). He went on to explain that this psychologically means that humans can make a choice of life, which relates to Ricoeur's emphasis on a "primary affirmation" of life. He also urged that such a decision should not be interpreted too narrowly as an existential decision of the moment that made eschatology a matter of the eternal now "at the expense of the temporal, historical, communitarian, and cosmic aspects contained in the hope of the Resurrection" (160). Such freedom in the light of hope "is nothing less than this creative imagination of the possible" (161).

The emphasis on resurrection, however, indicates the way that a testimony of faith moves beyond his general approximations of philosophy to ground hope. In very Kantian terms, he saw such affirmation as a *reasonable* hope or faith but not knowledge (although not Kantian in the sense of "religion within the limits of reason alone") (Kant 1960). As we have seen, the divide between faith and reason is elusive, less cavernous than he proclaimed at this point, but it does point to the way that faith and its theology can fill out and ground the philosophical possibility of hope, which it apparently did for him personally.

At the same time, in terms of his personal convictions, he apparently moved in a different direction or reframed his earlier perspective in terms of resurrection. In the interviews in *Critique and Conviction*, Ricoeur questioned a personal resurrection or afterlife and saw it rather as some theologians do as a symbol of hope in this life (Ricoeur 1998: 152–61). In the posthumously published notes of his later years, *Living Up to Death*, not prepared or perhaps even intended for publication, he reaffirmed his rejection of a personal afterlife in any kind of traditional sense. In these writings from his last few years, he ironically seemed to reject an afterlife strikingly as much for religious reasons as for philosophical reasons. Philosophically, he thought that a simple continuation of life is too simplistic. Theologically, one might say, or perhaps better, spiritually, he saw such an affirmation as selfish, as a contradiction to the call to give up one's life to follow Christ. He suggested that as infantile, selfish desire for continuation of life, it cannot be affirmed, leaving a dilemma between denial and selfish projection (Ricoeur 2009: 43ff.). In fact, several times as backing he refers to Jesus' phrase, "For those who want to save their life will lose it" (Matt. 16:25, NRSV) (Ricoeur 1998: 155, 2009: 45). It is also striking that there is no indication that he questioned the existence of God. He thus actually took up the theme of the true Christian spirit with a very Reformed accent, to which he attests that he came to as "a chance transformed into destiny by a continuous choice"

(Ricoeur 2009: 62), namely, to think of nothing for oneself but of God and others. He reflected, "This shift from the moral to the religious presumes a letting go of all the answers to the question 'Who am I?' and implies, perhaps, renouncing the urgency of the question itself, in any event renouncing its insistence as well as its obsession" (Ricoeur 1998: 156). He also rejected the diminishment of an emphasis on this life that is sometimes reflected in hope of an afterlife, perhaps a fruit of his immersion in the thought of Marx, who saw religion as the opiate of the people. Rather, Ricoeur emphasized in an impressive way the importance of living all the way "up to death" in this life and giving oneself for others in this life. He thus represents a way of renunciation that is impressively spiritual, especially for one facing the fading of the great energy and capabilities that had served him well, and who was obviously close to death. In speaking of such personal testimony, one can primarily listen and respect.

Ricoeur himself would be the first, however, to suggest that testimony calls for reflection if not criticism. Without desiring to diminish in any sense the respect one would give to anyone's last reflections and the penetrating insights of these religious reflections, I wish to take his explorations as "giving rise to thought." Realizing that these are notes in his journal, it is also true that they are consistent with his remarks in *Critique and Conviction*, a few years earlier, so they manifest some measured reflection. What is striking about the reasons given, for someone familiar with Barth and Moltmann, is how religious they are in terms of being sacrificial but yet also how limited they are in terms of a view of an afterlife. His critical remarks also about atonement as a crude penal-substitutionary model are actually widely shared but do not make much room for both reformulations and alternative models, which, for instance, can be found in Barth and Moltmann.[7] Both resurrection and atonement can be thought of not from the perspective of selfish human wish-fulfillment but in the context close to Ricoeur's own thought, in terms of gift, that is, God's gift (Ricoeur 1995b: 324). Rather than human desire, they can be seen as based on God's desire, a gift of love and even the desire of God for continued fellowship with God's creatures, an affirmation that both Barth and Moltmann in their Reformed background of God's sovereignty and grace extend to all people, and Moltmann to all of creation (Moltmann 1996: 70, 279). For Moltmann, particularly, it is essential in light of suffering and evil (92). Their affirmation of eternal life thus represents a logic of superabundance reflected in the parables and in Paul in Romans, as Ricoeur describes himself so well in another context, a logic of "how much more" (Ricoeur 1975: 110, 1980b: 164). In this light, eternal life is neither something natural as in the natural immortality of the soul nor something to which God should accede just because it is a selfish human wish. Rather, death represents the possibility of a real end. An afterlife must be a surprising gift of a gracious God upon which one cannot presume. It is more like the astonishing forgiveness of the father of the prodigal son. What the parables suggest is that the basis of a hope of eternal life is not human desire but God's surprising, extravagant desire, an "economy of the gift" beyond any economy of exchange exemplified in a crude theory of atonement (Ricoeur 1995b: 324, 326n14). Ricoeur's understanding of the gift thus may provide an alternative way of thinking about an afterlife.

In other words, one can well agree with Ricoeur's criticisms, but they are not exhaustive of ways to understand both of these admittedly mysterious aspects of Christian faith, as mysterious as the God that Ricoeur so emphasizes. It is also true that one could be cognizant of all of these alternatives, and perhaps Ricoeur was, and maintain his same perspective, as have other theologians. In short, there is a surplus of meaning, a broader horizon of hope, in relation to conceiving of resurrection and the afterlife that is significant for a wider theological, and perhaps philosophical, reflection on these issues.

Again, Ricoeur's emphasis on sacrifice for the other and focus on the good of this life is quite admirable and represents a significant shift in eschatology in contemporary theology. It is, one could argue, much more deeply Christian in attitude than much discussion of an afterlife that sounds very much like a reward that has little to do with self-giving love of God. It is striking that in a letter published in *Living Up to Death*, shortly before his own death Ricoeur is consoling a friend who was also approaching death. His expression is not totally clear, but when he is thinking of consolation of someone else rather than of his own well-being, he seemed to speak in a way that was more open to the hope of an afterlife.[8] This relates to Olivier Abel's observation of Ricoeur's "redoubling of concern detached from oneself so as to relate it to others. This may be the claim of a resurrection for others that I do not ask for myself" (Ricoeur 2009: xxi).

In the end, this somewhat controversial issue in Ricoeur's work exemplifies the value of a distinction between his philosophical work and his sometime religious reflections. His broad hermeneutical and incarnational philosophy represents a framework that can be appropriated in several ways. Ricoeur himself may have taken two major ways at different times in his life on this subject, both of which are consistent with his philosophy.

One other religious sentiment that Ricoeur expressed toward the end of his life relates to other world religions. As mentioned above, while Ricoeur did not expressly engage other world religions apart from his treatment of ancient approaches to evil in *The Symbolism of Evil*, he often remarked on connections. In *Living Up to Death* and at other times, Ricoeur expressed that his focus on "detachment" from his own concerns resonated with Buddhism.[9] Ricoeur stressed that one could not escape the particularities of one's history and one's own religion, but in the midst of these, perhaps especially in the midst of these, and in the face of death, "what the physician in the palliative care unit bears witness to is the grace granted some dying people that assures what I have called the mobilization of the deepest resources of life in the coming to light of the Essential, fracturing the limitations of the confessionally religious." Here is where the "barrier between religions" may be breached, even including the nonreligious, adding that he was here considering Buddhism.[10] Ricoeur suggested an approach that was open to dialogue with other religions, which he saw as similar to translation where one offers a kind of "linguistic hospitality" (Ricoeur 2010b: 38). No "super-religion" can be found. One must not forsake the particular for the general; rather, he insisted, it is often in the particular that the essential commonality can be found. He said:

> At the very depth of my own conviction, of my own confession, I recognize that there is a ground which I do not control. I discern in the ground of my adherence a source of inspiration which, by its demand for thought, its strength of practical mobilization, its emotional generosity, exceeds my capacity for reception and comprehension. (39)

This depth then opens up a breadth of humility and receptivity toward others. The threat of skepticism also looms. "The difficulty," he confessed, "is to hold myself on the crest where my conviction is at the same time anchored in its soil, like its mother tongue, and open laterally to other beliefs, other convictions, as in the case of foreign languages. It is not easy to hold oneself at this crest . . .."[11] For many theologians who consider the wideness of God's grace to extend far beyond the bounds of institutional Christianity, whether as inclusivist or pluralist, these reflections may be fruitful. Ricoeur did not claim to be a mystic but claimed to be "wary of the immediate, the fusional," and he added, "There is one exception, in the grace of a certain dying" (Ricoeur 2009: 16). Perhaps in these personal reflections, here is a place where he seemed not only to intimate but also to find the Essential.

The summoned self

Another instance of the delicate relationship between philosophy and theology that is pertinent at this point concerns the essay that Ricoeur had delivered with his Gifford lectures but published separately, "The Summoned Subject in the School of the Narratives of the Prophetic Vocation," which was an attempt to consider the self, as he put it, "formed and informed by the biblical paradigms," yet still in relation to the broader philosophical treatment of the relational self, published as *Oneself as Another* (Ricoeur 1995c: 262). Ricoeur said that he did not want to suggest that this biblically informed self

> crowns the self of our philosophical hermeneutics. This would be to betray our unambiguous affirmation that the mode of Christian life is a wage [wager, *sic*] and a destiny, and those who take it up are not led by their confession either to assume a defensive position or to presume a superiority in relation to every other form of life, because we lack criteria of comparison capable of dividing among rival claims. (262–63)

Perhaps more than Ricoeur allowed at that time, one can see how the Christian perspective influenced his general philosophical reflections. At the same time, the level of generality of his philosophical reflections stands on its own and can imply a variety of perspectives. They are not addressed specifically to Christians but the wider philosophical community, and they could be affirmed by non-Christians. One might also be able to say that such philosophical perspectives are also "a wager and a destiny"—but not necessarily based on the Scripture or theology. From that broader philosophical perspective, they do not lead ineluctably to the Christian conclusions that Ricoeur draws in this article. As he said toward the end of *Oneself as Another*:

> Perhaps the philosopher as philosopher has to admit that one does not know and cannot say whether this Other, the source of the injunction, is another person whom I can look in the face or who can stare at me, or my ancestors for whom there is no representation, to so great extent does my debt to them constitute my very self, or God—living God, absent God—or an empty place. With this aporia of the Other, philosophical discourse comes to an end. (Ricoeur 1992: 355)

In "The Summoned Subject," however, Ricoeur took his own route out of the aporia to show how he understood that his religious tradition concretizes and gives an intense description of the transcendent Other who is not external or tangential to the self but is in the dialogical relationship of "oneself as another."

At the outset, with the philosophical shadow hovering in the background, Ricoeur indicated that the self of which he speaks is the relational self, which is described in *Oneself as Another*. This self "diametrically opposes itself to the philosophical hubris of a self that absolutely names itself" (Ricoeur 1995c: 162). We should add the other aspects that Ricoeur assumed from his earlier work, namely, that the self is a fallible project, a tension between the finite and the infinite, the voluntary and the involuntary. The self for Ricoeur is "only human," as William Schweiker points out concerning Ricoeur, not "all too human" as in Nietzsche, or singly and autonomously human as in Descartes and Kant (Schweiker 2010). This self is a capable self that remains nevertheless a fragile and suffering self, a storied self whose autobiography is being written in relation to all the other stories that it encounters. It is not a solitary self but ineradicably moral and social, shaping and being shaped by others.

The tone that he added here to his philosophical reflection is that the self is a responding self, responding dialogically especially to the divine Other, reminiscent, though he does not mention him here, of Martin Buber and his emphasis on the I-Thou relation (Buber 1958). The paradigm case is that of the prophets in the Hebrew Bible. Ricoeur manifested here his perhaps surprising ability in biblical exposition, to which I can hardly do justice in a summary, which characteristically has rich theological portent but arises through exegesis and dialogue with primarily biblical scholars such as Gerhard von Rad, Claus Westermann, and Walther Zimmerli. These prophets' literary remains move them, as Ricoeur says, from a *Sitz-im-Leben* to a *Sitz-im-Wort* (a setting in life to a setting in word) and enable them thus to serve a paradigmatic function for the summoned self (Ricoeur 1995b: 264). Their dialogical style, however, is not the alternating I and we of the Psalms but is at first a personal response that in some sense uproots them from their communities to which they are eventually called or sent back (Ricoeur 1995c: 264). As Ricoeur said, "The call isolates; the commission binds" (266). This dissonance sounds out along with their role as "suffering mediators," as they also move from action to suffering for their critical words (263–64). They reveal thus both the capable self and the fragile self. Yet their role is always one in community. "The people, in fact, do not stop being the setting for the word" (266). And Ricoeur concluded this section on their role in terms of personal identity, "Thus it belongs to prophetic speech in its pain to conjoin an exceptional ipseity to a traditional community" (267).

Ricoeur then moved to the way the Apostle Paul made Christlikeness a part of the trajectory of the "commissioned self" of the prophets, which takes Christ as the suffering servant as the inversion of revelation of God's glory (Ricoeur 1995b: 267). Ricoeur thought that Augustine's idea of the "inner teacher" internalizes the mandated self even more. He is interested in Augustine because the biblical dimension remains dominant even in the context of a certain Christian neo-Platonism (268). Augustine spoke of illuminating wisdom of the soul, tying in with both the Platonic tradition of inner light and the Wisdom tradition of the Bible, yet saw Christ as the inner teacher who gives something to learn. Ricoeur said, "The metaphor of light cannot therefore be substituted for the figure of the teacher, for the simple reason that the light and the word are the same."[12]

Yet a further step is to take up the "most internalized expression of the responding self," namely, that of conscience (Ricoeur 1995b: 271). Here he rejoined the philosophical discussion to some extent,

saying that he did not reject the move to autonomy in Kant and
Hegel but thought that he could incorporate their shift in a further
dialectic of the summoned self that still connects to the prophetic
paradigm (271). He referred also to his discussion of the conscience
in *Oneself as Another* where he argued that conscience is an
internal dialogue, an address in part to itself, and that the testimony
of conscience precedes the accusation of conscience. "Through the
conscience, the self bears witness to its ownmost power of being
before measuring and in order to measure the adequation of its
action to its most profound being" (271). Again revealing his
Protestant inclinations, Ricoeur related this general characteristic
of the self into the way that justification for Paul must become
internalized rather than be an external act.[13] This inner dialogue
between the summoned, accused, and perhaps excused self calls for
interpretation. What makes this Christian reflection is that what
Ricoeur calls the great code of the Bible, following Northrop Frye,
"is inscribed in this space that we interpret insofar as it interprets
us" (273). In other words, this inner dialogue can take place within
the symbol system of the Bible, from the prophets to Christ, and one
should add, within the larger theology systems of the church. Such
a framework becomes the Christian framework for interpreting the
aporia of the Other to which Ricoeur referred at the end of *Oneself
as Another*. As such, it becomes a theological framework. Strikingly,
Ricoeur called it a "theology of conscience," while yet saying that
it is still to be achieved (273). Justification by faith is one way that
this call is expressed, in a highly textured Christian symbol system.
Ricoeur did not expressly say it but implied that justification by faith
is a contested account, one that is certainly variously interpreted in
various Christian traditions. It is difficult to improve on Ricoeur's
own words as a characterization of the delicate relationship between
philosophy and theology as he concluded:

> The Christian is someone who discerns "conformity to the
> image of Christ" in the call of conscience. This discernment is
> an interpretation. And this interpretation is the outcome of a
> struggle for veracity and intellectual honesty. A "synthesis" is
> not given and never attained between the verdict of conscience
> and the christomorphism of faith. Any synthesis remains a
> risk, a "lovely risk" (Plato). To the extent that the Christian
> reading of the phenomenon of conscience moves from being a

wager to being a destiny, Christians can say with the Apostle Paul that it is in "good" conscience that they stake their lives on this risk. (275)

This extended exposition of Ricoeur in this article reveals just how thoroughly Christian, even confessional, he could be and opens up for good or ill, depending on one's perspective, underlying assumptions of his philosophical thought. It is a philosophy of the self that allows at least for the self to be open to the call of God as a possibility. In Roman Catholic thought, one could relate it to Karl Rahner's notion that human beings are created as potential "hearers of the word "(Rahner 1969). In Protestant thought, one could relate it to Emil Brunner's idea of humans being born in the image of God as potentially open to God or to Wolfhart Pannenberg's view of the self as inherently exocentric, open outward to other people and to God (Brunner 1952: 57; Pannenberg 1970: Ch. 1). While Ricoeur recognized that even a philosophical attempt to defend such openness does not remove other religious possibilities (the voice of one's ancestors) or an atheistic possibility (a void or illusion), it is notable that he is willing to fill in the possibilities in such a thorough and concrete way as a person of faith, noticeably a Protestant one, to be more specific, though Augustine is richly present. It also reveals how much more dense or thick the wider context of faith can be; it can go deeper in part because it is not as broad as philosophy tends to be. For example, in a remarkable book concerning dialogue between Jews, Christians, and Muslims after 9/11, many of the writers point out, "The proper meaning of moral responsibility becomes fully intelligible only within our relationship with the Divine."[14] Of course, if one rejects any such transcendent reality or understands it as much more amorphous when it comes to ethics, this would not be true. The tendency of the religions of the Book, as they are sometimes called, is to see such ethical responsibility as grounded in God, not as something that one can rationally prove. If one has this conviction, it can be theologically developed in a rich way.

In an earlier article, Ricoeur himself is more specific in how Christ's cross and resurrection for the one who takes the risk of faith "give the word *God* a *density* that the word *being* does not contain" (Ricoeur 1991e: 98). There he related that the inherent textual nature of biblical faith "cannot be separated from the movement of interpretation that raises it to the level of language. The 'ultimate care' would remain *mute* if it did not receive the power of speech from an endlessly renewed interpretation of the signs and symbols that have, so to speak, educated and formed this care throughout the centuries" (99). The filling in offered by events such as the Exodus and the Resurrection "open and uncover the innermost possibility of my own freedom and thus become for me the word of God" (99).

Ricoeur's earlier essay on a faith on the yon side of atheism, which we considered in terms of a hermeneutics of suspicion in the previous chapter, filled out his own intuitions of how God must be reconceived after Auschwitz and after atheism. Richard Kearney aligns Ricoeur with Dietrich Bonhoeffer's similar reconceiving of God, which is also shaped by the trauma of the Holocaust and prison internment.(Kearney 2011) As we saw, Ricoeur called there for "a postreligious faith or a faith for a postreligious age" (Ricoeur 1974e: 440). The major shift was to reject the God of "ontotheology," so criticized by Martin Heidegger and a criticism now followed by many theologians, and move toward a postreligious (in this sense) faith, a more mature faith in a God who, explicitly referring to Bonhoeffer, "only through his weakness is capable of helping me" (460). This is a faith that emphasizes freedom more than accusation and in terms of consolation is "heir to the tragic faith of Job" (460). Such a view of God links with his reflection in other places to a God who "becomes," not just a God of being or pure actuality, which has been so dominant in the Christian tradition—a view that led to the denial of God's capacity to change or to suffer (Ricoeur 1998: 158). Ricoeur's former student, Kearney, has developed these ideas perhaps the most in ways consistent with Ricoeur in *The God Who May Be* and *Anatheism*, pointing to a God beyond the God of ontotheology.[15] Such reflections that have taken to heart the atheistic critique of the traditional Western metaphysical conception of God share in the direction of much theology that seeks to reclaim what one might consider a more Hebraic understanding of God as relational, passionate, suffering, mysterious, and on the move.

In his later work in 1998 with Pierre Changeux, Ricoeur offered a specific recommendation for theological change. His work at this time on the fragile and suffering self chimed in with his desire to give up the category of the "Almighty, to the extent that it is not a purely religious category but, I would say, a theological-political category" (Changeux and Ricoeur 2002: 271). He argued, similar to the earlier essay on atheism, that this view of absolute divine power was modeled on absolute political power. Combined with a traditional view of Hell as eternal torment by God, it makes the relationship to God one of fear. Ricoeur rejected this conception of God, which may mean "having to seek another idea of power— that of the word—and to link it to the all-weakness of a love that surrenders to death" (Changeux and Ricoeur 2002: 271). As he recognized, he joined here other theologians such as Moltmann who reconceive divine power in light of Christ's vulnerable suffering on the cross (Moltmann 1993a).

These articles also reveal up close the kind of interaction that might occur between philosophy and theology. Rather than the sharp lines that Ricoeur himself sometimes wanted to paint, they reveal more of an "interweaving" where the disciplines retain their coloring but move in and out of each other in colorful ways. This is the kind of relationship between the two for which I have argued in these pages, for which Ricoeur's thought provides a stimulating and provocative dialogue partner. Ricoeur's work nevertheless indicates that the pattern is not automatic or necessary. Even in his philosophy, he sees that convictions involve a risk, a wager. It is even more so when one moves to faith and theology. "A synthesis is not given." Any attempt is "a risk." Faith itself is a risk. Yet when one is summoned and one's critical interpretation of the wager made in response becomes in turn "a destiny," to use the fuller language of *Living Up to Death*, "a chance transformed into destiny by a continuous choice," it can be made "in good conscience."

NOTES

Chapter 1

1 (Reagan 1996: 5; Ricoeur 1998: 6–7). Ricoeur reflected at one point, "This kind of philosophical intrepidness has sustained me throughout my life" (Ricoeur 1998: 7).

2 For Ricoeur's life, see in these English sources, from which the following is largely drawn, (Ricoeur 1995a; Reagan 1996; Ricoeur 1998). The extensive biography in French is by (Dosse 1997).

3 Ricoeur commented poignantly in his autobiographical essay about the naming of Olivier as a sign of peace after World War II, "We could not foresee that less than forty years later this olive branch of peace would be replaced by a funeral wreath" (Ricoeur 1995a: 14).

4 See (Merleau-Ponty 1962) and (Hass 2008).

5 Ricoeur uses the phrase in (Ricoeur 1991d: 20).

6 On Gadamer, see (Gadamer 1991).

7 Ricoeur connected these themes also with Nabert, for example, see Ricoeur's preface to (Nabert 1969).

8 Ricoeur pointed out, "The discordant overthrows the concordant in life, but not in tragic art" (Ricoeur 1984: 43).

9 For a similar treatment of Ricoeur's thorough and sensitive treatment of other thinkers as a teacher, see (Peperzak 2010). Ricoeur was Peperzak's doctoral thesis director. Peperzak gave a stimulating version of this paper at the first annual Society for Ricoeur Studies meeting in Chicago in 2007, mentioned in the preface.

10 (Ricoeur 2006: vii, viii). There were exceptions. Ricoeur confessed not to be able to make sense of Jacques Lacan's work, even though he sat in his seminars for some time (Ricoeur 1998: 70–1). Commentators have also observed that he and Derrida, despite collaborating together earlier, did not always understand each other very well (Lawlor 1992; Pirovlakis 2011).

11 Two who deal with this are (Maddox 1992; Van den Hengel 1993).

Chapter 2

1 For example, on the more conservative side, see (Penner 2005). See also The Church and Postmodern Culture series by Baker Academic press, for example (Smith 2006). For more mainline, liberal perspectives, see the Religion and Postmodernism Series by the University of Chicago Press, for example (Taylor 2009). For overviews, see (Tilley 1995; Griffin, Beardslee and Holland 1989).

2 Graham Ward appropriates Derrida, who he argues can be interpreted in a nihilist direction but prefers to take him more positively as "a way of reading the signs that might enrich an understanding of, even as it reiterates, the Christian tradition." He mentions several other more positive, nonrelativistic appropriations of Derrida (Ward 2003: 91).

3 See (Ward 1997). Ward actually uses the terms "liberal" and "conservative." I prefer the terms deconstructive and constructive as more accurately descriptive. For instance, he places John Milbank in the "conservative" camp but is using "conservative" in a way that would potentially be confusing in a North American context. For more on my view of postmodernism, see (Stiver 1994, 2003a).

4 (Busch 1976: 145). This was the title of a journal that Barth and others began.

5 Besides the essays in On Grammatology, see the essay on Plato in (Derrida 1981: 61–171).

6 In theology, this turn is associated with the appropriation of virtue ethics and virtue epistemology. See, for example (Volf and Bass 2002; Murphy, Kallenberg and Nation 1997).

7 Ricoeur once expressed this relationship in the other way, "After doubting the thing, we have begun to doubt consciousness" (Ricoeur 1974f: 148).

8 (Klemke 1984: Ch. 10). See also my account of logical positivism in (Stiver 1996: 42–7).

9 He especially relates this idea to Gadamer and to Mikhail Bhaktin (1898–1975). His emphasis on the significance of genre is in part attributed to Ricoeur's seminal essay on the irreducibility of genre. He sees "canonical genres as canonical practices" themselves. See especially (Vanhoozer 2005: 273, 282, 310, 322, 327, 345).

10 See (Scott-Baumann 2009), for a careful treatment of this concept in Ricoeur, seeing its scope and limits.

11 (Comstock 1986). At this point, it is evident that a "school" of thought is overdrawn. None of the main figures in the controversy were well-understood in this conflict. See (DeHart 2006; Blundell 2010).

12 (Frei 1992: 1–7). For more analysis of the way his typology opens up affinity with hermeneutical philosophy, see (Stiver 2003b). For criticism of this typology, albeit in a context that shows how Ricoeur is closer to Barth than the Yale thinkers saw, see (Blundell 2010; Stiver 2003b: 176–7).

13 (Witherington III 1997). See Chapter 5, for further development of this theme in the context of Ricoeur's thought.

14 (Moltmann 1993). Ricoeur's journals, however, toward the end of his life on the other hand called into question a seeming earlier emphasis on resurrection as life after death. See Chapter 7.

15 For example (Kearney 2011).

Chapter 3

1 A common interpretation of Kant has been to see him thinking in terms of two realms, which has been taken up into theology as salvation history (*Heilsgeschichte*) that is immune to criticism from secular historiography (*Historie*), as in Karl Barth. See the book on Kant and theology in this series, however, which argues against the idea of two realms in Kant, although a distinction can still be made between scientific knowledge and moral reasoning (Anderson and Bell 2010).

2 (Ricoeur 1986b). Ricoeur also added that the excesses of utopia were countered by ideology in its positive senses. See Chapter 6, for further elaboration of his appropriation of ideology critique.

3 (Ricoeur 1981f: 202). A caveat to the powerful point that Ricoeur makes here, which I mentioned in Chapter 2, is that the distinction between face-to-face speech and writing is overdrawn, as Derrida and the later Wittgenstein underscored each in his own way. Even in face-to-face communication, there is not a presence that transcends the public nature of language that eludes authorial control—or perhaps better, domination.

4   (Ricoeur 1981f: 201). Gregory Laughery sees that Ricoeur still
    includes a place for the author but argues that appeal to the
    historical-critical method of illuminating the original situation of a
    text could be more strongly emphasized in Ricoeur (Laughery 2002:
    62). Ricoeur's practice, for instance, in *Thinking Biblically*, however,
    shows a great deal of sensitivity to the historical situation.

5   See (Derrida 1974, 1985: 3–27). See for discussion of the connections
    between Ricoeur and Derrida, (Lawlor 1992; Pirovlakis 2011).
    Lawlor, for example, says, "So close together that they are almost
    indistinguishable: Ricoeur and Derrida" (123). Nevertheless, the
    differences can loom large, as in Lawlor himself, although he
    overplays them at times, in my estimation. The contrast, however,
    between Ricoeur and Derrida in terms of imagination and chance is
    illuminating.

6   (Braithwaite 1971). See also my discussion of noncognitive
    approaches in (Stiver 1996).

7   For example, see Chapter 6, "The Curse of Choking and How To
    Avoid It" in (Syed 2010).

8   (Anderson 1998: Chs. 4–5). Anderson points out that Irigaray,
    however, goes beyond Ricoeur in putting more weight on
    refiguration. Referring to Irigaray, Anderson says, "Miming does not
    simply mean a configuration of reality or a prefiguration of sexual
    identity. Instead her distinctive miming collapses these distinctions
    in a mimetic refiguring; this refiguring aims to disrupt traditional
    discourse, to transform sexual identity and reality of all sex/gendered
    hierarchies" (195).

9   In general, he was clearer in *Time and Narrative* than earlier. See, for
    example (Ricoeur 1981b: 142, 143, 207, 219, 1988: 158, 164).

10 (Vanhoozer 2005). Vanhoozer, who wrote an earlier book on Ricoeur
    (Vanhoozer 1990), draws on Ricoeur in this book at numerous
    points, for example, 93 and 127. More precisely, his book represents
    an adaptation to some extent of Ricoeur to his approach that is
    a conservative reformed covenantal theology. (138–9) Thanks to
    Charles Scalise who pointed out the significance of the covenantal
    theology in this book.

11 (Pellauer 2007: 90; Ricoeur 1988: 244). Pellauer made this point
    more strongly in a paper he gave at the International Conference on
    Ricoeur Studies in Moscow, September 14, 2011, "Narrated Time,
    Narrated Action."

12 Ricoeur made this point especially in (Ricoeur 1988: 164).

13 (Pauw and Jones 2011). In Moltmann's case, the strong sense of sovereignty in his reformed tradition is behind his turn to a radical universalism, where God's will is able to redeem everything, humans, animals, and the universe. See (Moltmann 1996: 70, 92). One could add here Karl Barth's similar tendency as a reformed theologian toward universalism.

14 The story is told in a lively and humorous way in (Gilkey 1985).

15 Examples concerning atonement are (Green 2006; McKnight 2007).

16 In terms of the field of theology, this critique of foundationalism is seen from different perspectives, as in (Grenz and Franke 2001; Phillips 1995; Hauerwas, Murphy and Nation 1994).

17 This is true whether or not one agrees with them or agrees with all of the details (Moltmann 1993a, c). Frei's and Lindbeck's books, which we've discussed, similarly transformed the theological landscape.

Chapter 4

1 (Grant and Tracy 1984: 66). Their appeal to the literal sense included a historical sense, which precluded what some might think of today as a literal approach.

2 (Luther 1982: 189f.). This is not exactly fair to Origen's text criticism, a point made by Charles Scalise in writing, whose insights into patristic interpretation were helpful in this section.

3 The president was Charles Blanchard, president of Wheaton College from 1877 to 1925 (Marsden 2006: 220).

4 See (Marsden 1991, 2006; Larson 2006).

5 (Ricoeur 1977: 224). Janet Martin Soskice is rightly critical of a literal notion of two references because a reference is not even actually constructed at the literal level. Rather, people notice the problem of reference at the literal level and thus move on to metaphorical reference (Soskice 1985: 84–90). She is technically correct on this point, but there nevertheless is an implicit recognition at least of the tension at the literal level that leads to the metaphorical level, perhaps sometimes at an unconscious level. Ricoeur's phraseology, if not pressed too literally, is suggestive and quite useful when he applies it to narrative. Here one is reminded of the point of cognitive science that thought is mostly unconscious, an emphasis with which Soskice's tradition of analytical philosophy is not very comfortable. See (Lakoff and Johnson 1999: 3).

6   (Reagan 1996: 106–7). Ricoeur wanted to avoid at this point the criticism of Richard Rorty of philosophy's historic reliance on representation of the world as the goal, in other words, to mirror nature. Ricoeur says further, "I think that it is maybe after the book of Rorty that we may have more important reasons to drop the confusion of description, if it is true that the word 'description' commits us to a theory of representation as knowing the world" (Reagan 1996: 107).

7   For example, see (Barbour 1974, 1997; Hesse 1980).

8   (Polanyi 1962; Kuhn 1970; Lakatos and Musgrave 1974; Feyerabend 2010; Reagan 1996: 102; Ricoeur 1981f: 212). Kenneth Reynhout argues that while Ricoeur could have expressed himself on this point better at times, this tension in Ricoeur's thought is not a confusion but relates to different purposes in a convincing analysis. From a paper at the Society for Ricoeur Studies annual meeting in Philadelphia, October 22, 2011, "Ricoeur and the Natural Sciences." Perhaps David Pellauer is correct when he writes, "He [Ricoeur] was not really knowledgeable about the physical sciences and paid little attention to them, at least in his writing" (Pellauer 2010: 47).

9   An interesting example is the way that Jerry Gill indicates that Wittgenstein, a philosopher noted for his treatment of the meaning of univocal language, can hardly be understood apart from Wittgenstein's use of metaphor (Gill 1981).

10 (Ricoeur 1981e). See also (Ricoeur 1991c).

11 See (Damasio 1994; Nussbaum 2001; Johnson 1987).

12 For instance, in a recent article on Ricoeur's unpublished lectures on the imagination, given in 1975 at approximately the same period as his work on metaphor (and on ideology and utopia), George Taylor says, "In the Lectures, Ricoeur challenges the history of Western thought not only in its general failure to comprehend the interrelation of imagination and seeing but also in its almost singular emphasis . . . on the reproductive imagination to the exclusion of the productive imagination" (G. H. Taylor 2006: 96).

13 (McFague 1982). See also (McFague 1993).

14 (McFague 1982: 13). See also her earlier (McFague 1975). She does note that Catholic thinkers such as David Tracy and David Burrell use analogy similar to the way she uses metaphor (McFague 1982: 198–9n16).

15   See (Aquinas 1952: 1.13.3). David Burrell explicitly relates his
     Roman Catholic use of analogy to contemporary uses of metaphor
     (Burrell 1973: 259–60). Likewise, see (Tracy 1981).
16   The theologian Langdon Gilkey who was at the University of
     Chicago Divinity School, like Ricoeur and Tillich, and who was
     much influenced by Tillich, uses symbol in this Tillichian fashion
     instead of "doctrine" or "concepts" for such notions as Christology
     and anthropology. For a concise treatment, see (Gilkey 1979). For
     more elaborate treatment, see (Gilkey 1969, 1970).
17   See (Ricoeur 1981f, 1991d: 17).
18   (Ricoeur 1995d). See also (Goldberg 1982, 1989).
19   Alasdair MacIntyre and Charles Taylor have emphasized, even
     more than Ricoeur, the narrative frame for philosophy (although
     their narrative theory per se is not as developed as Ricoeur's). See
     particularly (MacIntyre 1990; C. Taylor 1989). John Milbank has
     also made a similar point in saying that one can only "out-narrate"
     one's opponents (Milbank 1993: 330).
20   For treatment of the way that Ricoeur appropriates the idea of the
     "schema" in Kant in relation to the imagination, see (Ricoeur 1981e).
     For wider reflection on this issue, see (Johnson 1987).
21   As Charles Scalise reminded, this description resembles the practice
     of controlled allegory in the church for over a millennium.
22   See also (Ricoeur 1980d).
23   See (G. Lindbeck 1984: 38, 136n5; Frei 1992: 6, 1993: 127, 139,
     163). Blundell traces out the conflation of Ricoeur with Tracy,
     along with its problems, in detail, for example (Blundell 2010:
     44n52).
24   Accounts of the contentious aspect of the conflict can be found in
     (DeHart 2006: 32–41).
25   See (DeHart 2006; Hunsinger 2003).
26   (Frei 1992: 3–4). Also see Tracy's sympathetic treatment of Lindbeck
     (Marshall and G. A. Lindbeck 1990: 35–68).
27   Ricoeur emphasized that he was not a theologian; Frei emphasized
     that he was not a philosopher (Blundell 2010: 45n55).
28   Blundell is so serious about this matter that he avoids using the
     nonphilosophical writings. (Blundell 2010: 6)
29   Ricoeur's language is that theology can make philosophical
     hermeneutics its *organon*; he also says that the experience of faith
     "escapes" hermeneutics (Ricoeur 1976b: 1, 19).
30   See for a fuller account, (Stiver 1996: Ch. 7).

Chapter 5

1 See especially (Ricoeur 2010a) and also the essay by Richard Kearney in this book, "Capable Man, Capable God, 49–61.

2 For further treatment of the biblical, theological, and philosophical background, see (Brown, Murphy and Malony 1998; Stiver 2009: Ch. 5).

3 A colorful introduction to both is (Zizek 2006).

4 Recall that the first volume was *Freedom and Nature*, and the second volume was published as two books, *Fallible Man* and *The Symbolism of Evil*. He had originally lined out a third volume on the poetics of the will that he never completed as such.

5 Merleau-Ponty, however, is influenced especially by the later Husserl's work on the lifeworld of the self, which some think was in part inspired by Heidegger's earlier *Being and Time* (Husserl 1970).

6 Erazim Kohák refers to this term in connection with these philosophers and sees them as representing a third force, a *tiers monde*, in French philosophy besides idealism and empiricism (Ricoeur 1966: xii–xiii).

7 Ricoeur dealt with it to some extent, or had an opportunity to do so, in his late dialogue with a neuroscientist (Changeux and Ricoeur 2002). Unfortunately, Ricoeur seemed on the defensive in rejecting a reductionist, wholly material approach so much that one does not see as much how he would integrate the two approaches—a physicalist and a phenomenological approach. Nevertheless, Ricoeur did call for a "third language" that would mediate between biological and everyday language. See (Ricoeur 1992: 319–29).

8 In another essay, published 12 years later, he refers to freedom's "power to *contract* habits." He adds, "Without the *acquired* nature of a character, we would not even be able to set about acquiring a personality" (Ricoeur 1974: 37).

9 (Arendt 1958: 247). For Ricoeur's connection with Arendt, see (Reagan 1996: 132). Note also that Ricoeur wrote a preface to the French translation of *The Human Condition* (Ricoeur 1992: 196n38).

10 On this point in relation to God, see (Moltmann 1993; Kearney 2001).

11 See especially (Damasio 2003) and (Nussbaum 2001). Garcia interestingly connects this emphasis also with Spinoza, so important to Ricoeur (Damasio 2003). Also note here the perception from cognitive science of (Lakoff and M. Johnson 1999) and (M. Johnson 1987).

12 For example, see (Gleick 1987; Prigogine and Stengers 1984).
13 In fact, Ricoeur says of the focus on negation, "Someone who remains at the level of negation remains in the adolescence of freedom" (Ricoeur 1974c: 31).
14 See, for example, (Beauregard and O'Leary 2007; Hagerty 2009).
15 (Changeux and Ricoeur 2002: 30, 69). I was greatly aided in considering the significance of a "third discourse" by an opportunity to read a draft of a dissertation on this subject by Michael Wong.
16 I use here the Marcellian term "mystery," which seems appropriate. Ricoeur refers to the Kantian term "marvel of time" to represent the general enigma of the way that the schema of the imagination relates percept and concept (Ricoeur 1986a: 42). The latter phrase is one that Ricoeur quoted from Kant, referring to the transcendental imagination but in connection with the way in which "respect" brings together character and happiness. (69)
17 For more on the fall, see (Stiver 2009: 225–36). Pamela Sue Anderson rightly discerns in Ricoeur a tendency to follow in this work in the 1950s a traditional conception of the roles of men and women (Anderson 1992: 19, 1998: 151). At the same time, Ricoeur somewhat balanced this with an emphasis on reciprocity. In his later work, he does not focus particularly on distinctive male and female experience, which can be seen as a weakness. On the other hand, his work, like Merleau-Ponty's, emphasized the importance of specific, embodied experience that is open to such development and does not rule it out or lock in traditional conceptions. For insightful treatment of the pros and cons of this issue in Merleau-Ponty that could similarly be applied to Ricoeur, see (Hass 2008: 94–7). Speaking of Luce Irigaray, Hass says, "Sexual difference isn't just one concern among many" (96). It is a major issue in itself, if not the major issue. This is something to which neither of the thinkers does justice; on the other hand, as Hass also indicates of Merleau-Ponty, his work points toward and does not contradict such a development. For an excellent account of the strengths and weaknesses of Ricoeur's approach for feminist philosophy (as well as Gadamer's), see (Derksen and Halsema 2011).
18 These may better be considered metaphors in light of his later work.
19 One might compare here the way the New Testament scholar Norman Perrin warns against reducing "tensive" symbols in the New Testament such as the Kingdom of God to literal concepts (Perrin 1976: 194, 196).

20   An excellent example is the way that Pamela Sue Anderson draws on mimesis in Ricoeur and Luce Irigaray to reconfigure philosophy of religion (Anderson 1998: Chs. 4–5).

21   He had already developed the categories in (Ricoeur 1988: 246).

22   An exception is (Ricoeur 1986b), based on lectures in the 1970s. Nevertheless, they remind us that Ricoeur was often lecturing on topics far beyond what he was publishing. There has been a flurry of activity in reflecting on the significance of these essays in Ricoeur conferences in recent years, which will likely find their way into published works, particularly in a conference in Moscow on Ricoeur's social thought and the Society of Ricoeur Studies annual meeting in Philadelphia, both in the Fall of 2011.

23   Two notable examples are works by the aforementioned Bernard Dauenhauer and David Kaplan (Kaplan 2003). See also the forthcoming works: *Paul Ricoeur and the Task of Political Philosophy*, edited by Greg S. Johnson and myself with Lexington Press, and *From Ricoeur to Action: The Socio-Political Significance of Ricoeur's Thinking*, edited by Todd Mei and David Lewin with Continuum.

24   (Ricoeur 2005: 245). For an exploration of the significance for this work in political and moral philosophy, see (Marcelo 2011)

25   On concerns of feminists for a loss of the self that in turns leads to the loss of the capacity to criticize, see (Benhabib 1992: 224–5; Hekman 1990: 80, 90; Anderson 1998: 54–6).

26   Hekman's summary referring to feminists such as Jane Flax (Hekman 1990: 80).

27   (Derksen and Halsema 2011: 221, 223). These authors especially note Ricoeur's article on sexuality and eroticism as being significant for feminists and the issue of embodiment. Ricoeur does not specify male or female approaches, but he offered a characteristically careful and provocative treatment of a postcritical view of sexuality with the possibility of "tenderness" being what marriage can sustain (Ricoeur 1964). Anderson's work also represents a way that much of Ricoeur's thought can be utilized in feminist philosophy of religion, especially through drawing upon his work of imagination and mimesis, yet not without seeing the limits of Ricoeur's more generalized thought for feminist self-understanding (Anderson 1997, 1998: 140).

28   (Hekman 1990: 94). A strong criticism of Ricoeur stems from a feminist perspective in (Farren 2011). While appreciative of Ricoeur's turn to the other, Farren does not see him doing as much justice to

the particularities and otherness of women's experience as Irigaray, which is a fair criticism. She goes further to say that Ricoeur's view is narcissistic, or at least contains "the seeds of pure narcissism" (205). More than she indicates, however, Ricoeur was more careful to emphasize that the other is not collapsed into the self. He did not say the self is an other or that the other is the self but sees the self as another, in relation to another. He said at one point, "This connection between self-constancy and narrative identity confirms one of my oldest convictions, namely, that the self of self-knowledge is not the egotistical and narcissistic ego whose hypocrisy and naiveté the hermeneutics of suspicion have denounced . . . . The self of self-knowledge is the fruit of an examined life" (Ricoeur 1988: 247). She is right to indicate, however, that his phrase, oneself as another, is open to an interpretation like hers.

29 (Anderson 2010: 146). She sets Ricoeur in dialogue with Spinoza on the affirmation of corporeality, conatus, imagination, emotion, and also reason in this rich article. In the same book, Scott Davidson and Maria del Guadalupe Davidson also find promise in Ricoeur's notion of the capable self for black feminist thought (S. Davidson and M. del G. Davidson 2010).

30 Italics in the original (Ricoeur 1992: 172).

31 (Ricoeur 1980: 166–80, 1988: 215).

32 I have generally argued that postmodernism does not necessarily lead to relativism or skepticism or to loss of the self, but it can, especially as in some interpretations of Derrida, Foucault, Lacan, or Bataille. I am referring to these latter interpretations here.

33 (Ricoeur 1992: 348–53). Heidegger's Nazi involvement is notoriously difficult to assess, not in terms now of what he did, but of extent. He was quite involved, but early and for a short time, resigning as rector of the University of Freiburg in 1935. Nevertheless, he never repudiated his morally gross involvement and continued to make questionable if not reprehensible statements. For critical but not dismissive treatment, see (Wolin 1993). Concerning Heidegger, one can think of Ricoeur's treatment of evil acts in *The Symbolism of Evil*, where evil is inherently irrational, something that befalls one, and something that one chooses—all at once. It is also significant to note that in Ricoeur's treatment there is of the slide from fallibility to fault that applies not just to grotesque actions but to everyone, reminiscent of Hannah Arendt's emphasis on the banality of evil. See (Arendt 2006; Neiman 2002).

34   See (Derrida 1994: 14–15). See also (Derrida 1995). For a helpful
     general treatment in a theological context, see (Webb 1996). For a
     very accessible account, see the treatment of the gift and forgiveness
     in (Caputo 2007: 69–75).
35   (Ricoeur 2004: 478). See also Gaelle Fiasse's treatment of Ricoeur on
     forgiveness, where she says, "Ricoeur does not want to start with an
     impossible forgiveness, as does Derrida, but neither does he adopt a
     naïve position" (Fiasse 2010: 85). In relation to Ricoeur's odyssey of
     forgiveness, see Paul Fiddes' journey of forgiveness (Fiddes 2000a:
     Ch. 6).
36   For a concise statement of human existence as communal in
     connection with society and church (and the Holy Spirit), see (Gilkey
     1979: 199–200)
37   (Ricoeur 1974a: 216). Ricoeur can often give a positive spin to
     eschatology, and he later affirmed quite positively Moltmann's
     eschatology, which is quite millenarian. It is fair to say, though, that he
     is implying an escapist millenarianism here that is foreign to Moltmann.
38   This is an emphasis of the appropriation of the value of the utopian
     being more of a rupture and gesture rather than a full-blown utopia
     in (G. S. Johnson 2011).
39   This is to use the dreaded phrase that Karl Barth rejected in Emil
     Brunner in an article entitled simply "*Nein*" (No) that raised the fear
     of a "correlation" that collapses the revelation into contemporaneity.
     For discussion, see (Busch 1976: 248–53, 476–7). For it is instructive
     here to recall that Ricoeur felt himself close to Barth's perspective
     and his care as a philosopher to protect the integrity of theology
     and revelation. One might also note here the analogy of faith and of
     relations (*analogia fidei* and *analogia relationis*) that Barth developed
     in connection also with his movement toward a more open attitude
     toward creation later in his theology (four volumes in the *Church
     Dogmatics* on the doctrine of creation) (316–17). For helpful
     treatment of Ricoeur and Barth, see (Blundell 2010).
40   See (Ricoeur 1974e: 452).
41   See the last chapter, for fuller treatment of the idea of the summoned
     self.
42   (Ricoeur 2002: 284). For further emphasis of this theme, see
     (Johnson, Michael A. 2006).
43   (Ricoeur 2003: 9). This quotation, as Ricoeur noted, appears at
     the head of the chapter on action in Hannah Arendt's *The Human
     Condition* (Arendt 1958: 175).

Chapter 6

1   For the irony of Descartes being the father of rationality going on a pilgrimage thanking God and having three dreams that he saw as coming from God, see (Stiver 2009: 13–16).

2   (Ricoeur 1965d: 24). Ricoeur mentioned this phrase once in connection with Marcel, "After all, I don't have the truth; I only hope (and I remind myself here of my master Gabriel Marcel) to be in truth" (Ricoeur 1997: 194).

3   (Ricoeur 1965f: 297, 303). He also speaks of this in Kant as "recuperative" reflection (301).

4   See (Kant 1966), especially the preface to the 2nd edition.

5   (Ricoeur 1980c: 138). See (Calvin 1960: I.VII.4).

6   Found in Studies 7–9 of (Ricoeur 1992).

7   (Kearney 1984: 45).

8   This is a point emphasized in (Scott-Baumann 2009).

9   One might compare Ricoeur's use of the term "archeology" (in 1965) to Michel Foucault's use at about the same time (1966) in *The Order of Things: An Archaeology of the Human Sciences* (Foucault 1973).

10   (Ricoeur 1986b: 182). Cf. (Ricoeur 1991: 318).

11   In one brief place, Ricoeur mentioned in passing a connection between the imaginative power of utopia that is like fiction (Ricoeur 1986: 309).

12   One can see here the more typical, domesticated version of the imagination as in Immanuel Kant. In a recent article on Ricoeur's unpublished lectures on the imagination, given in 1975 at approximately the same period as the lectures on ideology and utopia, George Taylor says, "In the Lectures, Ricoeur challenges the history of Western thought not only in its general failure to comprehend the interrelation of imagination and seeing but also in its almost singular emphasis . . . on the reproductive imagination to the exclusion of the productive imagination" (Taylor 2006: 96). Cf. also (Johnson 1987).

13   (Ricoeur 2004: 80). Ricoeur later connected this problem to narrative, "It was due to the mediating function of the narrative that the abuses of memory were made into abuses of forgetting. In fact, before the use, there was the abuse, that is the unavoidably selective nature of narrative. If one cannot recall everything, neither can one recount everything" (Ricoeur 2004: 448).

14 (Ricoeur 2000: 56) See also "the little ethic" in *Oneself as Another* (Ricoeur 1992). Also see (Ricoeur 2007: 60–2).

15 See (Wall 2005), for a helpful treatment of the importance of creativity in the moral and ethical spheres, especially dealing with ideology, and with a strong dimension of religion and theology.

16 (Ricoeur 1974e). For appreciation and elaboration of this reflection, see (Kearney 2011: Ch. 3).

17 (Dawkins 2006; Hitchens 2009). See for responses (Haught 2008; Stiver 2011; Kearney 2011: Conclusion).

18 (Ricoeur 1974e: 445, 448, 455, 459). For insightful treatment of tragedy and *phronesis*, see (Fisher 2011).

19 A classic text on this point is (Tillich 1957a).

20 A powerful emphasis of this point is (Westphal 1993).

21 For the significance of Ricoeur's emphasis on critique, see (Thompson 1981).

22 Martha Nussbaum argues that literature is indispensable to the formation of the practical judgment of judges in (Nussbaum 1995).

Chapter 7

1 (Ricoeur 2009: xx, 96). Referring to Etienne Gilson, Ricoeur mentions the Christian philosophy "that has given rise to so many polemics in France" (LaCocque and Ricoeur 1998: 353).

2 For discussion of how philosophy and theology can still be distinguished, see (Stiver 2001: 244–7).

3 (Changeux and Ricoeur 2002: 297). See below, for some further reflections of Ricoeur on interreligious relations.

4 For discussion, see (Pellauer 2007: 133–8).

5 (Ricoeur 1980). Paul Fiddes argues that "Moltmann's concept . . . has a more radical discontinuity with present reality than does Ricoeur." While Fiddes has sympathies with both in his view of the future and of God, he prefers the "link" that Ricoeur finds between the possibilities of the present and the "unexpectedness of new creation in the future" (Fiddes 2000b: 46–7). Fiddes points beyond Augustine's "eternal present" as does Ricoeur in the end, as we have seen in his development of a conception of a God of the possible, shared with Kearney (44).

6 For extended reflection on hope based on Ricoeur's thought, see (Huskey 2009).

7   (Ricoeur 2009: 53–5). Ricoeur was, however, quite aware of René
    Girard's significant reformulation of atonement as the abolishment
    of scapegoating (Ricoeur 1998: 152, 2010a: 32–5). At one point,
    Ricoeur gestured toward Alfred North Whitehead's process
    philosophy as a way that God may remember one without a personal
    afterlife (Ricoeur 1998: 158). In the preface, it is stated that he was
    chided by Olivier Abel for inconsistently holding on to that hope.
    Ricoeur responded somewhat humorously but also somewhat
    poignantly, "You mean I have to give up even that?" (Ricoeur 2009:
    xvii). In actuality, while that view of objective immortality is the
    main line of process thought, process thinkers have themselves
    affirmed subjective immortality in ways that they see consistent with
    Whitehead (Suchocki 1989; Griffin 2000: 3).

8   (Ricoeur 2009: 96). Here is the letter without the spacing, "Dear
    Marie, At the hour of decline the word resurrection arises. Beyond
    every miraculous episode. From the depths of life, a power suddenly
    appears, which says that being is against death. Believe this with me.
    your friend, Paul R."

9   (Ricoeur 2009: 49). See also (Ricoeur 1998: 156), where he related
    his detachment to Meister Eckhart and Flemish mysticism.

10 (Ricoeur 2009: 15). He spoke of this similarly in terms of the
    "fundamental" in (Ricoeur 1998: 160). See Richard Kearney's
    appropriation of Ricoeur and others in laying out a nuanced
    approach to other religions, and atheism, in the conclusion of
    (Kearney 2011).

11 (Ricoeur 2010b: 39). See also his interview with Hans Küng on
    the issue of Küng's championing a global ethic based on common
    affirmations of the world religions and Kearney's discussion of it
    (Ricoeur 1996; Kearney 2011: Conclusion).

12 (Ricoeur 1995c: 270). Ricoeur emphasized that learning is
    not Platonic reminiscence for Augustine because his Christian
    commitments caused him to reject the preexistence of the soul.

13 (Ricoeur 1995c: 272). One might note here the footnote in which
    Ricoeur explicated Rudolf Bultmann's view of Paul's use of
    conscience, complete with numerous biblical citations.

14 (Schweiker, Johnson and Jung 2006: 11). Schweiker was a student of
    David Tracy at Chicago who draws on Ricoeur.

15 (Kearney 2001, 2011). For a similar desire to learn from atheism by a
    Continental philosopher, see (Westphal 1993).

BIBLIOGRAPHY

Works by Paul Ricoeur

1964. "The Dimensions of Sexuality: Wonder, Eroticism, and Enigma." *Cross Currents* 14(2): 133–66.

1965a. "Christianity and the Meaning of History." pp. 81–97 in *History and Truth*, edited by Charles A. Kelbley. Northwestern University Studies in Phenomenology and Existential Philosophy. Evanston, IL: Northwestern University Press.

1965b. *History and Truth*. 2nd edn., edited by Charles A. Kelbley. Evanston, IL: Northwestern University Press.

1965c. "Objectivity and Subjectivity in History." pp. 21–40 in *History and Truth*, edited by Charles A. Kelbley. Northwestern University Studies in Phenomenology and Existential Philosophy. Evanston, IL: Northwestern University Press.

1965d. "The History of Philosophy and the Unity of Truth." pp. 41–62 in *History and Truth*, edited by Charles A. Kelbley. Northwestern University Studies in Phenomenology and Existential Philosophy. Evanston, IL: Northwestern University Press.

1965e. "The Political Paradox." pp. 247–70 in *History and Truth*, edited by Charles A. Kelbley. Northwestern University Studies in Phenomenology and Existential Philosophy. Evanston, IL: Northwestern University Press.

1965f. "True and False Anguish." pp. 287–304 in *History and Truth*, edited by Charles A. Kelbley. Northwestern University Studies in Phenomenology and Existential Philosophy. Evanston, IL: Northwestern University Press.

1966. *Freedom and Nature: The Voluntary and the Involuntary*. Evanston, IL: Northwestern University Press.

1967. *The Symbolism of Evil*. New York: Harper & Row.

1970. *Freud and Philosophy: An Essay on Interpretation*. New Haven, CT: Yale University Press.

1974a. "Adventures of the State and the Task of Christians." pp. 201–16 in *Political and Social Essays*, edited by David Stewart and Joseph Bien. Athens, OH: Ohio University Press.

1974b. "Existence and Hermeneutics." pp. 3–24 in *The Conflict of Interpretations*, edited by Don Ihde. Northwestern University Studies in Phenomenology & Existential Philosophy. Evanston, IL: Northwestern University Press.

1974c. "Nature and Freedom." pp. 23–45 in *Political and Social Essays*, edited by David Stewart and Joseph Bien. Athens, OH: Ohio University Press.

1974d. *Political and Social Essays*, edited by David Stewart and Joseph Bien. Athens, OH: Ohio University Press.

1974e. "Religion, Atheism, and Faith." pp. 440–67 in *The Conflict of Interpretations*, edited by Don Ihde. Northwestern University Studies in Phenomenology & Existential Philosophy. Evanston, IL: Northwestern University Press.

1974f. *The Conflict of Interpretations*, edited by Don Ihde. Evanston, IL: Northwestern University Press.

1974g. "The Hermeneutics of Symbols and Philosophical Reflection: I." pp. 287–314 in *The Conflict of Interpretations*, edited by Don Ihde. Northwestern University Studies in Phenomenology & Existential Philosophy. Evanston, IL: Northwestern University Press.

1975. "Biblical Hermeneutics." *Semeia* 4: 27–138.

1976a. *Interpretation Theory: Discourse and the Surplus of Meaning*. Fort Worth, TX: Texas Christian University Press.

1976b. "Philosophical Hermeneutics and Theological Hermeneutics." pp. 1–20 in *Protocol of the Colloquy of the Center for Hermeneutical Studies in Hellenistic and Modern Culture*, Center for Hermeneutical Studies in Hellenistic and Modern Culture, edited by James Wm. McClendon. Berkeley, CA: Center for Hermeneutial Studies in Hellenistic and Modern Culture.

1977. *The Rule of Metaphor: Multi-Disciplinary Studies of the Creation of Meaning in Language*. Toronto: University of Toronto Press.

1980a. *Essays on Biblical Interpretation*, edited by Lewis Mudge. Philadelphia: Fortress Press.

1980b. "Freedom in the Light of Hope." pp. 155–82 in *Essays on Biblical Interpretation*, edited by Lewis S. Mudge. Philadelphia: Fortress Press.

1980c. "The Hermeneutics of Testimony." in *Essays on Biblical Interpretation*, edited by Lewis Mudge. Philadelphia: Fortress Press.

1980d. "Toward a Hermeneutic of the Idea of Revelation." pp. 73–118 in *Essays on Biblical Interpretation*, edited by Lewis S. Mudge. Philadelphia: Fortress Press.

1981a. "Hermeneutics and the Critique of Ideology." pp. 63–100 in *Hermeneutics and the Human Sciences: Essays on Language, Action, and Interpretation*, edited by John B. Thompson. Cambridge, England: Cambridge University Press.

1981b. *Hermeneutics and the Human Sciences: Essays on Language, Action, and Interpretation*, edited by John B. Thompson. Cambridge: Cambridge University Press.

1981c. "Metaphor and the Central Problem of Hermeneutics." In *Hermeneutics and the Human Sciences: Essays on Language, Action, and Interpretation*, edited by John B. Thompson. Cambridge: Cambridge University Press.

1981d. "Science and Ideology." pp. 222–46 in *Hermeneutics and the Human Sciences: Essays on Language, Action, and Interpretation*, edited by John B. Thompson. Cambridge, England: Cambridge University Press.

1981e. "The Metaphorical Process as Cognition, Imagination, and Feeling." pp. 228–47 in *Philosophical Perspectives on Metaphor*, edited by Mark Johnson. Minneapolis, MN: University of Minnesota Press.

1981f. "The Model of the Text: Meaningful Action Considered as a Text." pp. 197–221 in *Hermeneutics and the Human Sciences: Essays on Language, Action, and Interpretation*, edited by John B. Thompson. Cambridge: Cambridge University Press.

1981g. "What Is a Text? Explanation and Understanding." pp. 145–64 in *Hermeneutics and the Human Sciences: Essays on Language, Action, and Interpretation*, edited by John B. Thompson. Cambridge: Cambridge University Press.

1984. *Time and Narrative*, vol. 1. Chicago, IL: University of Chicago Press.

1986a. *Fallible Man*. 2nd edn. New York: Fordham University Press.

1986b. *Lectures on Ideology and Utopia*, edited by George H. Taylor. New York: Columbia University Press.

1988. *Time and Narrative*, vol. 3. Chicago, IL: University of Chicago Press.

1991a. *From Text to Action: Essays in Hermeneutics, II*. Evanston, IL: Northwestern University Press.

1991b. "Ideology and Utopia." pp. 308–24 in *From Text to Action: Essays in Hermeneutics, II*. Northwestern University Studies in Phenomenology and Existential Philosophy. Evanston, IL: Northwestern University Press.

1991c. "Imagination in Discourse and Action." pp. 168–87 in *From Text to Action: Essays in Hermeneutics, II*. Northwestern University Studies in Phenomenology and Existential Philosophy. Evanston, IL: Northwestern University Press.

1991d. "On Interpretation." in *From Text to Action: Essays in Hermeneutics, II*. Northwestern University Studies in Phenomenology and Existential Philosophy. Evanston, IL: Northwestern University Press.

1991e. "Philosophical Hermeneutics and Biblical Hermeneutics."
    pp. 89–101 in *From Text to Action: Essays in Hermeneutics, II.*
    Northwestern University Studies in Phenomenology and Existential
    Philosophy. Evanston, IL: Northwestern University Press.
1992. *Oneself as Another.* Chicago, IL: University of Chicago Press.
1995a. "Intellectual Autobiography." pp. 3–53 in *The Philosophy of Paul
    Ricoeur.* The Library of Living Philosophers, vol. 22. Chicago, IL:
    Open Court.
1995b. "Love and Justice." pp. 315–29 in *Figuring the Sacred: Religion,
    Narrative, and Imagination,* edited by Mark I. Wallace. Minneapolis,
    MN: Fortress Press.
1995c. "The Summoned Subject in the School of the Narratives of the
    Prophetic Vocation." pp. 262–75 in *Figuring the Sacred: Religion,
    Narrative, and Imagination,* edited by Mark I. Wallace. Minneapolis,
    MN: Fortress Press.
1995d. "Toward a Narrative Theology: Its Necessity, Its Resources, Its
    Difficulties." pp. 236–48 in *Figuring the Sacred: Religion, Narrative,
    and Imagination,* edited by Mark I. Wallace. Minneapolis, MN:
    Fortress Press.
1996. *"Entretien Hans Küng-Paul Ricoeur."* Retrieved December 28, 2011
    (http://www.fondsricoeur.fr/index.php?m=54&dev=&lang=en&rub
    =3&ssrub=).
1997. *Tolerance between Intolerance and the Intolerable.* Providence, RI:
    Berghahn Books.
1998. *Critique and Conviction.* New York: Columbia University Press.
2000. *The Just.* Chicago, IL: University of Chicago Press.
2002. "Ethics and Human Capability: A Response." pp. 279–90 in *Paul
    Ricoeur and Contemporary Moral Thought,* edited by John Wall,
    William Schweiker, and W. David Hall. New York: Routledge.
2003. "Memory, History, Oblivion." Retrieved December 27, 2011 (http://
    www.fondsricoeur.fr/doc/BUDAPEST2003TEXTEANGL.PDF).
2004. *Memory, History, Forgetting.* Chicago, IL: University of Chicago Press.
2005. *The Course of Recognition.* Cambridge: Harvard University Press.
2006. *On Translation.* New York: Routledge.
2007. *Reflections on the Just.* Chicago, IL: University of Chicago Press.
2009. *Living up to Death.* Chicago, IL: University of Chicago Press.
2010a. "Asserting Personal Capacities and Pleading for Mutual
    Recognition." pp. 22–6 in *A Passion for the Possible: Thinking with
    Paul Ricoeur,* edited by Brian Treanor and Henry Isaac Venema.
    Perspectives in Continental Philosophy. New York: Fordham
    University Press.
2010b. "Religious Belief: The Difficult Path of the Religious." pp. 27–40
    in *A Passion for the Possible: Thinking with Paul Ricoeur,* edited by

Brian Treanor and Henry Isaac Venema. Perspectives in Continental
    Philosophy. New York: Fordham University Press.
Changeux, Jean-Pierre, and Paul Ricoeur. 2002. *What Makes Us Think?:
    A Neuroscientist and a Philosopher Argue about Ethics, Human
    Nature, and the Brain*. Princeton, NJ: Princeton University Press.
LaCocque, André, and Paul Ricoeur. 1998. *Thinking Biblically: Exegetical
    and Hermeneutical Studies*. Chicago, IL: University of Chicago Press.

Secondary literature

Anderson, Pamela S., 1992. "Ricoeur and Hick on Evil: Post-Kantian
    Myth?" *Contemporary Philosophy* 14(6): 15–20.
— 1997. "Re-reading Myth in Philosophy: Hegel, Ricoeur, and Irigaray
    Reading Antigone." pp. 51–68 in *Paul Ricoeur and Narrative: Context
    and Contestation*, edited by Joy Morny. Calgary: University of Calgary
    Press.
— 1998. *A Feminist Philosophy of Religion: The Rationality and Myths
    of Religious Belief*. Malden, MA: Blackwell.
— 2010. "Ricoeur and Women's Studies: On the Affirmation of Life and
    a Confidence in the Power to Act." pp. 142–64 in *Ricoeur Across the
    Disciplines*, edited by Scott Davidson. New York: Continuum.
Anderson, Pamela S., and Jordan Bell. 2010. *Kant and Theology*. New
    York: Continuum.
Aquinas, Thomas. 1952. *The Summa Theologica of Saint Thomas
    Aquinas*. Great Books of the Western World, vols. 19–20. Chicago, IL:
    Encyclopedia Britannica.
Arendt, Hannah. 1958. *The Human Condition*. Chicago, IL: University of
    Chicago Press.
— 2006. *Eichmann in Jerusalem: A Report on the Banality of Evil*. New
    York: Penguin Classics.
Aristotle. 1952. *On Poetics*. Great Books of the Western World, vol. 9.
    Chicago, IL: Encyclopedia Britannica.
Augustine. 1952. *The Confessions*. Great Books of the Western World,
    vol. 18. Chicago, IL: Encyclopedia Britannica.
— 1971. "The City of God." In *Saint Augustine's City of God and
    Christian Doctrine*, A Select Library of the Nicene and Post-Nicene
    Fathers of the Christian Church, vol. 2. Grand Rapids, MI: William B.
    Eerdmans.
Barbour, Ian G. 1974. *Myths, Models, and Paradigms*. New York:
    Harper & Row.
— 1997. *Religion and Science: Historical and Contemporary Issues*. Rev.
    edn. San Francisco: HarperSanFrancisco.

Barr, James. 1981. *Fundamentalism*. 2nd edn. Harrisburg, PA: Trinity Press International.

Beauregard, Mario, and Denyse O'Leary. 2007. *The Spiritual Brain: A Neuroscientist's Case for the Existence of the Soul*. New York: HarperOne.

Benhabib, Seyla. 1992. *Situating the Self: Gender, Community, and Postmodernism in Contemporary Ethics*. New York: Routledge.

Bernstein, Richard J. 1985. *Beyond Objectivism and Relativism: Science, Hermeneutics, and Praxis*. Philadelphia: University of Philadelphia Press.

Black, Max. 1981. "Metaphor." pp. 63–82 in *Philosophical Perspectives on Metaphor*, edited by Mark Johnson. Minneapolis, MN: University of Minnesota Press.

Blundell, Boyd. 2010. *Paul Ricoeur between Theology and Philosophy: Detour and Return*. Bloomington, IN: Indiana University Press.

Borg, Marcus J. 2002. *Reading the Bible Again For the First Time: Taking the Bible Seriously But Not Literally*. San Francisco, CA: HarperSanFrancisco.

Braithwaite, Richard B. 1971. "An Empiricist's View of the Nature of Religious Belief." In *The Philosophy of Religion*, edited by Basil Mitchell. Oxford Readings in Philosophy. Oxford: Oxford University Press.

Brown, Warren S., Nancey C. Murphy, and H. Newton Malony. 1998. *Whatever Happened to the Soul? Scientific and Theological Portraits of Human Nature*. Minneapolis, MN: Fortress Press.

Brunner, Emil. 1952. *Dogmatics*, vol. 2. Philadelphia: Westminister Press.

Buber, Martin. 1958. *I and Thou*. 2nd edn. Edinburgh: T. & T. Clark.

Burrell, David. 1973. *Analogy and Philosophical Language*. New Haven, CT: Yale University Press.

Busch, Eberhard. 1976. *Karl Barth: His Life from Letters and Autobiographical Texts*. 2nd edn. Philadelphia: Fortress Press.

Calvin, John. 1960. *Calvin: Institutes of the Christian Religion*. Library of Christian Classics. Philadelphia: Westminster Press.

Caputo, John D. 2007. *What Would Jesus Deconstruct?: The Good News of Postmodernism for the Church*. Grand Rapids, MI: Baker Academic.

Comstock, Gary L. 1986. "Two Types of Narrative Theology." *Journal of the American Academy of Religion* 55: 687–717.

Damasio, Antonio. 1994. *Descartes' Error: Emotion, Reason, and the Human Brain*. New York: G. P. Putnam's Sons

—2003. *Looking for Spinoza: Joy, Sorrow, -and the Feeling Brain*. Orlando, FL: Mariner Books

Dauenhauer, Bernard P. 1998. *Paul Ricoeur: The Promise and Risk of Politics*. Lanham, MD: Rowman & Littlefield Publishers.

Davidson, Scott, and Maria del Guadalupe Davidson. 2010. "Ricoeur and African American Studies: Convergences with Black Feminist Thought." pp. 165–80 in *Ricoeur across the Disciplines*, edited by Scott Davidson. New York: Continuum.

Dawkins, Richard. 2006. *The God Delusion*. Boston, MA: Houghton Mifflin.

DeHart, Paul. 2006. *Trial of the Witnesses: The Rise and Decline of Postliberal Theology*. Malden, MA: Wiley-Blackwell.

Derksen, Louise D., and Annemie Halsema. 2011. "Understanding the Body: The Relevance of Gadamer's and Ricoeur's View of the Body for Feminist Theory." pp. 203–25 in *Gadamer and Ricoeur: Critical Horizons for Contemporary Hermeneutics*, edited by Francis J. Mootz and George H. Taylor. Continuum Studies in Continental Philosophy. New York: Continuum.

Derrida, Jacques. 1973. *Speech and Phenomena: And Other Essays on Husserl's Theory of Signs*. Evanston, IL: Northwestern University Press.

—1974. *Of Grammatology*. Baltimore, MD: John Hopkins University Press.

—1981. *Dissemination*. Chicago, IL: University of Chicago Press.

—1985. *Margins of Philosophy*. Chicago, IL: University of Chicago Press.

—1994. *Given Time: I. Counterfeit Money*. Chicago, IL: University of Chicago Press.

—1995. *The Gift of Death*. Chicago, IL: University of Chicago Press.

—2001. *On Cosmopolitanism and Forgiveness*. New York: Routledge.

Descartes, René. 1952. "Discourse on the Method." pp. 41–67 in *Descartes, Spinoza*, Great Books of the Western World, vol. 31. Chicago, IL: Encyclopedia Britannica.

Dewey, John. 1929. *The Quest for Certainty*. New York: Capricorn Books.

Dosse, François. 1997. *Paul Ricoeur: les sensd'une vie*. Paris: La Découverte.

Evans, Jeanne. 1995. *Paul Ricoeur's Hermeneutics of the Imagination*. New York: P. Lang.

Farren, Katrina M. 2011. *Narrative Identity in Paul Ricoeur and Luce Irigaray: The Circularity between Self and Other*. Ann Arbor, MI: ProQuest, UMI Dissertation Publishing.

Feyerabend, Paul. 2010. *Against Method*. 4th edn. New York: Verso.

Fiasse, Gaëlle. 2010. "The Golden Rule and Forgiveness." pp. 77–89 in *A Passion for the Possible: Thinking with Paul Ricoeur*, edited by Brian Treanor and Henry Isaac Venema. Perspectives in Continental Philosophy. New York: Fordham University Press.

Fiddes, Paul S. 2000a. *Participating in God: A Pastoral Doctrine of the Trinity*. Louisville, KY: Westminster John Knox Press.

—2000b. *The Promised End: Eschatology in Theology and Literature*. Malden, MA: Wiley-Blackwell.

Fisher, David H. 2011. "Is *Phronēsis Deinon*? Ricoeur on Tragedy and *Phronēsis*." pp. 156–77 in *Gadamer and Ricoeur: Critical Horizons for Contemporary Hermeneutics*, edited by Francis J. Mootz and George H. Taylor. Continuum Studies in Continental Philosophy. New York: Continuum.

Foucault, Michel. 1973. *The Order of Things: An Archaelogy of the Human Sciences*. New York: Vintage Books.

Frei, Hans W. 1967. *The Identity of Jesus Christ: The Hermeneutical Bases of Dogmatic Theology*. Philadelphia: Fortress Press.

—1974. *The Eclipse of Biblical Narrative: A Study in Eighteenth and Nineteenth Century Hermeneutics*. New Haven, CT: Yale University Press.

—1981. "An Afterword: Eberhard Busch's Biography of Karl Barth." In *Karl Barth in Review: Posthumous Works Reviewed and Assessed*, edited by H. Martin Rumscheidt. Pittsburgh, PA: Pickwick Press.

—1992. *Types of Christian Theology*, edited by George Hunsinger and William C. Placher. New Haven, CT: Yale University Press.

—1993. *Theology and Narrative: Selected Essays*, edited by George Hunsinger and William C. Placher. New York: Oxford University Press.

Froehlich, Karlfried, (ed.) 1984. *Biblical Interpretation in the Early Church*. Philadelphia: Fortress Press.

Gadamer, Hans-Georg. 1991. *Truth and Method*. 2nd edn. New York: Crossroad.

Gilkey, Langdon. 1969. *Naming the Whirlwind: The Renewal of God-Language*. Indianapolis, IN: Bobbs-Merrill.

—1970. *Religion and the Scientific Future: Reflections on Myth, Science, and Theology*. New York: Harper & Row.

—1979. *Message and Existence*. New York: The Seabury Press.

—1985. *Creationism on Trial: Evolution and God at Little Rock*. Minneapolis, MN: Winston Press.

Gill, Jerry. 1981. *Wittgenstein and Metaphor*. Dallas, TX: University Press of America.

Gleick, James. 1987. *Chaos: Making a New Science*. New York: Penguin Books.

Goldberg, Michael. 1982. *Theology and Narrative: A Critical Introduction*. Nashville, TN: Abingdon.

—1989. "God, Action, and Narrative: Which Narrative? Which Action? Which God?" pp. 348–65 in *Why Narrative? Readings in Narrative*

Theology, edited by L. Gregory Jones and Stanley Hauerwas. Grand Rapids, MI: William B. Eerdmans.

Gorospe, Athena E. O. 2006. "The Ethical Possibilities of Exodus 4:18–26 in Light of Paul Ricoeur's Narrative Theory: A Filipino Reading." Center for Advanced Theological Studies, School of Theology: Fuller Theological Seminary.

Grant, Robert M., and David Tracy. 1984. *A Short History of the Interpretation of the Bible*. 2nd edn. New York: Fortress Press.

Green, Joel B. 2006. "Kaleidoscopic View." pp. 157–85 in *The Nature of the Atonement*, edited by Paul R. Eddy and James K. Beilby. Downers Grove, IL: InterVarsity Press.

Grenz, Stanley J., and John R. Franke. 2001. *Beyond Foundationalism: Shaping Theology in a Postmodern Context*. Louisville, KY: Westminster John Knox Press.

Griffin, David R. 2000. "Process Theology and the Christian Good News: A Response to Classical Free Will Theism." pp. 1–38 in *Searching for an Adequate God: A Dialogue between Process and Free Will Theists*, edited by John B. Cobb and Clark H. Pinnock. Grand Rapids, MI: Wm. B. Eerdmans.

Griffin, David R., William A. Beardslee, and Joe Holland, (eds) 1989. *Varieties of Postmodern Theology*. Albany, NY: State University of New York Press.

Hagerty, Barbara B. 2009. *Fingerprints of God: The Search for the Science of Spirituality*. New York: Penguin Group.

Hass, Lawrence. 2008. *Merleau-Ponty's Philosophy*. Bloomington, IN: Indiana University Press.

Hauerwas, Stanley. 1991. *After Christendom: How the Church Is to Behave If Freedom, Justice, and a Christian Nation Are Bad Ideas*. Nashville, TN: Abingdon Press.

—2001. *With the Grain of the Universe: The Church's Witness and Natural Theology*. Grand Rapids, MI: Brazos Press.

Hauerwas, Stanley, Nancey C. Murphy, and Mark Nation, (eds) 1994. *Theology Without Foundations: Religious Practice and the Future of Theological Truth*. Nashville, TN: Abingdon.

Haught, John F. 2008. *God and the New Atheism: A Critical Response to Dawkins, Harris, and Hitchens*. Louisville, KY: Westminster John Knox Press.

Hawkes, Terence. 1977. *Structuralism and Semiotics*. Berkeley, CA: University of California Press.

Heidegger, Martin. 1962. *Being and Time*. New York: Harper & Row.

Hekman, Susan J. 1990. *Gender and Knowledge: Elements of a Postmodern Feminism*. Boston, MA: Northeastern University Press.

Van den Hengel, John. 1993. "Jesus Between History and Fiction." in
    Meanings in Texts and Actions: Questioning Paul Ricoeur, edited
    by William Schweiker and David E. Klemm. Studies in Religion and
    Culture. Charlottesville, VA: University Press of Virginia.
Hesse, Mary. 1980. *Revolutions and Reconstructions in the Philosophy of
    Science*. Bloomington, IN: Indiana University Press.
Hitchens, Christopher. 2009. *God Is Not Great: How Religion Poisons
    Everything*. New York: Twelve.
Hobbes, Thomas. 1947. *Leviathan*. 2nd edn. New York: Macmillan.
Hunsinger, George. 2003. "Postliberal Theology." pp. 42–57 in *Cambridge
    Companion to Postmodern Theology*, edited by Vanhoozer, Kevin J.
    New York: Cambridge University Press.
Huskey, Rebecca K. 2009. *Paul Ricoeur on Hope*. New York: Peter Lang.
Husserl, Edmund. 1965. *Phenomenology and the Crisis of Philosophy:
    Philosophy as Rigorous Science, and Philosophy and the Crisis of
    European Man*. New York: Harper & Row.
—1970. *The Crisis of European Sciences and Transcendental
    Phenomenology: An Introduction to Phenomenological Philosophy*.
    Evanston, IL: Northwestern University Press.
Iser, Wolfgang. 1974. *The Implied Reader: Patterns of Communications in
    Prose Fiction from Bunyan to Beckett*. Baltimore, MD: John Hopkins
    University Press.
Jenkins, Philip. 2002. *The Next Christendom: The Coming of Global
    Christianity*. New York: Oxford University Press.
Johnson, Greg S. 2011. *Elements of the Utopian*. Aurora, CO: Davies
    Group.
Johnson, Mark. 1981. "Introduction: Metaphor in the Philosophical
    Tradition." in *Philosophical Perspectives on Metaphor*, edited by Mark
    Johnson. Minneapolis, MN: University of Minnesota Press.
—1987. *The Body in the Mind: The Bodily Basis of Meaning,
    Imagination, and Reason*. Chicago, IL: University of Chicago Press.
Johnson, Michael A. 2006. "Creation and Initiative: A Reading of
    Ricoeur's Ethics of Originary Affirmation." in *Humanity Before God:
    Contemporary Faces of Jewish, Christian, and Islamic Ethics*, edited by
    William Schweiker, Michael A. Johnson, and Kevin Jung. Minneapolis,
    MN: Fortress Press.
Kant, Immanuel. 1960. *Religion Within the Limits of Reason Alone*,
    edited by Hoyt H. Hudson. New York: Harper & Brothers.
—1966. *Critique of Pure Reason*. Garden City, NY: Anchor Books.
Kaplan, David M. 2003. *Ricoeur's Critical Theory*. Albany, NY: State
    University of New York Press.
Kearney, Richard. 2001. *The God Who May Be*. Bloomington, IN:
    Indiana University Press.

—2002. *Strangers, Gods and Monsters: Interpreting Otherness*. New York: Routledge.

—2011. *Anatheism: Returning to God after God*. New York: Columbia University Press.

Kearney, Richard. (ed.) 1984. *Dialogues with Contemporary Continental Thinkers: The Phenomenological Heritage*. Dover, NH: Manchester University Press.

—2004. *Debates in Continental Philosophy: Conversations with Contemporary Thinkers*. New York: Fordham University Press.

Kelsey, David H. 1999. *Proving Doctrine: The Uses of Scripture in Modern Theology*. 2nd edn. Harrisburg, PA: Trinity Press International.

Kerr, Fergus. 1986. *Theology after Wittgenstein*. Oxford: Basil Blackwell.

Kierkegaard, Soren. 1941. *Concluding Unscientific Postscript*. Princeton, NJ: Princeton University Press.

Kittay, Eva F. 1987. *Metaphor: Its Cognitive Force and Linguistic Structure*. Oxford: Clarendon Press.

Klemke, E. D. (ed.) 1984. *Contemporary Analytic and Linguistic Philosophies*. Buffalo, NY: Prometheus Books.

Kliever, Lonnie D. 1981. *The Shattered Spectrum: A Survey of Contemporary Theology*. Atlanta, GA: John Knox Press.

Kuhn, Thomas. 1970. *The Structure of Scientific Revolutions*. 2nd edn. Chicago, IL: University of Chicago Press.

Küng, Hans. 1976. *On Being a Christian*. Garden City, NY: Doubleday.

Labron, Tim. 2009. *Wittgenstein and Theology*. New York: Continuum.

Lakatos, Imre, and Alan Musgrave, (eds) 1974. *Criticism and the Growth of Knowledge*. New York: Cambridge University Press.

Lakoff, George. 2008. *The Political Mind: Why You Can't Understand 21st-Century Politics with an 18th-Century Brain*. New York: Viking.

Lakoff, George, and Mark Johnson. 1980. *Metaphors We Live By*. Chicago, IL: University of Chicago Press.

—1999. *Philosophy in the Flesh: The Embodied Mind and Its Challenge to Western Thought*. New York: Basic Books.

Larson, Edward J. 2006. *Summer for the Gods*. 2nd edn. New York: Basic Books.

Laughery, Gregory J. 2002. *Living Hermeneutics in Motion: An Analysis and Evaluation of Paul Ricoeur's Contribution to Biblical Hermeneutics*. Lanham, MD: University Press of America.

Lawlor, Leonard. 1992. *Imagination and Chance: The Difference between the Thought of Ricoeur and Derrida*. New York: State University of New York Press.

Levinas, Emmanuel. 1969. *Totality and Infinity*. Pittsburgh, PA: Duquesne University Press.

Lindbeck, George. 1984. *The Nature of Doctrine: Religion and Theology in a Postliberal Age*. Philadelphia: Westminster Press.

Locke, John. 1952. *An Essay Concerning Human Understanding*, edited by Robert Maynard Hutchins. Chicago, IL: Encyclopedia Britannica.

Luther, Martin. 1982. *The Babylonian Captivity of the Church*. Grand Rapids, MI: Baker Book House.

MacIntyre, Alasdair C. 1984. *After Virtue: A Study in Moral Theory*. 2nd edn. Notre Dame, IN: University of Notre Dame Press.

—1988. *Whose Justice? Which Rationality?* Notre Dame, IN: University of Notre Dame Press.

—1989. "Epistemological Crises, Dramatic Narrative, and the Philosophy of Science." in *Why Narrative? Readings in Narrative Theology*, edited by Stanley Hauerwas and L. Gregory Jones. Grand Rapids, MI: William B. Eerdmans.

—1990. *Three Rival Versions of Moral Enquiry: Encyclopaedia, Genealogy, and Tradition*. Notre Dame, IN: University of Notre Dame Press.

Maddox, Timothy D. F. 1992. "Paul Ricoeur's Time and Narrative as a Model for Historical Reference in Biblical Narrative." Th.M. Thesis. Southern Baptist Theological Seminary.

Marcel, Gabriel. 1956. *The Philosophy of Existentialism*. Secaucus, NJ: Citadel Press.

Marcelo, Gonçalo. 2011. "Paul Ricoeur and the Utopia of Mutual Recognition." *ÉtudesRiceourienne/Ricoeur Studies* 2(1):110–33.

Marsden, George M. 1991. *Understanding Fundamentalism and Evangelicalism*. Grand Rapids, MI: Wm. B. Eerdmans Publishing Company.

—2006. *Fundamentalism and American Culture*. 2nd edn. Oxford: Oxford University Press.

Marshall, Bruce, (ed.) 1990. *Theology and Dialogue: Essays in Conversation with George Lindbeck*. Notre Dame, IN: University of Notre Dame Press.

Marx, Karl. 2011. "Theses on Feuerbach." *Marx/Engels Internet Archive*. Retrieved September 30, 2011 (http://www.marxists.org/archive/marx/works/1845/theses/theses.htm).

McClendon, James Wm. 1974. *Biography as Theology: How Life Stories Can Remake Today's Theology*. Nashville, TN: Abingdon.

McFague, Sallie. 1975. *Speaking in Parables: A Study in Metaphor and Theology*. Philadelphia: Fortress Press.

—1982. *Metaphorical Theology: Models of God in Religious Language*. Philadelphia: Fortress Press.

—1987. *Models of God: Theology for an Ecological, Nuclear Age*. Philadelphia: Fortress Press.

—1993. *The Body of God: An Ecological Theology*. Minneapolis, MN: Fortress Press.

McKnight, Scot. 2007. *A Community Called Atonement*. Nashville, TN: Abingdon.

McSweeney, John. 2008. "The Singularity of Self in the Later Foucault: Reconsidering the End(s) of Poststructuralist Thought." *The Global Spiral*. Retrieved September 4, 2010 (http://www.metanexus.net/magazine/ArticleDetail/tabid/68/id/10497/Default.aspx).

Merleau-Ponty, Maurice. 1962. *Phenomenology of Perception*. New York: Humanities Press.

Milbank, John. 1993. *Theology and Social Theory: Beyond Secular Reason*. Cambridge: Blackwell.

Moltmann, Jürgen. 1993a. *The Crucified God: The Cross of Christ as the Foundation and Criticism of Christian Theology*. 2nd edn. Minneapolis, MN: Fortress Press.

—1993b. *The Trinity and the Kingdom: The Doctrine of God*. Minneapolis, MN: Fortress Press.

—1993c. *Theology of Hope: On the Grounds and the Implications of a Christian Eschatology*. Minneapolis, MN: Fortress Press.

—1996. *The Coming of God: Christian Eschatology*. Minneapolis, MN: Fortress Press.

Mumford, Lewis. 1962. *The Story of Utopias*. New York: Viking Press.

Murphy, Nancey C. 1990. *Theology in the Age of Scientific Reasoning*. Ithaca, NY: Cornell University Press

—1996. *Beyond Liberalism and Fundamentalism: How Modern and Postmodern Philosophy Set the Theological Agenda*. Valley Forge, PA: Trinity Press International.

Murphy, Nancey C., and Brad J. Kallenberg. 2003. "Anglo-American Postmodernity: A Theology of Communal Practice." pp. 26–41 in *The Cambridge Companion to Postmodern Theology,* edited by Kevin J. Vanhoozer. Cambridge, [Eng.]: Cambridge University Press.

Murphy, Nancey C., Brad J. Kallenberg, and Mark Thiessen Nation. 1997. *Virtues and Practices in the Christian Tradition: Christian Ethics After Macintyre*. Harrisburg, PA: Trinity Press International.

Nabert, Jean. 1969. *Elements for an Ethic*. Evanston, IL: Northwestern University Press.

Neiman, Susan. 2002. *Evil in Modern Thought: An Alternative History of Philosophy*. Princeton, NJ: Princeton University Press.

Niebuhr, Reinhold. 1949. *The Nature and Destiny of Man*. New York: Charles Scribner's Sons.

Nussbaum, Martha C. 1995. *Poetic Justice: The Literary Imagination and Public Life*. Boston, MA: Beacon Press.

—2001. *Upheavals of Thought: The Intelligence of Emotions.* New York: Cambridge University Press.

Ogden, Schubert M. 1977. *The Reality of God, and Other Essays.* New York: Harper & Row.

Pannenberg, Wolfhart. 1970. *What Is Man?* Philadelphia: Fortress Press.

Pauw, Amy P., and Serene Jones, (eds) 2011. *Feminist and Womanist Essays in Reformed Dogmatics.* Louisville, KY: Westminster John Knox Press.

Pellauer, David. 2007. *Ricoeur: A Guide for the Perplexed.* New York: Continuum.

—2010. "Remembering Paul Ricoeur." pp. 41–8 in *A Passion for the Possible: Thinking with Paul Ricoeur,* edited by Brian Treanor and Henry Isaac Venema. Perspectives in Continental Philosophy. New York: Fordham University Press.

Penner, Myron B. 2005. *Christianity and the Postmodern Turn: Six Views.* Grand Rapids, MI: Brazos Press.

Peperzak, Adriann. 2010. "Ricoeur and Philosophy: Ricoeur as Teacher, Reader, Writer." pp. 12–129 in *Ricoeur across the Disciplines,* edited by Scott Davidson. New York: Continuum.

Perrin, Norman. 1976. *Jesus and the Language of the Kingdom: Symbol and Metaphor in New Testament Interpretation.* Philadelphia: Fortress Press.

Phillips, Dewi Z. 1995. *Faith After Foundationalism: Critiques and Alternatives.* Boulder, CO: Westview Press.

Pirovlakis, Eftichis. 2011. *Reading Derrida and Ricoeur: Improbable Encounters between Deconstruction and Hermeneutics.* New York: Suny Press.

Placher, William C. 1987. "Paul Ricoeur and Postliberal Theology: A Conflict of Interpretations." *Modern Theology* 4:35–52.

—2007. "Review of The Trial of the Witnesses: The Rise and Decline of Postliberal Theology – By Paul DeHart." *Conversations in Religion & Theology* 5(2): 136–45.

Plantinga, Alvin. 1984. "Advice to Christian Philosophers." *Faith and Philosophy* 1(3): 253–71.

Plato. 1952. "The Seventh Letter." pp. 800–14 in *The Dialogues of Plato and the Seventh Letter.* Great Books of the Western World, vol. 7. Chicago, IL: Encyclopaedia Britannica.

Polanyi, Michael. 1962. *Personal Knowledge: Towards a Post-Critical Philosophy.* 2nd edn. Chicago, IL: University of Chicago Press.

Prigogine, Ilya, and Isabelle Stengers. 1984. *Order Out of Chaos: Man's New Dialogue with Nature.* Toronto: Bantam Books.

Pui-lan, Kwok. 2005. *Postcolonial Imagination & Feminist Theology.* Louisville, KY: Westminster John Knox Press.

Rahner, Karl. 1969. *Hearers of the Word*. Montreal: Palm Publishers.
Reagan, Charles E. 1996. *Paul Ricoeur: His Life and His Work*. Chicago, IL: University of Chicago Press.
Richards, Ivor A. 1981. "The Philosophy of Rhetoric." pp. 48–62 in *Philosophical Perspectives on Metaphor*, edited by Mark Johnson. Minneapolis, MN: University of Minnesota Press.
Rorty, Richard. 1981. *Philosophy and the Mirror of Nature*. Princeton, NJ: Princeton University Press.
Scalise, Charles J. 1994. *Hermeneutics as Theological Prolegomena: A Canonical Approach*. Macon, GA: Mercer University Press.
Schweiker, William. 2010. *Dust that Breathes: Christian Faith and the New Humanisms*. Malden, MA: Wiley-Blackwell.
Schweiker, William, Michael A. Johnson, and Kevin Jung. 2006. *Humanity Before God: Contemporary Faces of Jewish, Christian, and Islamic Ethics*. Kindle ed. Minneapolis, MN: Fortress Press.
Scott-Baumann, Alison. 2009. *Ricoeur and the Hermeneutics of Suspicion*. New York: Continuum.
Smith, James K. A. 2006. *Who's Afraid of Postmodernism? Taking Derrida, Lyotard, and Foucault to Church*. Grand Rapids, MI: Baker Academic.
Soskice, Janet M. 1985. *Metaphor and Religious Language*. Oxford: Clarendon Press.
Stiver, Dan R. 1994. "Much Ado about Athens and Jerusalem: The Implications of Postmodernism for Faith." *Review and Expositor* 91: 83–102.
—1996. *The Philosophy of Religious Language: Sign, Symbol, and Story*. Cambridge: Blackwell.
—2001. *Theology After Ricoeur: New Directions in Hermeneutical Theology*. Louisville, KY: Westminster John Knox Press.
—2003a. "Baptists: Modern or Postmodern?" *Review and Expositor* 100: 521–52.
—2003b. "Theological Method." pp. 170–85 in *Cambridge Companion to Postmodern Theology*, edited by Vanhoozer, Kevin J. New York: Cambridge University Press.
—2009. *Life Together in the Way of Jesus Christ: An Introduction to Christian Theology*. Waco, TX: Baylor University Press.
—2011. "A Common Table: The Hermeneutics of Atheism and Faith." *Liberal Arts and Sciences* 15(2): 120–40.
Suchocki, Marjorie H. 1989. *God, Christ, Church*. New York: Crossroad.
Surber, Jere P. 1997. *Culture and Critique: An Introduction to the Critical Discourses of Cultural Studies*. Boulder, CO: Westview Press.
Syed, Matthew. 2010. *Bounce: Mozart, Federer, Picasso, Beckham, and the Science of Success*. New York: Harper.

Taylor, Charles. 1989. *Sources of the Self: The Making of the Modern Identity*. Cambridge: Harvard University Press.

—2007. *A Secular Age*. Cambridge, MA: Belknap Press of Harvard University Press.

Taylor, George H. 2006. "Ricoeur's Philosophy of Imagination." *Journal of French Philosophy* 16: 93–104.

—2010. "Ricoeur and Law: The Distinctiveness of Legal Hermeneutics." pp. 84–101 in *Ricoeur Across the Disciplines*, edited by Scott Davidson. New York: Continuum.

Taylor, Mark C. 2009. *After God*. Chicago, IL: University of Chicago Press.

Thiselton, Anthony C. 2009. *Hermeneutics: An Introduction*. Grand Rapids, MI: Wm. B. Eerdmans Publishing Company.

Thompson, John B. 1981. *Critical Hermeneutics: A Study in the Thought of Paul Ricoeur and Jürgen Habermas*. Cambridge, [Eng.]: Cambridge University Press.

Tilley, Terrence W. 1995. *Postmodern Theologies: The Challenge of Religious Diversity*. Maryknoll, NY: Orbis Books.

Tillich, Paul. 1957a. *Dynamics of Faith*. New York: Harper & Brothers.

—1957b. *Systematic Theology*, vol. 1. Chicago, IL: University of Chicago Press.

—1963. *Systematic Theology*, vol. 3. Chicago, IL: University of Chicago Press.

Tracy, David. 1979. *Blessed Rage for Order: The New Pluralism in Theology*. New York: Seabury Press.

—1981. *The Analogical Imagination: Christian Theology and the Culture of Pluralism*. New York: Crossroad.

—1985. "Lindbeck's New Program for Theology: A Reflection." *The Thomist* 49: 460–72.

Vanhoozer, Kevin J. 1990. *Biblical Narrative in the Philosophy of Paul Ricoeur: A Study in Hermeneutics and Theology*. Cambridge: Cambridge University Press.

—2002. "First Theology: Meditations in a Postmodern Toolshed." pp. 15–41 in *First Theology: God, Scripture, and Hermeneutics*. Downer's Grove, IL: InterVarsity Press.

—2005. *The Drama of Doctrine: A Canonical-Linguistic Approach to Christian Theology*. Louisville, KY: Westminster John Knox Press.

Vanhoozer, Kevin J. (ed.) 2003. *The Cambridge Companion to Postmodern Theology*. Cambridge: Cambridge University Press.

Volf, Miroslav, and Dorothy C. Bass. 2002. *Practicing Theology: Beliefs and Practices in Christian Life*. Grand Rapids, MI: William B. Eerdmans.

Wall, John. 2005. *Paul Ricoeur and the Poetics of Moral Life*. Oxford: Oxford University Press.

Wallace, Mark I. 1990. *The Second Naiveté: Barth, Ricoeur, and the New Yale Theology*. Macon, GA: Mercer University Press.

Ward, Graham. 1997. "Postmodern Theology." pp. 585–601 in *The Modern Theologians: An Introduction to Christian Theology in the Twentieth Century*, edited by David F. Ford. Malden, MA: Blackwell.

—2003. "Deconstructive Theology." pp. 76–91 in *The Cambridge Companion to Postmodern Theology*, edited by Kevin J. Vanhoozer. Cambridge: Cambridge University Press.

Webb, Stephen H. 1996. *The Gifting God: A Trinitarian Ethics of Excess*. New York: Oxford University Press.

Werpehowski, William. 1986. "Ad Hoc Apologetics." *Journal of Religion* 66: 282–301.

Westphal, Merold. 1993. *Suspicion and Faith: The Religious Uses of Modern Atheism*. Grand Rapids, MI: William B. Eerdmans.

Whitehead, Alfred N. 1953. *Science and the Modern World*. New York: The Free Press.

Witherington III, Ben. 1997. *The Jesus Quest: The Third Search for the Jew of Nazareth*. 2nd edn. Downers Grove, IL: InterVarsity Press.

Wittgenstein, Ludwig. 1958. *Philosophical Investigations*. 3rd edn. New York: Macmillan.

—1963. *Zettel*. Berkeley, CA: University of California Press.

Wolin, Richard. 1993. *The Heidegger Controversy*. 2nd edn. Cambridge, MA: MIT Press.

Wood, Charles. 1981. *The Formation of Christian Understanding*. Philadelphia: Westminster Press.

Zizek, Slavoj. 2006. *How to Read Lacan*. London: Granta Books.

INDEX

wager   42–3, 109, 148, 152–4,
    158–9, 161–2, 164
Wall, John   178n. 15
Wallace, Mark   32, 87–8
Walzer, Michael   15
Ward, Graham   19, 166n. 2
Webb, Stephen H.   176n. 34
Weber, Max   137
Werpehowski, William   32
Westermann, Claus   160
Westphal, Merold   178n. 20,
    179n. 15
Whitehead, Alfred North   27,
    134, 179n. 7

Witherington, Ben, III   167n. 13
Wittgenstein, Ludwig   14–15, 24,
    28, 32, 39, 85–6, 119,
    149, 167n. 3, 170n. 9
Wolin, Richard   175n. 33
Wolterstorff, Nicholas   39
Wong, Michael   173n. 15
Wood, Charles   64

Yale School   31–3, 63–5,
    84–9, 149

Zimmerli, Walther   160
Žižek, Slavoj   92, 172n. 3

* 20, 30, 31, 33-34 94(approx) 102

114 (Rahner), 131 (marks of phil), 135 (recur + faith)

New alleys 142, 149, 152

key on distinction as productive

— framework for this

what I hope to do is for N skch of which ground an account which Ric is faithful for embosh rely beyond cannc crits

while for Audpris a way of useing how Ric laen proned, as DS puts it, a firm work for Analyg o its renewal.

term Ricua

— text B

— not authored relat

— but a rene of interprets projected in front" of a text

World of text 45-46

Bib add FTA — p.56

God not a concept 56

Feeling: 124

Ad hoc: 145